4

Facing the Congo

Facing the Congo

JEFFREY TAYLER

Ruminator Books
St. Paul, Minnesota

Published by Ruminator Books
1648 Grand Avenue
St. Paul, MN 55105
www.ruminator.com

First Ruminator Books printing 2000
Cover design by Randall Heath
Cartography by Patricia Isaacs, Parrot Graphics
Photographs by Jeffrey Tayler
Book design by Wendy Holdman
Typesetting by Stanton Publication Services
St. Paul, Minnesota

Library of Congress Cataloging-in-Publication Data

Tayler, Jeffrey.
    Facing the Congo / Jeffrey Tayler.
        p.   cm.
    ISBN 1-886913-44-7
        1. Congo River—Description and travel. 2. Congo River
Region—Description and travel. 3. Tayler, Jeffrey—Journeys—
Congo River. I. Title.

DT639.T37 2000
916.75104′34—dc21   00-034211

Printed in Canada

*Author's note: To protect the privacy of certain people
in this book, I have changed a few names and minor
identifiying characteristics.*

To Tatyana

"La nuit n'est pas longue à tomber dans les contrées sans crépuscule."

—ALAIN ROBBE-GRILLET

Contents

Acknowledgments   xi

Prologue: Visions of a River   xiii

Brazzaville   3

The Beach   17

Kinshasa   31

The Colonel   43

Shoving Off   59

Stowaways   77

Dancing on the Equator   87

Into the Great Forest   93

Upriver   113

Kisangani   129

Alone on the River   139

Land without Evenings   155

The Woes of SNIP   169

Omens   177

Danger   191

Lisala   209

Crisis   223

Chasing the *Ebeya*   241

Mbandaka Again   249

Epilogue   257

List of Illustrations   261

Acknowledgments

I WOULD GRATEFULLY LIKE TO ACKNOWLEDGE THE ASSISTANCE of the following people who helped me with my travel and in the composition of this book: Mike Edwards and Charles E. Cobb Jr., of *National Geographic* magazine, for their counsel; Dr. Erin Eckert, for her recommendations and guidance in matters African and French; Simon Lelo, for his Lingala lessons, and Tom Crubaugh and the rest of the staff of the Peace Corps in Brazzaville, for their hospitality; Pierre Lokengi of Marsavco, Zaire, for arranging my travel upriver; Marc J. M. Delmage, George Kotsovos, and André of Stanbic Bank/Zaire, for making me feel at home in Kinshasa and helping me outfit myself for the barge trip; Dr. Sam Shaumba and Linda Melesi of the Sapelli Clinic in Kinshasa, for their encouragement and advice on malaria medication; Mfimbo Nsamba of the U.S. Embassy in Kinshasa for telling me of his experiences on the river; Nze, Captain Mopai, Jean, and the rest of the staff of the *Laetitia* for all their support and patience; Roger and Leslie Youssef of Kisangani, for their hospitality; Papa Jean of the *Colonel Ebeya,* for his solicitousness; Yuri and Lilia Filchagin of Kiev, for finding me the apartment in which I wrote the first draft; the director and staff of the Hotel Spina in Istanbul, where I wrote the second draft, for their attentiveness; my mother, father, Mary Dent Crisp, and Paul Hesse, for their reading of the manuscript and comments; my editor, Brigitte Frase, for her sharp eye; my agent, Sonia Land, for her tireless work (as always); and, wherever they are and most of all, Colonel Ekoondo Nguma and Désiré Mundele, for ushering me safely into and out of a world in which, without their help, I might not have survived.

Prologue: Visions of a River

IN THE RAINY, MUCKY AUTUMN OF 1994 IN MOSCOW, MY adopted home city, at the age of thirty-three, I found myself suffering the rejections and dismay familiar to many first-time authors. I had left my work at the Peace Corps in Uzbekistan and had written a book about traveling across Russia, but I could not sell it. To make ends meet I had taken another nonwriting job: that of co-manager of a Russian-American company providing security services (bodyguards and the like) to Western businessmen in Moscow trying to fend off the Russian mafia. I gave the job my all, but I was miserable. It wasn't only the risk of being blown up or gunned down that bothered me—it was the thrumming frustration that corporate life engendered in me, even in such an unorthodox position as my own, and, with my book not selling to a publisher, I had no way of knowing if I would ever find a way to escape it. I searched the faces of those around me in the office for solace and saw that most of my colleagues were diminished and oppressed by their work, which they disliked as much as they feared losing. Everyone was settling for the humdrum and embracing the routine (as hazardous as it occasionally was, in our case), and I felt pressured to do the same.

Time was passing, of which my Russian friends reminded me at every opportunity. "You're thirty-three already! That's *vozrast Khrista* [the age of Christ]!" Allusions to Golgotha notwithstanding, I understood what they meant: at thirty-three one's direction in life should be clear, and mine was not. If anything, it was growing murkier. As I slipped out of youth and into adulthood, doors were slamming shut before me as paths back to what I had grown up with were being cut off. In the preceding eight years all my grandparents, to whom I had been very close, had passed away; letters from friends in the States yellowed and then many of the friends had drifted away. The wanderlust that had impelled me to travel happily throughout my twenties made me a miserable misfit in my thirties. And then there was my writing, which was going nowhere. More and more, with no prospect of a satisfying vocation, and feeling ever more alone, the romantic notions that had led me abroad—that one must write one's own life and never settle for solutions scripted by others; that one must pursue a destiny based on one's unique talents and never surrender to convention— prompted me to get up and take action, but I could not conceive of *what* action.

I spoke of these things to Tatyana, my girlfriend. She sympathized, to a point, but my complaints started to wear on her. She saw little wrong with my remunerative job and the comfortable future it offered us. We talked of marrying, but I could not take that step yet. To be ready for marriage, I needed to know who I was and what I was good for, and I did not.

The rains of autumn went on and on, reds and oranges washed into grays and browns. By November, snow was falling on bare trees standing against bare sky, and I could find no answers. Had I thought that I might raise my spirits by packing up and heading to a warmer climate, I might have done so. But there was Tatyana, whom I did not want to leave, and my doubts, I knew, would follow me wherever I went.

Idly I began sketching alternatives and drafting plans; I let my pen wander across the pages of my journal. I read a lot about the Middle East and North Africa, where I had traveled and lived in the past, thinking that those places would offer me something for my future. But they did not, and as time passed I grew more and more agitated, desperate even, and my desperation focused my thoughts on a truth as stark and chilling and inevitable as the winter that was deepening around me: our days are numbered and our time runs out. Whether we succeed or fail in our professional or family lives, our time runs out. The imperative is to accept the frightening yet liberating fact of our finitude, to keep our eyes on the truth of time, and not to succumb to the illusion, comforting though it may be, that our days will go on and on. I also believed that in life, as in literature, there are climaxes, decisive moments that resolve our doubts and answer our questions, that determine who we are and what we are worth.

It was during this stretch of musing and searching that I chanced upon V. S. Naipaul's novel *A Bend in the River*. Naipaul's Indian protagonist, Salim, comes to Kisangani (the town is never named but its identity is clear) on the Congo River to set up shop and establish a new life. It was a mesmerizing story and seemed to promise me something, though I did not know what exactly. But what it definitely did do was limn a Congo motif in my life; it connected disparate impressions and linked morsels of information that I had imbibed about the river. With its sonorous *o*'s, the word *Congo* resonated with the power of a village drum to conjure up visions of jungles and thrashing crocodiles along a great African river.

Soon after, I came across the navigation charts for Zaire (as the Democratic Republic of the Congo was known then) published by the Defense Mapping Agency. To cover the river at a scale of 1:1,000,000 it took four unwieldy, four-by-five-foot charts, crinkly sheets of green paper crisscrossed by longitudinal lines and latitudinal etchings, veined with meandering streams and marked with POSITION APPROXIMATE notations by jungle villages with names like Busala and Kikongo, Bosango and Matari. POSITION APPROXIMATE. Maps or no, it seemed you could never be quite sure where you were in Zaire, even in our unromantically precise age of satellite photography and precision cartography. That appealed to me.

I laid out the charts on my living room floor and they stretched from wall to wall. Zaire is roughly a quarter the size of the United States. In its monotonous green expanses, what catches the eye, like some monstrous, half-extended claw, is the three-thousand-mile-long Congo River (which was known in Zaire, in 1994, as the Zaire River), that winds north from near Zambia and crosses the

equator. Near Kisangani, in the heart of the continent, it veers
west through some of the densest jungle on earth to dip below the
equator again before cascading into the Atlantic over thirty-two
gigantic cataracts. In many parts, especially in the middle stretches
between Lokutu and Mbandaka, it appears to be less a river and
more a crescent swath of rain forest cut and slashed by currents
pouring in from dozens of tributaries; it is a labyrinth stretching
fourteen miles wide in places and composed of hundreds of islands. Away from the cities of Kinshasa and Brazzaville, only a
few dirt roads, rained into quagmires for much of the year, reach
the settlements on the Congo's banks, and the people dwelling in
its wilderness are, to this day, some of the most isolated in Africa.

Intrigued by the charts, I started reading up on Zaire's history.
Although a Portuguese navigator traveled the river as far as the
cataracts at Matadi in the late fifteenth century, the rest of the
Congo remained, as far as the West was concerned, one of the last
great terrae incognitae on earth until the arrival in the 1870s of the
British explorer Henry Morton Stanley. Stanley, accompanied by
a crew of hundreds of Africans and three Europeans, trekked his
way inland from Zanzibar, on the Indian Ocean coast, to Nyangwe,
on the upper Congo, then sailed downriver in pirogues, or dugout
canoes, fighting cannibal tribes all the way. By the time he reached
the Atlantic, half of the Africans and all of his European companions had perished in battles or died of disease, drowning, or
starvation.

Stanley's expedition opened up Central Africa for European
exploitation, slaving, and despoilment. In 1885, King Léopold II
of Belgium took over the territory through which Stanley had
traveled, named it the Congo Free State, and ran it as his private
rubber plantation. The atrocities of the "Free State," which resulted in five to eight million deaths and included the routine
maiming, enslavement, and murder of local tribes, provoked outrage among Europeans, and in 1908 the king was forced to hand
over the Congo to the Belgian government, which continued,
however, to exploit it as a colony. As far as colonial powers went,

Belgium proved to be lackadaisical: it built primary schools and a few roads, but not much else.

Pondering this history, poring over these maps, I began to be intrigued by Zaire for the same reasons that I had been by Russia: it was a land of tragedy, hope, and great drama; it was vital to its continent, huge and primal and rich in resources; and it was still largely untrammeled by outsiders.

But it was the Congo River, Zaire's dominant geographic feature, that possessed me. I studied my navigational charts, I read accounts of those who had traveled it by barge, I tried to decide what specifically it offered me, what I could do with my fascination by it. Finally in February of 1995, as I was driving to work, with the pale orange orb of the sun ahead of me sending its frigid blue light through a powder of falling snow, I hit upon an idea: I would make a solo descent by pirogue of the Congo's longest navigable stretch, from Kisangani to the capital, Kinshasa—a distance of 1,084 miles, or 1,736 kilometers. This would be a partial re-creation of Stanley's historic journey. Confronting and vanquishing a tropical river would be my defining achievement. Traveling its jungle waterways, I would strip myself of encumbering personal concerns, remake myself. I hoped that the expedition would settle once and for all my doubts about who I was and what I could accomplish.

The expedition looked broadly feasible. I would sail with the current so that I would not exhaust myself; at thirty miles a day I would cover the route in forty-five days, including rest stops. I would not get lost: the current would carry me of its own accord toward my destination. It would not cost much: I would travel in an inexpensive pirogue that I could buy in Zaire and leave behind when I left. I would take staples such as rice and beans and barter for fish and meat from villages. No special clothing would be required for the tropical climate. I spoke French, the former colonial tongue, and was sure that I could master the rudiments of Lingala, the Bantu language that served as the lingua franca of the linguistically diverse country. Malaria medications and vaccinations would take care of significant health risks. To be sure of success (and survival), I had to plan carefully, but I was not an inexperienced traveler and I relished the challenge.

And as I read on, I learned that there would be challenges beyond those deriving from the river, challenges stemming from the violent history of the land and the legacy of the Cold War. (Zaire's minerals interested both the United States and the Soviet Union.) In 1960, the Belgians, in response to rioting in the Congolese capital and a rebellion in the east, granted the Congo independence. Five years of secessionist chaos, political instability, and Soviet intervention led to the covert Belgian military action that resulted in the murder of Patrice Lumumba, the democratically elected prime minister, and the ascension to power of an obscure army officer, Joseph-Désiré Mobutu.

When Mobutu took over, copper, cobalt, and diamonds had replaced rubber as the Congo's most valuable resources. Copper prices were rising, and as a result, the Congo had the potential to become one of the richest countries in Africa. Yet Mobutu's ascension to power initiated an era of corruption and widespread plunder that was to see no equal on the continent. Assuming a role akin to that of national chief, he devised a system of patronage that enriched himself and his tribe, the Ngbandi, and collaborating local chieftains, at the expense of everyone else. By offering lucre in return for loyalty, he brought potential rivals to his sumptuous table; many of those who refused to partake in his repast were hanged, poisoned, shot, or imprisoned.

Mobutu cut a flamboyant figure and set about elevating himself to godlike status. He dubbed himself the Messiah, the Sun-President, the Guide. In processions he had himself carried on a throne on the backs of his subjects. His portrait—which showed a stern bespectacled face topped by a leopardskin hat—hung everywhere, even in churches, where he had his name substituted for God's in hymns. Among Zaireans it was rumored that bullets could not pierce his skin, that he consorted at night with identical twin beauties, that he was a sorcerer possessed of irresistible magi-

cal powers. In the garage of his residence in Tshatshi, outside
Kinshasa, he maintained a fleet of Mercedes-Benzes and Rolls-
Royces; he built eleven palaces for himself around the country;
he acquired estates all over Europe, South America, and North
Africa. His private fortune, consisting mainly of revenues stolen
from the state treasury and diverted foreign aid (during the Carter
years, for example, Zaire received almost half of all foreign aid the
United States allotted to Africa), was eventually estimated at between $5 billion and $8 billion, while per capita income among his
subjects dropped to the equivalent of $135 a year.

As Mobutu impoverished his people, he realized that he
needed a compensating ideology to justify to them his continued
reign, and found it in a campaign for African *authenticité*. He
dumped the colonial-era name Congo and rechristened the country Zaire, an appellation that was, however, hardly more "authen-
tic" than Congo (which at least derived from the name of the
Bakongo tribe in the southwest); Zaire was a Portuguese corruption of the Kikongo word for "large river," *nzadi*. He forced all
Zaireans to adopt African names and created a new Lingala title
for himself—Mobutu Sese Seko Koko Ngbendu wa za Banga
(which is usually translated as "The All-Conquering Warrior
Who, Because of His Endurance and Inflexible Will to Win, Will
Go from Conquest to Conquest Leaving Fire in His Wake," but
which literally means "The Cock Who Jumps on Anything That
Moves"); he outlawed Christmas and neckties on the grounds that
they were non-African. "Mobutuism," a loose collection of his
anticolonialist sayings and "wisdom" strung together into dogma,
became the official state ideology. He expropriated the prominent
Indian, Greek, and Belgian trading and plantation-owning com-
munities and handed over their businesses to his cronies, who
bankrupted them. As the campaign for *authenticité* gathered pace,
what infrastructure the Belgians had left behind crumbled and the
country returned to bush: roads decayed, telephones stopped
working, electricity and running water disappeared. However (and
most important), Mobutu's anti-Soviet foreign policy conformed

with the Cold War dictates of his Western backers, and as late as 1989 he visited the White House as an honored guest.

The copper boom ended, and the Cold War drew to a close. The Western aid on which Mobutu partially relied to finance his government and fill his private coffers dried up. In 1991 (and later in 1993), his army, unpaid, ran amok and took to looting the cities, and the civilian population joined in. Mobutu, protected by his loyal, well-equipped, and Israeli-trained Division spéciale présidentielle, retreated to safety on his helipad-equipped yacht in the middle of the Congo River and watched his country burn. Hyperinflation rendered worthless the national currency, the zaire; revolts and disturbances began afflicting the land as regularly as the seasonal rains; what government there had been withered; and at least 40 percent of Zaireans came to suffer from chronic malnutrition. Zaire, just twenty-five years earlier one of the most promising countries in Africa, had become one of the poorest on earth. Yet Mobutu's wealth continued to increase, coming now largely from black market trade in minerals.

By 1995 Mobutu was forcing Zaire through its darkest days ever, pillaging the remnants of wealth from a depleted land and an exhausted populace.

I called an Africa-wise friend of mine from the Peace Corps, which had maintained a mission in Zaire until the violence of 1991, and asked her if she knew of anybody who might have attempted an expedition similar to the one I had in mind. She made some inquiries and learned that once, in the late 1980s, a few volunteers had set out in a pirogue from Kisangani but had capsized in a storm soon after departure; they spent a long time stranded on a jungle island and almost starved. The river was dangerous, she said, the currents were strong, and the Peace Corps had not stationed personnel in the outback regions where I was heading, where people were considered unfriendly to outsiders. Other aid agencies had withdrawn their staff from Zaire under fire in 1991. I also spoke to the National Geographic Society, but their writers and photographers had not been in Zaire since the revolts began,

and they warned me of the risks. From everyone to whom I spoke
the response was basically the same: renegade soldiers, the collapse of the state, civil unrest, and possibly hostile locals would
put me in danger of being robbed or murdered. I searched and
searched for evidence that someone else had completed a descent
of the river by pirogue, but I could find nothing. Should I succeed, it appeared, I would most likely be the first Westerner to do
so since Stanley.

I could find only one guidebook that covered Zaire: the Lonely
Planet guide to Central Africa. It said nothing about piroguing the
Congo, but it explicitly detailed how the post-1991 breakdown
of the state affected travelers: "Because of the ongoing chaos in
Zaire . . . security is a major problem throughout the country. . . .
In terms of danger, Kinshasa is unrivaled in Central Africa. . . .
Groups with knives and guns have attacked travelers in broad
daylight, so even walking around Kinshasa during the daytime
poses serious risk. . . . Foreigners have been dragged at gunpoint
from their cars at major intersections and murdered. . . . Try to
avoid arriving in Kinshasa airport during the night. . . . Riding in
a taxi from there to the city center is very risky as you could easily
be stopped along the way by bandits and robbed, if not killed,"
and so on.

These warnings unsettled but did not dissuade me. In other
unstable parts of the world where I had traveled, I had heard dire
warnings and found them exaggerated. And in Zaire, long infa-
mous in the West as the "heart of darkness" (from Joseph Con-
rad's novel of the same name), I reasoned that the tendency to ex-
aggerate would be especially pronounced. I would rationally assess
risks and surmount them; if necessary, I would hire a guard to protect me. In any case, I was desperate to effect a change in my life, to
force upon it a climax, a denouement. I felt I was weak. If I survived, I would be all the stronger for it, I would be transformed.
The Congo River filled my dreams and flowed through my waking
hours, and my expedition took on a fated aspect.

I spent the winter in Moscow, reading, making calls, examining

maps, and consulting weather charts. My enthusiasm aside, I recognized that I had no experience in sub-Saharan Africa. The warnings convinced me that I had to learn all I could about the Congo
before getting in a pirogue, so I decided to take a barge from
Kinshasa upriver to Kisangani. By gathering information on the
way up I would be able to formulate a plan to confront the dangers
on the way down. I also decided to spend some time in Brazzaville,
the capital of the Republic of Congo (just across the river from
Zaire), studying Lingala. From Brazzaville I could take a ferry to
Kinshasa when I was ready.

The best time for my expedition would be the driest season
(driest near Kinshasa, that is; where the river parallels the equator
it rains all year), from June through August, so when spring came
I set about burning bridges. I fired off a letter of resignation to my
employer. I said a wrenching good-bye to Tatyana. I gave up my
Moscow apartment and returned to the States, where, after buying a tent and other camping gear and getting the necessary vaccinations and malaria medication and running a thousand other
minor but somehow vital errands, I exchanged farewells with my
family and friends, and left for London, from where I would fly to
Brazzaville.

On the long flight toward the equator from London I felt guilty
for causing my loved ones distress; they saw my obsession with the
river as some sort of ruinous, even absurd, idée fixe. They were
right: I was obsessed. During the week before departure I could
hardly sleep for all my newfound nervous energy and excitement
and, yes, fear—but I would let nothing stop me. As I neared
Brazzaville my past fell away, as if into an abyss; ahead, for me,
was only the Congo.

Facing the Congo

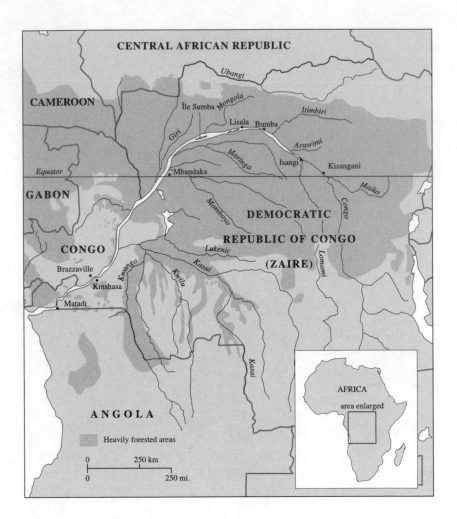

CENTRAL AFRICAN REPUBLIC

CAMEROON

Ubangi

Île Sumba *Mongola*

Lisala Bumba

Itimbiri

Giri

Aruwimi

Maringa

Isangi

Kisangani

Equator

Mbandaka

Maiko

GABON

Momboyo

DEMOCRATIC

Congo

REPUBLIC OF CONGO

CONGO

(ZAIRE)

Lukenie

Lomami

Brazzaville

Kwango

Kasai

Kinshasa

Kwilu

Matadi

Kasai

ANGOLA

AFRICA

area enlarged

■ Heavily forested areas

0 ———— 250 km

0 ———— 250 mi.

Brazzaville

THE SQUAWKS OF PARROTS FILTERED DOWN INTO THE BLACK well of sleep and slowly called me up into the lighter realms of wakefulness. There was a whir, as of an air conditioner, and the muffled, hollow echo of voices in the corridor. I opened my eyes and looked around me at the white room and its shutters, where the timid light of dawn was creeping in between the slats. Still exhausted from the flight and the hectic preparations of the previous week, I shut my eyes again and drifted back into memories of the past twenty-four hours.

There had been only a few people on the plane. Sometime during the night we crossed the equator into the Southern Hemisphere, and the captain announced our descent toward Brazzaville. Through my window I could discern no city, only stars in an indigo sky above the sweeping, pitch-black expanse of the earth. A minute before landing, dimples of yellow appeared below: lamps in house windows diffusing pale light onto nearby palms. The capital of the Republic of the Congo looked like a tiny settlement from the air.

Maya Maya Airport was dark and dank, with mosquitoes whining in warm mists and gaunt-cheeked soldiers loitering in unlit corridors. A woman in a banana colored scarf sitting in an illuminated booth peered at my yellow fever vaccination certificate, a red-eyed official yawned and stamped my visa. Next, a man in sandals and a tan uniform stopped me abruptly, gave my passport a supercilious look, and asked me if I was a resident. No. "Ah. *Attendez*." But he occupied himself with other passengers, so I walked on down the corridor.

Customs was a dimly lit green-and-blue chamber streaked

3

with dirt and filled with the rustling shadows of greeters, taxi
drivers, policemen, porters. White spots danced toward me out of
the gloom: a lanky youth in a blue-white calico print jumpsuit
sauntered up and pulled me toward the baggage conveyor belt.
"How much will you give me?" he asked in French.

"For what? I don't have my bag. The conveyor belt isn't working yet."

"Ah-haa!"

He grabbed the belt and, throwing his weight into it, started
pushing it along by hand, his sandals scuffing and sliding on the
dusty floor. Other porters joined in, heaving and hoing, and the
thing creaked to life. But an attendant in khaki shouted in Lingala
and came running over to the calico fellow; grabbing my bag, he
shoved him aside. He was an official porter, he said; the man I had
hired was a hustler. Using my bag as a ram he forced a passage
through the crowd, and I followed him to the customs desk, where
officers sat slumped with their berets slanted low over half-closed
eyes and waved us on toward the doors. The hustler skulked along
behind us, pleading, *"Monsieur! Monsieur!"* I gave him a few
francs. He nodded, and he and his white spots danced back into
the dark of the terminal.

We walked out into the moonless night. There were no lights
on the street, and the inky, close air rang with crickets and smelled
of fruit and sweat. Moist palms landed on my forearms and pulled
me in this direction and that; an incantation arose from figures
bobbing faceless in the black: *"taxi . . . taxi . . . vous cherchez un bon
hôtel . . . eh, monsieur . . . taxi . . ."* My porter pushed on. I followed
the white address label on my bag, stumbling over an unseen curb,
stomping flat-footed into a pothole, not knowing whether I was
about to trip on a fender or step on a body. Then he halted and a
driver was quoting me a fare to a hotel. *D'accord.* They hustled me
into the car. The porter asked for five dollars. I pulled out a dollar,
slapped it in his hand, and we were off.

In Brazzaville a couple of years before there had been con-
tested elections followed by riots and looting, and a serious prob-

lem with crime remained. As my taxi trundled through the city's outskirts—pitch-black warrens overgrown with bush—I remembered this and found I could not help but be afraid. When the driver hit the brakes at bumps I worried he was stopping for robbers; when we crashed through branches hanging out into the road I thought he might be taking a detour and I was about to get my throat slit. Once we slowed to creep around a crater and people came running up to the car: there were white T-shirts in the dark, there were shouts, there were fists pounding on our hood. But we rolled on, unharmed, down more mud lanes, careened around a circle, bounced onto a boulevard, and turned off onto a side street.

Ahead of us a bare lightbulb dangled on a wire over a hand-painted sign: Hôtel Les Bougainvillées. As we drove up, a gray-haired man with a goatee and a bow tie popped his head into the receptionist's window and swatted at a mosquito on his neck. I got out.

"You want a room?" he asked.

"Yes."

"Well, *pas de chambre!* We're full!"

I reluctantly started to turn back to the taxi, sinking inside at the thought of more cruising in the dark.

He swatted his neck again. "Okay, okay. We have a room."

I set down my bag and filled out a registration form.

✕✕✕

The light outside my window was getting stronger, the parrots were bickering more and more raucously. I did not want to get up. I was still nervous, so I stayed in bed for a long time more. But eventually music with a salsa beat—drums and tinny electric pianos and guitars—percolated in and set me at ease. I arose, dressed, and headed out, my destination the Peace Corps office.

How silly and irrational my fears seemed now! Palms shot up like geysers of emerald green into drifting layers of cottony mist; winding tar roads were flanked by shoulders of cream-colored sand; old French colonial homes sat placidly behind whitewashed walls, the foliage of the broad trees above them forming a dark canopy splashed here and there with the flitting red and gray plumage of parrots. My hotel was in the high part of town; the rest of Brazzaville sloped downward in lazy tiers laced with lanes that ended in a sea of fog. Now and then a battered taxi would putt by. Crowds ambled along the shoulders, crowds of young people dressed in navy slacks and gray skirts, laughing, relaxed kids carrying the floppy checkered *cahiers* of students in France; they mixed French and Lingala and headed on down the road. The fear of the night having dissipated, I fell in with them and strolled along as though seeing the world for the first time. Gradually I found myself lower and lower on the hillside, nearing the more modern buildings of the center. I was fresh, ready for anything.

There was a promontory. I left the crowd and walked out onto it, feeling compelled, for some reason, to keep my eyes on the sea of fog below. I stared into the fog: two dark stick figures in the white resolved themselves into men, then a pirogue sifted into view beneath them. Fishermen on water. One man was hurling a net while the other rowed against the current, putting his back into his strokes. The Congo River. Here at Malebo Pool the Congo's waters, glistening expanses of pearl only a shade darker than the fog, were wide, but they poured with a powerful hiss out of a hazy realm of islands and trees to the northeast, carrying toward the Atlantic sheets of water hyacinth, chunks of chartreuse plant matter that looked like it had been vomited up by a great jungle, a jungle sickly fertile and spilling out of itself. Across the water there was no trace of Kinshasa—only a mat of fog and water speckled in its lower reaches with the green of the water hyacinth. My gaze returned to the pirogue. The current was strong; the paddler was leaning into his strokes, struggling to keep his craft from being swept downriver.

I remembered where I was going. I returned to the street and rejoined the crowds.

Tom Crubaugh, the director of the Peace Corps mission in Brazzaville, sat behind his desk listening to me explain my plan to study Lingala and travel the river. He had a frank face and his hair was long and pulled back in a ponytail. He wore a tie, it seemed, as a concession to convention. He had spent years in Lower Zaire as a Peace Corps volunteer and had left only with the evacuation during the revolt of 1991.

After I finished telling him my plans, he drummed a pencil on his desk and leaned back, smiling. "Going to Kisangani, eh? The heart of darkness!"

"Isn't that a bit of an exaggeration?"

"Well, Zaire's always been the Wild West. People have to work hard there to make ends meet. They haven't been softened by socialism like the Congolese here."

"What do you think my chances are of making it?"

"Don't know, really. Bad idea to go alone, though. You'll need a guide if only to keep from getting lost in all the islands. And the people upriver—they could be another problem. We didn't put volunteers up there. Alone, you'll be quite a target. Life's tough in Zaire, a lot tougher than in Brazzaville, where people have retained their humanity. You'll see this at the Beach."

"The Beach?"

"The Kinshasa port. Ngobila Beach. It's hell. All police and soldiers demanding bribes. You'll see. But let me introduce you to Simon. He's one of our Lingala instructors. You can talk to him about your lessons."

✦✦✦

Simon had humorous eyes, a soft demeanor, and an even softer handshake. He was self-assured in a calm, egoless way. He agreed to give me an eight-hour-a-day, weeklong intensive course in Lingala through French. We sat under a twirling fan in a second-floor classroom of the Peace Corps office. When I got something right he would exclaim, "Ah-*haa!*" and lean back, his eyes smiling.

But he lowered his eyes when I raised mine to his—a courtesy in this part of Africa.

Lingala is the Bantu *langue de passage,* the lingua franca of both Congo and Zaire. Besides Lingala there are 220 languages in use in Zaire by 250 different ethnic groups; only Lingala and, to a lesser extent, French unite them. With so little time, we concentrated on basic grammar and vocabulary I would need to know on the river. Although its nouns had no gender or case and its sounds were open and easy to imitate, the grammar was formidable. My head ached at the end of each of our sessions. As with any language, the vocabulary of Lingala told a lot about the life of those who spoke it: for example, animals were referred to as *banyama,* the plural of *nyama,* or "meat," for almost all wildlife in the forest could be turned into a meal. Interestingly, Simon did not fully understand me when I asked him for the Lingala for *soir;* in Lingala there is no word for "evening," only words for "day" (*moi,* which is synonymous with "sun") and "night" *(butu),* because there is no evening in Central Africa—a characteristic of the equatorial latitude I was only later to appreciate.

Although Simon said that only *"les imprudents"* get eaten by crocodiles, he was reticent about Zaire and grew concerned when I told him of my plans to pirogue the Congo alone from Kisangani to Kinshasa. I would need a local with me to smooth the way, he thought, or people along the remote reaches of the river might greet me, a *mondele* ("white person"), with suspicion or even hostility. At least this was what he thought. He, like all the other Congolese I was to speak to during my stay in Brazzaville, had never been on the river except to travel, in better times, across Malebo Pool to Kinshasa.

Our lessons proceeded apace. Under Simon's tutelage, I found myself beginning to adapt to the unfamiliar language, although the concept of my expedition, especially after seeing the river surging out of the jungle beyond the town, became no less intimidating than it had been before my arrival.

I studied and studied; one day flowed into the next. At night, however, I found myself lurching awake in a cold sweat, unable to remember my dreams.

✂✂✂

"Halt! Eh, *monsieur!* Halt!"

On my way back to the hotel one afternoon a man called out to me from a café. He got up, his sandals scraping the dirt, his mud-splattered blue trousers baggy around his ankles, and started toward me, teetering, correcting his steps, and teetering again. His eyes were red. When he made it to me he stopped and paused. His pause suggested some sort of authority: he was too important to be concerned with my time. Then I noticed he wore the top half of a tan uniform.

Slitting his eyes, he raised his chin. "You remember me, *monsieur?*"

"No, I don't."

He smirked and swayed; his cheeks puffed out slightly with a restrained belch. "Well, *monsieur,* my name is Jean Claude. I settled the matter of your papers."

"What matter?"

"I examined your passport, *monsieur,* at the airport. I stamped your visa, *monsieur.* I verified your accommodation certificate"— here he burped again— *"monsieur."* He bared his teeth and leaned toward me. "I helped you, *monsieur.*"

I vaguely recognized him from Maya Maya.

He leaned into me and steadied himself, then stood erect. "I'm hungry, *monsieur.* I have no money to eat."

He had money to get drunk though, but I could think of nothing to say to his words about hunger, which caught me off guard. Reflexively, I handed him a few francs. He examined them, said *"Merci, monsieur,"* turned, and teetered back to his café.

As I watched him walk away it dawned on me who he was. At Maya Maya he had done nothing except ask me if I was a resident, and he had not collected a bribe for letting me pass, as I now surmised must have been his custom. I had overreacted to his declaration of hunger: he showed me I was vulnerable to a ruse based on pity. I felt I should not have given him anything.

I started across the street. An explosion of honking and shouting startled me, and I jumped back. Four or five open-back trucks shot by, filled with scowling, helmeted soldiers in navy-blue uniforms, holding their guns high in the air.

✦✦✦

I spent that evening sitting in the veranda restaurant at Les Bougainvillées. The veranda was a serene place hung with oil paintings that showed Africa as a European romantic might have imagined it: idylls with pirogues on the river at sunset, the jungle at dawn, villagers gathering on the riverbank in the moonlight. They were false images of Africa, Africa as a primitive paradise. I could imagine a Parisian fleeing here to escape the confines of urban life, a failed love, or even the law, and painting these scenes because he needed to see Africa this way. But the paintings were beautiful and evocative nonetheless.

Grumbling to himself, the old hotelier walked onto the veranda in his bow tie and flicked on the television set by the bar. *"Les actualités,"* he said. The news was about to start. He sat down, his face strict and joyless.

"Is that a Congolese station?" I asked him, wanting to be polite.

"Zairean," he muttered and swatted a mosquito on his neck.

"I'm going to Zaire."

He leapt from his seat. "You *are?* Zaire! Ha! The homeland of Mobutu!"

As if he had conjured up the dictator by exclamation alone, Mobutu appeared on the television addressing a delegation of Zairean officials. He was in his leopardskin hat and his own version of the Mao jacket, the abacost. The camera showed him large in the foreground and the others small in the background, standing in a submissive row. He was speaking Lingala, his chin held high, his eyes half-closed, his hands clasped behind his back. Most notably, his head was turned away from his audience, as though they were unworthy of his gaze. He seemed to be reprimanding them.

The hotelier raced to the screen. "That is Mobutu! Ha! You will see the result of his despotism at the Beach! You are going to Zaire alone or with a guard?"

"Alone."

"Then listen, remember you're entering the homeland of Mobutu. Mobutu! He made Lingala the official language of the country. Not French, Lingala!" He was clenching his fists, he was electrified. "But listen! No matter. At the Beach it can be dangerous, oh, *que c'est dangereux!* When those soldiers set upon you, you must wave your passport and shout, 'American diplomat going to the American Embassy! Diplomat! American diplomat! Embassy!' Only this way will you get past them! You must make them *fear* you, you understand? They fear the American Embassy! They must be made to tremble! Make them *tremble!*"

Tremble? Thoughts of my expedition and the dangers of Kinshasa hit me like a wave of nausea. Fear—I felt it rush through me now. It was I, to be sure, who would fear the soldiers. He ranted some more, and I told him my plans.

He harrumphed and swatted at a mosquito. "I don't know about upriver. But Kin, as we call Kinshasa, is violent. The Zaireans are more primitive, more brutal than we are," he said, examining the squashed bug on his palm. "But you are going to Zaire. You must never forget that you are going to the homeland of Mobutu. Only by instilling fear in the soldiers, FEAR"—his voice shot up—"will you survive."

When Mobutu left the screen, the hotelier, his finger darting into the air, quit the veranda, shouting, "FEAR! Remember, FEAR!"

I was alone again with the idylls, a film of cold clammy sweat covering my palms.

✧✧✧

Brazzaville was so agreeable that I began to wonder if I should leave. My days passed easily with Simon. It was fun learning a new language. The Peace Corps volunteers to whom I had spoken loved the country. Why not remain here? Why not admit, for the first time, that life can be a joy where I am? Why search more, go farther? Just thinking about Kinshasa, of which I still had not managed to catch sight owing to the fog, turned my stomach; the river and the jungles that I could see from the promontory evoked in me a foreboding, a primal fear, and I hardly wanted to look at them. Brazzaville, on the other hand, offered an easy world of new sensations, of tame pleasures. Maybe I should stay put.

I thought about this as I shuffled down the sandy road late one afternoon to the port, slipping into the casual rhythms of the people around me, wanting to do nothing more than inhale the scents of the vines and flowered bushes and listen to the rippling, trilling calls of the birds.

I dropped into a store to buy some nuts. Inside I recognized a young Peace Corps volunteer I'd met in the office. He was wearing loose African pants, a calico-print dashiki, and slipper-style Congolese shoes. *He's gone native,* I thought, at first perceiving him as vaguely ridiculous. But why ridiculous? In this humidity, my American clothes, though they were loose and of cotton, felt tight and sticky on me. His dress looked more comfortable.

We talked. Like many Peace Corps volunteers (I had been one myself, so I knew), he was concerned to show that he had raised his consciousness through assimilation in his adopted land. He said he had lived for years in an upcountry village—no big deal; he had suffered malaria a few times—no big deal; he had had his first bout of diarrhea only recently. Also no big deal—for one who had gone native, no native problems were big deals, even if natives died from them by the thousands, as the Congolese died from diarrhea and malaria. The drunk official who begged money from me, the air of violence that filled the night, the passion of the hotelier at the mere sight of Mobutu—indicators of fundamental flaws in the society, of coming tragedy—were also no big deal, he said; they were part of the culture. I asked him questions about his Peace Corps life; he asked nothing about where I was from or how

I happened to end up in Brazzaville, though there were few non-Africans here indeed, aside from aid workers. Like many Peace Corps volunteers, he was, in a way, the star of his own show, at least when outsiders were around.

I grilled him about Zaire. He had been there, but not since 1991 and the troubles. The Beach was hell, I would have to run a gauntlet of drunk soldiers, I would have to sleep with my camera gear or it would be stolen, and so on and so forth, or that, at least, was what he had heard. He didn't ask me why I was going there, so I told him. What problems could he foresee? He couldn't say. My plans for adventure were, he implied, as incomprehensible to him as they might be to a Congolese local selling manioc root on the street corner. We parted and I walked on to the river.

For the first time since my arrival the air over Malebo Pool was clear and Kinshasa was visible. It stood mighty and tall across the water, a phalanx of soaring skyscrapers and crisscrossing dock cranes that recalled the copper boom of decades past. It was an energizing sight.

That energy galvanized the port, where pandemonium raged. Traders grabbed at my arms, offering bundles of manioc and bunches of bananas and plantains; money merchants hawked sheaves of zaires, greasy, string-tied bricks of bills bearing Mobutu's portrait. Boys pushed carts laden with sacks of rice at breakneck speed through the mud; gangly soldiers with darting eyes circulated with their fingers on the triggers of their rifles. People were tussling and arguing over everything. Big-bellied Zairean men wearing silk shirts and gold rings yelled in baritones at grunting porters walking briskly under heavy crates. Children were running helter-skelter, and everyone was shouting. This, too, was a scene of great energy, and all the energy flowed toward a ferry about to cross the river to Kinshasa.

I forced my way to a mud-yellow building where tickets were being sold. The polite clerk said I could come at any time for the boat to Zaire: there were many. And four ferries a month ran from Kinshasa to Kisangani, leaving at eleven in the morning on

Mondays. It would be that easy to go to Zaire, and no problem getting upriver. A wheelbarrow almost knocked me over as I listened to him.

I thanked him and headed back to the hotel, thinking that things could not be so simple. Zaire, the port showed, evoked in people all the peace and tranquillity of an onrushing tornado; it *energized,* and that energy reminded me that Zaire was where I had to be. The benumbing security enjoyed by the Peace Corps volunteer suddenly seemed repugnant and absurd and phony, part of a routine as suffocating as any office job, and I abandoned thoughts of staying on in Brazzaville. I would depart for Kinshasa the next afternoon and do what I had come to Central Africa to do.

Night was falling over the town and the sky flushed with lavender. Burning middens scented the air; egrets wandered in looping flight through rising smoke. I passed the university campus and came upon students memorizing their lessons, strolling along, reciting from their *cahiers,* squinting at their notes in the failing light, then looking up and reciting again. When I got back to Les Bougainvillées I sat out on the veranda and wrote long letters to Tatyana and my family. There was nothing more to be gained by sitting here under the painted idylls. I would leave the next day. It would be better to cross the river and get on with it.

When the old hotelier showed up to watch the news, I paid my bill and went to my room to pack.

The Beach

IT WAS TIME TO LEAVE. I BROUGHT MY BAGS OUT TO THE FRONT door, and the hotelier arranged a taxi for me. The afternoon air smelled of blossoms, nectarous and fruity; every trill, squawk, and screech from the palms rang loud and distinct. In my gut a wire was growing tauter and tauter. As on my first morning here, it was as if I were seeing and hearing everything for the first time. Only now it was fear, not novelty, that was sharpening my senses: ahead was the Beach and Kinshasa and the river.

I stood near the receptionist's booth, hoping to chat with the hotelier, but he kept his eyes averted and fussed with his papers. The taxi rolled up the driveway. He swatted a mosquito on his neck and looked up. "*Bon*. Be careful."

"I'll remember what you said about shouting 'American diplomat.'"

His face went blank as though he had no idea of what I was talking about. I felt my stomach turn.

We shook hands and I got in the cab. He stared at me as we pulled out, his eyes as joyless as they were the first night we met, then turned crisply and walked back inside. Les Bougainvillées fell away in the rearview mirror.

We rolled down toward the river, passing the Voix du Congo radio station, the university, the Peace Corps office. Words from what the guidebook said about Kinshasa flitted in and out of my thoughts, as did the warnings about the Beach. I tried to focus on what I was likely to encounter, and how I would behave with the drunken soldiers.

We rattled onto the corniche leading to the port. Ahead, skeins of dust were hanging in the sunlight, dust kicked up by porters pushing bags of cement in wheelbarrows; farther on, the exhaust of pickups and the acrid fumes of scooters added a noxious blue to the browned-out air. We slowed, easing our way into a great bottleneck, into a jostle of sweaty bare backs and shaved heads, honking a path through the tide of shouldered burlap sacks of grain and bobbing bushels of sugar cane, among which moved shouting, commanding, kingly men: fat-cat Zairean businessmen in lavish gold bracelets and designer sunglasses. Everyone was hurrying to make the last ferry before nightfall; no one wanted to land in Kinshasa after dark. We forded the crowd; my driver leaned out of his window and scolded and shook his fist and gunned his engine and pounded his horn, and the porters went bug-eyed and stumbled under their loads as they bumped into each other to get out of our way, but we came up against the pickups and could go no farther.

We were still some way from the steel gates at customs and border control. I paid the driver and forced open the door. In a crush of bare backs, slick with sweat and hot, I struggled to stand up; grain was sifting out of sacks, people were shouting in Lingala and Kikongo; I shouldered my way through the hurly-burly of scratchy burlap and sweaty torsos and bony elbows and plantains.

Next to me popped up a bony fellow in a green BRAZZAVILLE PORT smock. He pointed at my bag. I nodded okay. He hoisted it to his left shoulder and with his right hand beat apart the bodies and shoved through them, looking back to make sure I was keeping up. Lingala and Kikongo were tumbling out of mouths in basso profundo diatribes; soldiers were using their rifle butts to bully the crowd away from the gates. Loaded carts creaked along and threatened my feet, my porter kicked and pushed and ripped his way to the gates and dragged me through.

They slammed behind me. I was free, panting and soaked in perspiration not my own.

"Halt! *Vos papiers!*"

An officer in a navy beret, short and stout as a fire hydrant, stomped up and held out his hand. I gave him my passport. He snarled, his ivory teeth set in an ebony mask, his voice a comedian's parody of a growl. "Big problem! You have no entry stamp!" I did have one and I showed him. He gave me a sly look. "Well, okay, but there are many . . . aah . . . formalities here—will you buy me a beer?"

"If you get me to the ferry without any problems, yes."

Forget about the immorality of rewarding the corrupt. I wanted to get out of Brazzaville and through the Beach as quickly and smoothly as possible. I was, after all, a walking bank: I had almost two thousand dollars' worth of cash (in dollars and French francs) concealed in a pouch under my belt, and two thousand dollars in traveler's checks in my knapsack, plus camera gear. The tactics of intimidation that the hotelier suggested I employ seemed like they could backfire on me, so I decided I would pay police and soldiers *matabiches* (as bribes were locally known) on both sides of the river for their good offices, as I had heard Zairean businessmen did, and lessen the risk of conflict. I would try to look bored, blasé, and basically good-natured, as though I made this sort of trip every day and sympathized with the valiant and underpaid men in blue and green, and was happy to help them out with a buck or two here and there, as long as I was paying for services rendered. Toward this end, I had folded in half a dozen one- and five-dollar bills, plus some French francs, and positioned them in my pants pockets so that I could withdraw them one at a time and not have to produce a tempting wad of banknotes.

The officer disappeared with my passport into a corrugated steel shed marked IMMIGRATION. Kinshasa loomed large in the keen afternoon light. Smoke was rising from somewhere beneath the towers and cranes—was something on fire in the city?

Congo pop blared tinny-sounding from the loudspeakers of the bar past passport control. The porters awaiting new customers were swaying to this music. A couple of them smiled at me. I found my face frozen into its affected expression of casualness, and their smiles took an instant to register with me. When they did, I smiled back.

My porter looked at Kinshasa. "Zaire," he said, almost wistfully. "The land of the great gamble. Wealth, minerals, diamonds— anything is possible there. In Zaire you can win big."

"You've been?"

"No, I don't have the money. Zaire is for big-money men. Just look at the Zairean businessmen around here."

The officer came back. He glanced at the bar and smiled. Wasn't it beer time?

"So where's my passport?"

"Ahh!"

He swelled his chest and stomped over to the shed and barked something into the barred windows. Inside my passport was fluttering from one set of hands to the next. An officer yelled from between the bars: "Come here! We must examine your face!"

I put my face up to the bars. A wincing man, the chief, apparently, shifted on his haunches, snorted, and cleared his throat. He slowly turned his eyes to the picture in my passport, then back to my face, then again to the picture. *Bon.* He assiduously inscribed my name and number in his ledger. Then he asked for the first name of my father and country of birth of my father and then of my mother and so on, writing them all down, licking his lips, furrowing his brow, clearing his throat. This was demanding work, and I would just have to be patient.

My officer pounded on the wall with his fist. The chief handed me my passport. The song changed. I gave my officer a dollar and he nodded thanks and salsaed off to the bar. I paid the porter and moved on to customs. Customs was a plank shed the size of a phone booth, with tattered curtains for a door. I flung them open and walked in. A man in a T-shirt and baggy shorts rose from a stool. He snatched my passport. "Ah, a relative of Mr. Clinton! How much money do you have?"

"Two thousand dollars."

He gulped. "Show me those dollars."

I took out my traveler's checks. He slumped back onto his stool and waved me on.

From his booth, a wobbly ramp, slime-coated, rust-red, and about ten yards long, led out over the churning azure river to a dock, where two double-decked, tugboat-sized ferries were lashed together and rocking in the current. I trod carefully, my smooth-soled shoes slipping on the ramp. Hurried by the sacks and crates on their shoulders, porters, in ragged shorts, their bare feet affording them reliable purchase, rushed by me shouting, *"Attention!"* bouncing the ramp and disrupting my balance, compelling me to clutch the rail. However, slippery as it was, the ramp was well staffed with document specialists: one officer demanded my passport, another inspected my yellow fever vaccination certificate, the next scrutinized my ticket. *Bon. Passez.*

Finally, when I was one last dainty step from the dock, a rail-thin martinet with bug eyes, a sort of red-bereted Congolese Don Knotts, stopped me and ordered me in a squeaky voice to show all of my documents again and I'd better be *tout de suite* about it! He grabbed my yellow vaccination booklet and shuffled its pages. *"Mais c'est trop!* Too many vaccinations! What's in your bag?"

Clothes, I told him.

"Clothes? Let me see your *clothes."* He was swaying, and his eyes were red.

I opened my bag to an Updike novel and a roll of underwear, and *Ho!* A porter tripped and tumbled down the ramp, his sack scraping across the metal, his bare back sliding in the slime, his shins slamming into the railing. He clutched his legs and howled. Don Knotts blew his whistle and brandished his baton—how dare this witless boob slip on *his* ramp!—and made a step onto the ramp, nearly slipped, stepped back and whistled and excoriated the downed man in shrill Lingala.

I shot past him, jumped aboard the ferry, slipped through the crowd on deck, and found a place. A tricycle wheelchair with loaded wagon attached swerved and bounced as it sped down the ramp toward the water, having broken free of its porter; its driver, a polio victim sitting on shriveled legs, was helpless to direct its course. The porter raced to catch up and slipped, the ramp bounced,

the ferry's deck heaved with the current. It would either be too high
or too low for the wheelchair. In spasms of furious maneuvering,
the other wheelchair drivers aboard, and there were many, lurched
their chairs out of the way. The free-rolling wheelchair rebounded
off a mooring post, swerved, and sailed over the foot-wide gap between dock and deck to land on the ferry, its cart losing grain,
shocks of maize, and a jumble of cooking pots as it crashed and rattled to a halt. But the driver kept his seat. Laughing, he raised his
thumbs in victory, and everyone applauded.

As the loading went on, a warm fog dropped between us and
Kinshasa. We were a half hour, then an hour late. I began to per-
spire, as much from the rising humidity as from nerves. Legless
women merchants dragged their boxy torsos over the deck, their
hands shod in plastic sandals, careful to keep their shawls wrapped
around their upper bodies. Properous-looking Zairean men twirled
gold chains and bullied their porters. The porters, I noticed, were
a rugged and handsome lot—men with meticulously shaved heads
and brawny knotted backs—who worked tirelessly.

Finally, when we had carts on top of carts, a dozen limbless
merchants stuffed among sacks of grain and bushels of cane, when
not a free inch remained on deck, a bell started ringing as if for a
two-alarm fire, then a three- then a four-alarm fire, faster and
faster. The captain marched aboard in dress whites and climbed
the stairs to the bridge. The engine hacked and coughed into
steady chugs, smoke belched from the stern, and the boat began
vibrating and rocking. We honked, cast off, swung round, and motored out into the rushing blue currents, heading diagonally across
the river, cutting through the fog, listing hard, with the rafts of
water hyacinth bearing down on us, green in the blue water, hissing as they swept against our sides, hissing and speeding on into
the mists. When we reached midriver a breeze blew over us, a
breeze fresh if not cool, and for the first time since boarding we all
relaxed.

But not for long. Half an hour later the fog fell away and revealed the skyscrapers and cranes of Kinshasa, with smoke at their

bases. The passengers rustled back to life, and a knot formed in my gut. As we drew near, the city that looked so grand and modern from Brazzaville turned into a vision of ruin and charred shells and rot: tin-shack slums huddled along the banks under a shroud of smoke; heaps of warped steel and buckled beams—rusted-out barges and the wrecks of ancient riverboats—crowded the shallows, the current churning through their gutted lower chambers. They were alive, these wrecks, with squatters: eyes peered at us from glassless windows, cooking fires from braziers released pungent aromas into the breeze. On a few of the sterns people stood naked, facing away from us, men and women in separate circles, lathering and scrubbing themselves down, rinsing themselves off.

"Ngobila Beach!" said an old porter next to me in cutoff jeans, his hair a fine dusting of silver on his bony cranium. He hoisted my bag atop his head. At Ngobila Beach was a rusted ramp, down which a crowd was sprinting. Behind them, soldiers, shouldering their rifles, were jogging our way; legless beggars with sandals on their hands began loping in our direction, swinging their torsos along.

We started docking, a laborious bobbing maneuver of lurches and swings in the surging current. There were shouts from the Beach. The soldiers were gesturing—I saw, to my sudden consternation—to *me*, the ragged youths were waving at *me*, even the legless ones were gyrating and motioning to *me*. *Mondele! Le blanc! Ey, le blanc!*

Why?

The ferry crowd stirred and scrimmaged and shoved toward the edge. With a yard of water between our deck, which was heaving in the current, and the dock, which was stable but jammed with rifle-toting soldiers and hailing beggars, the ambulatory contingent of our passenger load started leaping ashore. My porter made the jump. I would have waited, but people pressed at my back; I leapt over the divide, smacking into the backs and arms of those ahead of me, catching my balance to avoid plunging into the narrowing gap between the boat and the dock. But I was ashore.

I pressed ahead, following my porter.

"Halt in your tracks!" a crisp voice commanded in English. "I am from SNIP. Documents!"

A tall man in Ray-Ban sunglasses, strong of jaw, dressed in a shimmering green sports jacket, a starched white shirt, and pressed navy trousers, stood ramrod straight amid a swirl of porters and soldiers, holding out a laminated ID card. I scrutinized it: SNIP stood for Service national de investigation et protection. I took out my passport and he snatched it. The soldiers, black-bereted, in green fatigues, brandishing their rifles, their eyes fogged red, flooded past him and grabbed at me. He waved his arm and they scattered like frightened dogs. "*You* come with *me!*"

He turned and started into the crowd. Looking away from the pairs of wild red eyes, I tried to follow him, but the rush of bodies closed as soon as he passed, and I had to wrench my way through scuffling forearms and gun butts and sweat-stained fatigues. My porter, agile and thin, kept up with me.

We reached an iron gate and the SNIP officer slipped through, but people thronged against the gate on the other side and it slammed in my face, striking me in the cheek; my eyes watered from the pain and my head rang. At my back the crowd heaved and shoved, thrusting me against the bars. The bars indented my cheek; I tried to cry out but I had no breath. My porter was jammed beneath my underarm. I managed to think, *He has my passport!* Then the gate swung open and the SNIP man yanked me and my porter through. "*Viens!*" he said, pulling me by the arm, like an apprehended felon.

Here the soldiers came on harder than ever. "Open those bags!" "Give me money!" "Show me your documents!" From right and left, beer-breathed commands in French were shouted into my face; a soldier grabbed my belt and yanked, pulling me backward and off-balance. My officer kicked him in the shin and the soldier relented, his face a mess of bony cheek and gnarled brow, his eyes red with booze.

"*Viens!*" The SNIP man forced his way ahead, shoving aside

khaki, pummeling his way through berets and rifles. He was heading toward a large blue shed—Immigration and Customs.

Near the shed a woman soldier touched my forearm. She had
long straightened hair done up in a bun and was wearing loopy
gold earrings, and her beret was set way back, like a stylish French
bonnet. She was chewing gum. *"Ouvrez vos bagages!"* she ordered,
smiling and showing me her gum wad.

The SNIP man thrust himself in her face. "The American must
be addressed only in English!" He placed his palm against her
chest and propelled her into the shed wall.

We walked inside the Immigration shed. My porter was still
with us, my bag was still in one piece, my knapsack was intact. But
here there were hallways, corridors of peeling blue paint, and dark
little rooms. I had heard about the little rooms. The little rooms
were to be avoided, no matter what. In those little rooms the officers could shake you down in privacy. You could get beaten up if
you failed to cough up the right bribe. They could strip you down
and find every cent you had, wherever you had hidden it.

"Come!" He strode down the corridor. He stopped by a little
room. He snapped the dust off his lapels and adjusted his Ray-
Bans. "Now, how much money you have?"

I said sixteen hundred dollars, lessening my sum instinctively
and planning to show only my traveler's checks, then thinking I
had still said too much.

"What?"

"One six zero zero dollars."

"One hundred six dollars?" He looked at the little room. "You
come to Zaire with so little money?"

Now was I to counter his suspicion that I was lying by correcting his mistake, or should I hope he believed I was somehow not
worth his trouble? It was easiest to just agree with him.

"Yes. So little money."

He wrote "106" down on a chit and led me by the arm down the
corridor. At the end, outside, we met a chubby man, barefoot and
jovial, whose face was slick with sweat and oil and covered with

pimples. *"Bonsoir!"* he said to me, jingling car keys in his pocket. He looked like a roly-poly inflatable figure—if you hit him he would bounce back up.

Along this side of the shed there were barred-off rooms open to the street, rooms like cages. In the cages were desks stacked with rat-chewed files, pyramids of green and red and blue passports, reams of yellowed papers, scattered banana peels, shards of beer bottles, piles of coffee-stained documents. Behind them were men who looked like prisoners. The SNIP man tossed my passport through the bars and one of the inmates snatched it out of the air. A dispute broke out in Lingala with my precious blue booklet being bandied from criminal to criminal.

The SNIP man exchanged a few words with them, then turned to me. "There is a problem. *Un grand problème.*" His features settled into a mask of the gravest concern. "This is your first time in Zaire. *C'est vrai?*"

"Yes."

"Well, they want to know why you've come."

The driver's oily faced mimicked his suspicion. This was serious, oh, *très trrrès sérieux!* they agreed, rolling their *r*'s in an un-French way and chortling and shaking their heads.

"I'm . . . I'm a tourist."

This sounded ridiculous even to me. But something stopped me from saying anything about my plans—they sounded too ambitious for $106 and might provoke a search or further interest. I looked back at the inmates who had my passport and saw that Zairean businessmen were passing them dollar bills and retrieving their documents.

SNIP shook his head, and the driver waggled his oily noggin as well. SNIP frowned. "*Que c'est sérieux!* You must give the chief of immigration five dollars to solve your problem."

I looked away. I reached into my pocket and fingered through the bills, locating a prefolded five. But as I retrieved it a fifty, which I must have included by mistake, slipped out and fluttered to the ground. SNIP and I both lunged for it, nearly knocking heads, but I got to it first and thrust it back in my pocket. He took the five and marched over to the cage. An unshaven young man in a denim shirt and stained trousers stuck his arm through the bars and took the bill.

Further expostulations in Lingala followed, and both of them scrutinized my passport. My driver jingled his keys. SNIP came back jumpy and apoplectic.

"You lie! *Quelle est votre mission ici?* You are no tourist!"

"I told you, I *am* a tourist."

He stamped his foot. "You are *not!* We have no tourists here! The chief of immigration demands to know your true purpose. What is your mission? Gold? Diamonds? What are you searching for in Zaire?" Veins stood out on his forehead, and he stamped his foot again. "You *must* give fifty dollars to the chief or he won't let you go!"

I turned away. I couldn't think fast enough to retort, but my silence, I hoped, would be taken as expressive of the hauteur of a man who was above it all—a man with a mission, in fact, a mission authorized from somewhere on high. He only said fifty because he'd seen the bill. I would not give him fifty, even to expedite my passage—that was too much. And that unshaven lout behind the bars didn't look like the chief.

The SNIP officer reached inside the bars, grabbed my passport off the desk, and flipped through the pages to my visa. "Look here. You have a six-month, multiple-entry visa. You can come and go for six months. Tourists don't get such visas. You are on a mission, and we must know what it is."

"I know the Zairean ambassador to the United States." This was a lie, but I turned away as though that said it all.

Night would soon come on. The fear of having to drive across Kinshasa in the dark stole over me. The lot was teeming with porters and soldiers and lorries; the smoke, wherever it was coming from in the city, was thickening. I reached into my other pocket and fished out a fifty-franc (ten-dollar) note and handed it to SNIP. He smirked and looked away, then took it and gave it to the "chief," who started yelling in Lingala. But he gave me back my passport.

The porter hoisted my bag to his shoulder, the driver flipped his key chain, and we set off for his cab—a lopsided, 1950s station wagon with busted side windows and a cracked windshield. I paid and parted with my porter. The SNIP man was close on my heels; I got in the front seat, and he jumped in the back.

"Now is the biggest problem of all," he declared, leaning over my ear. "Ahead there are ten police checkpoints. The cost is ten dollars each. You must give me one hundred dollars so that I can give the bribes to each checkpoint, or you will be turned back."

"No."

He launched into another round of histrionics and accusations of espionage and diamond dealing, but the driver started the engine.

"No," I repeated.

When SNIP repeated his demand I held up a ten-dollar bill. He laughed, he shook his fists, he screeched, he begged, and he bellowed; he kicked the back of my seat. The driver pulled his station wagon out a few feet and stopped. SNIP shut up, plucked the bill out of my hand with his thumb and forefinger, hopped out, and leaned into my window. "So," he smiled, "when will we see each other again?"

"*Allons!*" I told the driver.

He pressed his bare foot to the accelerator, and we lurched out of the lot.

I settled back into my seat, incredulous. All that had to have been an act, an act performed with the intent to fleece me—or had it been? What would the soldiers have done to me had SNIP not shown up? Nothing? Or would I have been robbed and beaten to a pulp?

Fifteen yards on, at a crossbar, a soldier leapt into the road. Puffing up his cheeks, he blew his whistle and thrust out his arm.

"Halt! *Arrêtez-vous!*"

His gesture was so exaggerated that I had to laugh, and he laughed, too, laughed and bared his teeth and put his face through my window. "Passport! Ah, America! A great power! Give me a big American present!"

I laughed and said no. In my pockets I had only tens and the fifty left, and I was not going to part with them. But his smile dropped away and his voice turned hoarse. "I said give me a present. How much money do you have?" Two other soldiers came out of the hut behind him, their rifles swinging from their shoulders.

The driver whipped a half-dozen zaire notes out of his pocket and handed them to him. When the soldier stepped aside to count, we shot past them. "The soldiers are dangerous," the driver said flatly. "You should not play with the soldiers."

There were no more checkpoints. The sun was going down, and fast. We swung out onto an avenue of cracked tar, skirting the jagged bidonvilles of the Cité, the old town. On every corner glowed burning middens four and five feet high, and smoke hung in layers, gilt in patches by the fires, and we rattled through the smoke. The traffic lights were dark. The driver kept his bare foot pressed on the accelerator; we jostled for position amid honking trucks with lean young men hanging off the sides, trucks that whirled the smoke into giant curlicues that hung in the air and slowly fell away. Here and there pairs of women in dashikis sauntered by, swinging their bottoms, balancing baskets on their heads, laughing and talking loudly, their bare feet raising lazy trails of ashen dust; emaciated children raced along, pushing wheels with sticks, kicking soccer balls made of rags, all amid a vista of palm trees and middens, bombed-out neighborhoods of cinder block huts and steel shacks. Everything was an apparition, dim under a pall of smoke, smoke that was now suffused with the molten hues of the dying sun.

The sky went black. Cooking fires flared up on the corners, illuminating faces and figures; the smoke caught hues of red and orange from the fires.

A half hour later, we pulled into the sandy lot by the Afrique Hôtel.

Kinshasa

THE MANAGER AT THE AFRIQUE HÔTEL WAS A TALL WOMAN WITH the graceful, loping gait of a lioness and the sculptured cheekbones and aquiline nose of an Ethiopian princess. Or at least I *thought* she resembled an Ethiopian princess. My guidebook, which highly recommended the hotel, described her as a "friendly Ethiopian woman," so after asking her for a room, to be friendly myself, I made an inquisitive remark about Addis Ababa.

"Addis *what?*" She looked puzzled. I explained myself. She shook her head languidly. "I don't know the Ethiopian manager you speak of. I'm from Rwanda. Maybe she was here before, but the *pillages* changed everything." *Les pillages* was how people referred to the army looting sprees of 1991 and 1993 that decimated the country.

She led me down the hall to a room and opened the door. I peered inside. The air conditioner had been torn off the mold-mottled walls; all that remained by way of appliances was a sparking bare bulb dangling on a rat-chewed wire. The bed was a mess of sweat-splotched sheets that recalled a former occupant's sleepless night passed in battle with mosquitoes, which must have been many: the windows wouldn't shut, and if they had, it wouldn't have mattered. they had no glass. The cracked knob on the bathroom door cut my thumb when I grabbed it. The toilet had no seat and the shower no head. Toad-sized roaches scratched their way across fruit-peel rubbish on the concrete floor.

The manager looked at me. "Well?"

"I'll take it."

I wasn't about to set out into Kinshasa at this late hour. She gave me the key and scuffed out. I stripped the bed and erected my mosquito net atop it—a sort of tent with gauze walls and a solid nylon base—and resolved to make do.

All that night I writhed in and out of sleep, languishing in the damp heat, listening to the crickets chirp, the moths flutter, the rats squeak. The room swarmed with mosquitoes; whenever one of my limbs brushed the net, it was set upon and bitten to the point of pain. Now and again I grabbed Nabokov's *Lolita,* which I had found in the Peace Corps office, and tried to read it. But I kept looking up from the pages and marveling: I had arrived.

In the morning the sun oppressed the palms and heated the mists into steam. I arose early and decided to go into the center, my first task being to change money. Outside the hotel lopsided trucks and rattling jitney cabs, crammed with people and stirring up clouds of ashen dust, sputtered and honked down the broken black macadam. They looked unsafe, so I waited for a regular taxi.

With a *toot-toot,* a wheeled contraption of smoking steel and protruding wires was slowly swerving off the road onto the dusty shoulder and bearing down on me. By the traces of yellow paint on its rusted sides I recognized it as a cab.

"À la Banque du Zaïre!" I shouted at it. The driver, an old fellow in rags, slowed but did not stop, and he feebly waved for me to get in. Jogging along, I pulled on the door handle but it was stuck; he fumbled with the latch on the inside and yanked. The door swung open—and the motor went dead. I climbed aboard.

The driver's face was patchy pink and brown with pellagra; his arms were spindles of bone sheathed in flaccid skin. He sat for a moment looking down, as if recovering from a tragedy. Then he reached under the dashboard and pulled out two wires, which he pressed together, and after a couple of minutes of sparks and zaps, the engine cranked back to life. I tried to settle into my seat. Springs popped up through shreds of upholstery; the window handles had fallen off; the windshield was a spider's web of cracks, and it would take just one nudge to cave it in.

The driver coughed, and pressing his bony toes to the accelerator, turned the wheel, which rotated with a squeak. We slowly rolled off the shoulder and joined the caravan of weaving jalopies heading for the center. He rocked back and forth in his seat, as if by doing so he could hurry his vehicle along. Perhaps his motions weren't deliberate—maybe he had a nervous disorder or suffered from spasms—but they accorded with our ever more dubious progress. The cab was now filling with exhaust, but it didn't matter—there was no glass in the side windows, and the fumes whirled out. Still, by any standard, it would not have been an exaggeration to say we were "on fire," but judging by the wheezing, smoking array of similarly ancient vehicles in our caravan, all of them mobile assortments of wires, bald tires, rust, and dangling youths, such a state of ignition was nothing extraordinary, and I tried to relax about it.

The traffic lights were dead, and every intersection was an impromptu pedestrian market made up of jaunty, lean young men circulating in the sun with cigarette displays mounted on their heads; lean young men selling manioc root sheathed in leaves, known in Lingala as *shikwanga;* lean young men sporting twenty wristwatches on each arm or peddling gray-red parrots in cages, the same birds one saw in the trees everywhere. The high cheekbones and well-trimmed haircuts of these merchants gave them a spiffy aspect; despite looking thin enough to be hungry, they moved along with a kind of *joie de vivre* and grace I had not seen in more prosperous Brazzaville.

There was suddenly a staccato rapping on the rear of the car. A soldier was strutting up to the driver's window, candy-stripe baton in hand. My driver slumped in his seat and groaned, "The Garde civile."

The soldier thrust his mug into the open window, his white helmet fastened low over his red eyes by a too-tight chinstrap. He shrieked, *"Tes papiers! Tes papiers tout de suite!"*

The driver reached for the glove compartment and rummaged through shreds of yellowed documents, greasy wrappers, and pencil stubs, his breathing raspy, his eyes blinking and watery, his fingers trembling.

"*Tes papiers!*" *Rap-rap-rap!*

Smoke from the idling engine was filling our cabin. The driver found his license but held it over my lap, and, thinking he meant me to take it for some reason, I grasped it, but he pulled it out of my hands.

"*Pesa ngai ton permit!*"

The soldier shrieked and leaned through the window and snatched at the license, his long-nailed fingers whizzing by my eyes like claws, *snatch, whizzz, snatch*. The driver yanked it out of his reach, emitting tiny grunts and coughs with the exertion, his toes splaying on the floor.

The traffic jam eased. The driver pressed the accelerator and we lurched ahead, with the soldier's head and shoulders still in the cab. Seconds later he dropped away and tumbled in the dust, his baton flailing.

"The Garde civile. They never give you your license back if you let them have it," he said, looking back to see that the soldier was not following us. "They want money. They are *méchants*." *Méchant*. Vicious, mean. I was to hear the word over and over in Zaire. Men in uniform, be they soldiers from the Garde civile or gendarmes or policemen, were always *méchants*. They were considered, in a way, a tribe apart, as different from ordinary people as weasels or jackals, with innumerable nasty traits.

Ahead rose the modern apartment and office towers I had seen from Brazzaville. Beneath them, on Boulevard du 30 Juin, between the palms, faded billboards promoted Miki skin-lightening cream and Shabair, Primus beer and Scibé-Airlift, all with cheery, 1950s-style painted advertisements. Men—little more than skeletons in rags—wandered down sun-bleached, trashed-out side streets, stirring up ash-colored dust. In the garbage heaps, which were still smoldering from last evening, starvelings scavenged on their knees, or twitched and groaned, prostrate in the offal and debris, too weak to move.

I could not stomach the sight and turned away.

"We are sick here," the driver said, setting his filmy yellow eyes on mine. "We are a sick people. Sick with malaria and other diseases."

I did not know what to say, and I could not bear to look into his eyes. My gaze fell to the creases in his hands, the skin on his forearms. Maybe he was not so old; maybe hunger and disease had desiccated him, wasted him away, made each of his years the equivalent of ten of mine.

We rolled along Boulevard du 30 Juin. That the city had been the showpiece of Mobutu's Zaire was impossible to forget: the twenty-two-story glass-and-concrete Sozacom building, head-quarters to the country's once-thriving mining industry, still towered above Boulevard du 30 Juin, which was a multilaned thoroughfare of banks and ramshackle office buildings, many closed or abandoned, and embassies. But the smoke of burning garbage floated under the palms; the sun was flooding down razor-sharp, bleaching away colors and lending the city the incin-erated look of Hiroshima after the blast. Dust, decay, crazed men in uniforms, starvelings, and cripples—it all hit me and I nearly broke. I felt nausea rising within me; pity and revulsion and shock swamped me and kept at bay the fear I had thought I would feel. Although I had expected to see poverty, I had no idea it would upset me so thoroughly, so viscerally.

The cabbie dropped me off at the Bank of Zaire. The bank seemed like a logical place to seek Zairean currency, but the em-ployee I approached scoffed at me with a mix of outrage and incredulity ("*Money?!* The bank has no money! It hasn't had money since the *pillages!*"), and told me to try a big hotel, so I next visited the Intercontinental. But the Intercontinental was out of cash as well. The receptionist, who at least said he was sorry not to be able to help me, came out from around the counter. "Money is a problem here. You could try Wall Street. That's what we call the black market for money changers. But it's dan-gerous. There are thieves and soldiers there, so you shouldn't go alone. For now you might try paying for something cheap with a big bill in an Indian store. That should work."

On a nearby corner I found an Indian-owned grocery store and paid for a candy bar with a fifty-dollar bill. The cashier, a Hindu with dark circles under his sympathetic eyes, handed me my change in zaires—almost two thousand banknotes—and gave me a paper bag to carry them in.

Next I had to see about a boat upriver.

⌁⌁⌁

Hundreds of people were camped out by the docks at the main Congo River shipping company, Marsavco. It was late afternoon by the time I made it there. Women in floral dress were frying bananas and dough balls over charcoal braziers; naked children were chasing each other in circles; elderly men were sitting and waiting amid a profusion of blankets and cardboard suitcases. Beyond them spread the river, a pane of bluish silver and glare dotted with moving clumps of water hyacinth. Far, far on the other bank, like a vision from another life, was Brazzaville.

The guards at the gate directed me to the administration building. There I explained my needs to a clerk. She said there was a boat leaving in a few hours, a cargo barge, and a spot on deck would cost thirty dollars. No bed, no food, no bathroom, no water provided. In fact, even the spot on deck was doubtful, but the ticket would give me the right to board, and I could jostle with the rest of the passengers for space. The trip could take two weeks, a month, or six weeks. I had to decide now.

I told her no: I wasn't yet equipped. But what about the state-owned ferries that plied the river? The *Colonel Ebeya,* I had heard in Brazzaville, still made the trip. She told me that the *Ebeya* hadn't run in four years, and all the other ferries had broken down long ago. It was doubtful that they would be repaired. Ever.

Dispirited, I thanked her and walked out to a balcony overlooking the dock. I looked at the campers. What was I to do?

There was a tap on my shoulder. "You look at the people?" A

young man with a very flat nose and a sweaty forehead, dressed in a pink Oxford shirt, a blue tie, and cream trousers leaned against the railing next to me. "They have been waiting a week for the boat. But the boat doesn't go." He was speaking English, English that was measured and a touch pedantic. "Excuse me if I bother you. My name is Luv. May I help you?"

Luv said he was an English instructor for the shipping company; he wiped his brow and gripped the rail, his face turning gray, and asked what I was doing here. I told him I was here to find out about boats.

"Then you should talk to my student, Pierre, director of transportation. Come." He led me back inside, past the clerk's desk.

Pierre sat behind a sturdy desk in an immaculate, air-conditioned office where a cell phone served as a paperweight and a green computer screen showed boat routes and schedules. He wore a checkered shirt and a tailored blue blazer, and his mustache and broad forehead recalled Martin Luther King's, as did his frank baritone. His thick shoulders suggested strength, the strength to get the job done. This comforted me—at least someone here was healthy—and I relaxed in his presence. Speaking in French, he welcomed me to his office and asked me to take a seat. I wanted to get down to business and ask him about boats, but Luv, sweating and changing color again, interrupted and explained my request in English. Pierre, whose English was weak, took a while to get the drift.

Pierre's cell phone rang and he answered. While he was talking, Luv leaned toward me. "I apologize: I'm ill with malaria, I think. Eighty percent of our people are starving and ill. If you go to the hospital you will see the corpses of the young, the mature, and the old. Their families have not the money to bury them so they leave it to the state, but the state has not the money, so it dumps the bodies in the river. The politicians, the top few percent, steal from the people, who can do nothing but die." He coughed; fresh beads of sweat popped out on his forehead. "Yes, the only recourse the people have is death." He stood up. "Please excuse me. I think I shall go to the hospital. My student will help you."

He shook my hand with a feverish palm and walked out.

Pierre finished his phone conversation and looked at me. "Well, about boats. We had a barge going to Kisangani today—the *Forestière*. But I've just learned it's broken down. I will see about a boat for you later this week or next. I will arrange a cabin for you, a luxury cabin. But why do you want to go to Kisangani?"

I told him my pirogue plans. As I spoke, he pressed his hands together and listened. I finished, and he studied my eyes, saying nothing.

He leaned forward and cleared his throat. He said that he had never heard of anyone trying such a descent, and he thought I would need a motorboat. I insisted that, no, I would go by pirogue. In fact, I *had* to go by pirogue: that was the point. He looked at me, letting a moment of silence pass. After straightening his collar and adjusting his sleeves, he spoke again. "Well, this is a serious matter. You cannot go alone. You will need two men, one to paddle and one to guide. The river is wide, wide! The wind raises waves and the storms are fierce. In the great forest you will travel for days without seeing a village, and there are many animals. You will need a gun." His diction was precise, his manner poised. "From Kisangani to Mbandaka you will face the dangers of the jungle: the crocodiles and hippos and leopards. But from Mbandaka to here you'll face another problem, which can be worse: the soldiers. You see, that part of the river is the border with the Congo Republic, and there are patrols looking for smugglers. The soldiers are hungry. They are not paid, and they are often drunk or stoned. They will loot you." He leaned back. "Yes, they will loot you, certainly they will loot you. What's more, without permission from the military, you will be taken for a spy."

"A spy?"

"A spy, certainly. No whites travel that way, except, perhaps, mercenaries. You will need permission from the military."

At the mention of the military I froze. Mobutu's elite came to mind, as did political killings and black-market diamond deals, copper trading and corruption. It could be dangerous getting in-

volved with such men, and I had nothing but a visitor's visa; I had
no sponsor or official contacts to establish who I was or to protect
me. Trying to change the subject, I said that for now I was most
interested in getting a cabin on a barge upriver; the rest I would
decide later.

"Even on a barge you should be protected," Pierre insisted.
"You must have permission for your pirogue trip. Without permission and guards, you will not be able to travel. I will arrange
this for you tomorrow. Be here at nine sharp. You will be taken to
see a colonel who is close to Mobutu."

Close to Mobutu? "But . . ." I didn't know what to say. "But
I . . ." Then I shut up, needing time to think.

Pierre rose. "I'm sorry, I must go home. It's getting late."

He walked out with me. Islands, unseen earlier in the glare, had
appeared on the horizon and were breaking up the expanses of the
river, which was now shimmering with orange and pink, reflecting
the sky inflamed by the setting sun. Families were settling in for
the night—the dock now looked like a refugee camp. The mosquitoes were already swarming. I asked Pierre how people who had no
nets dealt with them.

"Ils sont habitués." They're used to them. He shook my hand
curtly, said *à demain,* and walked off, and I caught a taxi back to
my hotel.

✐✐✐

Near my hotel that evening I discovered a posh, Japanese-owned
restaurant and went there to eat. Its interior gleamed white. On
television the *Baywatch* team cavorted on a California beach for
the coiffed Zairean diners, who sipped iced colas and speared
cheese-glazed french fries on polished forks. Pamela Andersen,
dubbed into French, aroused no specific comment, even among
the men; rather, the scenes of beaches and healthy bodies worked
on the audience as a sort of narcotic, suppressing the need for conversation: the diners simply chewed their food and stared at the
screen.

At the table next to mine a cell phone rang. A Zairean in black leather pants and a purple silk shirt, his fingers covered in gold rings, put down his fork and answered *oui*. He rose and walked a few feet away from the noise of the television, picking at his gold-brocaded belt with one hand and holding his phone in the other. *"Oui . . . oui . . . tout est en règle! Tout est en règle!"* he shouted, switching from French to Lingala and back. The date was set: they would meet at the Belgian Club. He walked back to his table, tucked in his napkin, blew the dust off his fork, and plunged it into a chunk of freshly grilled beef. Whenever the restaurant door opened, beggars sitting on the steps in the humid, mosquito-infested blackness outside, their legs shriveled with polio, extended their bony hands and whined at the diners.

Listening to their whining it was tough to eat my food. What would stop, *should* stop, the poor here from murdering the rich? Here, where the rich stole everything and left the poor to starve, who could blame the looters and the bandits? The wealthy in Zaire raped the poor; the poor had the moral justification to do the same to them. These were hardly novel notions, but they suddenly seemed new and self-evident and incontrovertible to me, made cogent by what I had seen during the day and what I was seeing now as I tried to eat. I thought back on the Cold War, about how Western countries justified aiding Mobutu, about how, from the States or Europe, it had often appeared that the Cold War had had few victims and was largely a matter of perceived threat and high defense expenditures. But it did have victims, millions of them, and it had victors; and both were right in front of me, all around me. Zaireans were either one or the other, rarely anything in between, and mostly the former.

It was my country that had helped create this hell (for that was what Kinshasa had shown itself to be, a wrecked, malarial hell), and my primitive musings on the right of the poor to plunder had to mean something for me as well—for who and what was I? I was not one of the poor. I had everything I needed to survive in either Moscow or the States; but I was preparing to risk my life amid people who had nothing. What mercy would I deserve from a bandit who might jump me as I walked back to my hotel, steal my last dollar, and slit my throat?

None.

None. But I was here now, having quit my job and left my loved ones; I had come too far to turn back. I was not a Zairean; I told myself that my presence here would hurt no one, just as my absence, should I pack up and leave, would help no one.

If I dwelled on the misery around me I would end up letting my guard down, but I could expect no leniency from any hungry thug or vicious soldier who might come at me as a result. In order to succeed in my venture—indeed, in order to live through it—I was going to have to stop reacting to my heart and start obeying the dictates of survival. If this place was hell, I would get one of the devils to take me through it. I grabbed my fork and ate. I thought back on Pierre's promise of help. I knew what I had to do, and now I would do it.

The Colonel

THE COLONEL'S SECRETARY DROVE FAST, BARRELING THROUGH the rubbish on Boulevard du 30 Juin, speeding unhindered through gendarme checkpoints, pulling into opposite lanes to skirt blocked traffic, leaning on the horn to scatter beggars and peddlers. Somewhere behind the Marché Central he turned down an dirt alley that led into a neighborhood of cement walls and faceless low buildings. By a pair of steel gates, a guard in plain clothes slouched in his chair, an automatic rifle on his lap. As we pulled into the driveway he stood up and opened the gates, and we drove onto an enclosed lot with more guards milling about. One of them rushed to open the car door for me and I stepped out. Ahead of us stood a single-story white stucco building.

The secretary led me inside. Enthroned behind an oak desk was the Colonel. Sturdily built and well perfumed, dressed in black trousers and a silk shirt of midnight blue that bulged at the belly, he looked to be in his early forties. His jaw and nose pointed forward in a way that called to mind a fox. His darting eyes filled the room with the tense energy of a predator, and that energy gave him an unsettling, vaguely threatening charisma. Above him hung a portrait of himself in full dress whites; on another wall was Mobutu in a leopardskin cap; and a third picture showed Mobutu and the Colonel greeting each other at some sort of ceremony. Beneath the portraits a dozen or so supplicants sat sunk in deep sofas, their knees jutting up to their chests. The Colonel didn't acknowledge me when I entered. I took a seat on a sofa, and my knees jutted up to my chest.

In a patois of high-pitched Lingala and French, the Colonel was discussing a business deal with a man sitting in a chair in front of his desk. The Colonel was adamant: the man had no idea of how to propose a profitable venture. "I'm in this to make money," the Colonel hissed, slitting his eyes. "You fail to understand that. You talk like a child, and I have no time for children."

Hands cupped together, the supplicant began pleading, but the Colonel turned away to a hulking young man standing behind him and said something about the *mondele* and the Secrétariat Général. Stepping forward, the young man pulled out a set of car keys and nodded to me. He was trimmer than the Colonel but resembled him. His shoulders rippled under a starched collarless white shirt; his baby-blue Italian jeans bulged with muscles at the thighs and calves. He wore mirrored sunglasses and a gold bracelet; gold rings adorned his thick fingers. I freed myself from the grasp of the sofa and followed him out. Despite his size he walked with grace, trailing a scent of Italian cologne.

He preceded me into the lot. Parked at one end was a boat-sized silver Mercedes, freshly washed, with black-tinted windows. He raised his keys, clicked, and the doors unlocked.

As we backed out he spoke in French, his bass voice lilting with the cadences of Lingala. "I am the brother of the Colonel. The Colonel has put me in charge of you. First we're going to the Secrétariat Général du Tourisme to get your photo permit." The Mercedes hummed, the air-conditioning purred. Behind the tinted windows Kinshasa slipped by like a silent movie. We pulled onto the boulevard and he forded the crowds, driving with one hand on the wheel, his gold bracelet jingling with the turns. "Taking pictures is illegal here without a permit, *tu vois.*"

A ways on he swerved up onto the sidewalk and stopped. We entered a nondescript government building. Patting his gelled coiffure, he strode ahead of me. There was a guard at the end of the hallway.

"I am the brother of Colonel Ekoondo," he announced. The guard stepped aside. We walked past him and headed up the stairs to the director's office.

The brother interrupted a conversation between the director

and another man and introduced me as "the tourist who wants to go from Kisangani to Kinshasa by pirogue . . . who must have a photo permit."

"Come back tomorrow and it will be ready," the director said, half-rising from his seat and bowing to us. I wrote down my passport details for him and we left.

Back at the compound, we found the Colonel walking out. "You come!" he commanded, looking at no one in particular, as we passed at the door. The brother continued on his way inside. Thinking the Colonel must have been addressing me, I followed him to the black BMW he was approaching and got in with him.

We drove back out into the city. After a while he spoke. "I'm going to take you on my boat all the way to Kisangani. I'm doing this as a favor to Pierre, my great friend. I will ask the Chief of Military Intelligence in the Office of the President to issue you a *lettre de recommandation* for your journey. This will grant you the right to aid from military bases up and down the river. And it will give you the right to an armed escort. You must have armed guards, or you will not survive."

The Office of the President—that meant Mobutu! I did not know what to say. I felt sudden anxiety: Why was this Colonel doing this for me? What would he expect of me in return?

He anticipated the question. "You will pay me nothing."

We arrived at the docks. It was a cloudy day. The gray river spread away from us, fused by nacreous mist to the gray sky. The pirogues on the water looked tiny, the fishermen aboard them puny. They poled and paddled hard against the current, which seemed ever about to pull them away into the mist.

The Colonel got out and, without looking at me, started walking, taking long, easy steps. I followed along, trying to keep up. "My boat!" he announced, as if to the river, gesturing broadly.

A barge of rusted steel, about fifty yards long, with a set of orange cabins on both ends, rocked ten feet beneath the dock (the river was low), lashed at its stern by oversize cables to the bow of a blue-and-white tugboat. Here and there workmen on board hammered

metal, sawed wood, carted around buckets of paint. A foot-wide
plank, shifting with the motion of the boat, led from the dock
down to the deck at a forty-five-degree angle. The Colonel jogged
down it, and it wobbled wildly with his weight.

"Viens!" he shouted, for the first time turning to look at me.

Catching sight of the water rushing violently between the hull
and dock, I placed a foot on the plank and felt it wobble. I froze.

"Ah, ha! You are afraid!" He roared with laughter. Nearby, a
ladder led down to the deck. I used that instead. "Come, I'll show
you around," he said, turning away from me again. He led me off
the barge and onto the tugboat, which he called the *pousseur,* or
pusher. We climbed a ladder to the upper deck, and he threw open
a door.

"My cabin!"

His cabin had a bed and a shower in the back room, and workmen were outfitting the front room with bookshelves, a VCR, and
a stereo system. All in all, it was a comfortable, even homey, white-
walled apartment.

We descended the ladder, made our way along the side of the
pousseur, and climbed back onto the barge. The Colonel ripped
open a hatch. The hold. *"Viens!"*

He climbed down inside and so did I. We found ourselves
standing below deck in a unlit dungeon of sorts that squeaked
with rats, a half-inch of river water sloshing at our feet. A shudder
of claustrophobia ran through me.

"You can sleep here," he said, gesturing into the black. As he
climbed out he stole a look at my face. "Ha-ha-ha!"

Next he wandered over to one of the cabins at the stern and
opened the door: it was a windowless, rusted-out, lizard's-nest
scullery of steel with a pair of wooden bunks and hardly room
enough to stand. "Or you can sleep here," he said. This time he
did not laugh. He walked away and started talking with the workers. Then, without notice, he sprang back up the gangplank to the
dock. The tour was over. I climbed the ladder and followed him to
his BMW.

Once we were moving again, he spoke, looking ahead, interrupting me when I tried to ask questions. This was to be the maiden voyage of the barge. The eleven-hundred-mile trip upriver would take two weeks and not a day more; the engines were powerful and brand-new. He had a servant and provisions; I would have to bring all my own food and water and cook for myself. Was I strong? I would have to be: there would be much malaria and dysentery, and no doctors along the way.

I mustered as much spirit as I could and said I was strong and ready. But I was suddenly nearly sick with fear. The huge river, the rusted craft, the water in the hold, the dank cabin—how could I stand it all? And the *lettre de recommandation* from the Office of the President—I still did not know what to make of it. What had I done—or what was I supposed to do—to deserve it?

~~~

The next day I returned to the Colonel's office, and the guards told me to wait outside for his brother—he was taking me somewhere important. Soon the silver Mercedes drove up, and I got in.

Half an hour later we were on the forested outskirts of Kinshasa, coasting down a gravel driveway toward a gate and a crossbar. On either side there were high walls crowned with barbed wire. Headquarters for Military Intelligence, the brother said. A cluster of red-bereted guards emerged from a hut. They were gangly, hyped-up, and wild-eyed; they swaggered over to us on lanky legs, swinging their rifles, and shouted something in Lingala.

The brother slowly turned his head toward them. "I am the brother of Colonel Ekoondo."

They straightened up and backed off. We drove through, parked, and walked up to a door with more guards.

"I am the brother of Colonel Ekoondo."

The guards parted and we entered. The brother strutted along, flipping the keys on his chain, patting his hair, leaving in his wake the aroma of Gucci perfume. Down the hall more soldiers scurried out of his path, and he flung open a door.

"I am the brother of the Colonel."

A clerk jumped from behind his desk and motioned us into yet another office, a cool, wainscotted room in which heavy red curtains kept out the light and an air conditioner was humming. A half-dozen guards in camouflage uniforms were standing around the desk of a small man in civilian clothes.

"This American must have a soldier," the brother announced. "He is going on a dangerous mission."

The small man politely asked for my passport and noted down the details, then handed it back to me. He cleared his throat and looked up: "Are you willing to pay for his food?"

I said I was.

"Bon. Pas de problème."

The brother turned and walked out. I thanked the man and followed the brother back to the lot. There, after the air-conditioning, the humidity hit me hard. When we drove out through the compound gates, black clouds were massing above the forest.

◢◢◢

Pierre suggested that I move out of the Afrique Hôtel (it was, he said, a den of thieves) and proposed I stay a few blocks away from the shipping company at the hotel compound of the Centre D'Accueil Protestant, in the placid old colonial quarter of Kinshasa known as the Ville. The receptionist at the Centre, a dowdy young Zairean in a clip-on tie and church blazer, frowned when I walked in. *"Ici, pas de putains, pas d'alcool!"* he declared right away, as though suspecting that I had chosen his mission for a mad debauch. That was fine with me. He assigned me an expensive but clean Spartan room just off the manicured garden. The other guests were Zairean pastors from all over the country—a smiling lot who appeared to have adopted a dress code mandating no African color, spirit, or natural fabrics. But the Centre was quiet and salubrious and granted me sound sleep, so I was glad to be there.

Later in the parking lot I met an American, Jim. He was a pasty fellow with a musty air who worked for an American evangelical

organization in Zaire, but his thick hands told me he did something other than flip the pages of a Bible all day. In fact, he was an
agriculture specialist and spent most of his time in the bush. He
asked me to have brunch with him the next day, and I accepted.

Sunday brunch at the American Club was a tradition for many of
Kinshasa's expatriates. Walled off and well guarded, with its own
tennis courts, game room, and bar, the club was set in the Ville,
not far from the Centre. You were never farther away from the
chaos of Kinshasa than inside the club's walls. Although it was not
affiliated with the Centre D'Accueil Protestant, it had the same
atmosphere: bloodless, buttoned up, and Anglo-Saxon. Jim introduced me to our lunchmates—an overfed Canadian couple in their
mid-forties and their teenage son, and a pudgy, pallid American
named Bob, whose bald, egg-shaped head sprouted curlicues of
mouse-brown hair over the ears. They were all missionaries and
had been in Zaire a long time.

We ordered burgers, fries, Cokes, and milkshakes. Some
church business was discussed, a bit of gossip was passed along,
and Jim explained what I was doing in Zaire. The husband nodded mutely, the wife buttered a roll. Smiles. Then the son farted
like a foghorn. They all thought this hilarious and worthy of com-
mentary. ("*That* was sure polite! Whoa, what a stinker!") Bob, recovering from his guffaws, turned to me. "Oh, *my!* Well, anyway,
you're going to learn a *lot* about Zaire on your trip. And I know
what you're going to learn. I like to say I'm not a racist, just a realist That's how I like to put it. You see, I've done some work upriver myself."

I suppressed a jumble of negative reactions and asked, "How
was it?"

"Tough. They've had a terrible problem with people getting
hacked to pieces up there"—here he chomped through a french
fry in multiple, squirrel-like bites—"with machetes and so forth.
Hacked into *little* pieces."

"I've heard they've got a lot of bandits around Pimo," said Jim.

"Yeah," Bob answered. "They'll slit your throat for a buck up there. Say, you taking a barge upriver? Well, a lot of people don't make it all the way."

"What do you mean?"

"The Zairean passengers on the barge—they're something. You'll have hundreds of 'em with you. They'll piss in the water and drink it and get cholera." He gurgled down some cola and smacked his lips. "That's how smart they are. Like I said, I'm not a racist, just a realist." *Burp.*

The son slurped his drink through his straw. They stared at him with mock disgust. He laughed and snorted cola out of his nose. More laughter and pounding on the table. Oh, *my!*

Bob continued. "So, like I was saying, they get cholera and die and they just toss the bodies overboard. And you can die of malaria, too. It's a horrendous problem up there. You may have to be medevacked." He chomped into his burger. "Ever been medevacked?" he asked, showing me a mouthful of burger.

The Canadian said the river was a labyrinth, "and many of the waterways end in marsh. You'll get lost without a guide."

"How do I get one?" I asked.

Bob answered for him. "Talk to Frère Franky in Kisangani. If he's still there, of course. Frère Franky had a drinking problem. He may be drying out in Europe by now."

The Canadian salted his fries. "I'm afraid most of the missionaries along the river have already left. They got tired of paying bribes on bribes. You won't have much company."

"Yeah," said Bob, examining the bite hole in his burger. "Only Zaireans are left up there, so you'll have a *lot* of fun. Like I said, I'm not a racist, just a realist."

The Canadian kept to the subject. "Sadly, these are not the days to canoe around Zaire. It's just too dangerous with the soldiers on the loose. A revolt can start up in no time."

I explained that a Zairean colonel was helping me. I told them about the barge, the permit I was going to receive, the trip to

Military Intelligence, and the offer of armed protection. They put down their forks and shared a moment of disbelief.

Jim broke the silence. "Why would this colonel help *you?*" Do you have some sort of official connections or something? If you don't mind me asking, who the heck are *you?* They don't give a hoot here about expats."

"Not a *hoot,*" Bob said, scarfing down his last chunk of burger.

I couldn't answer. Why *was* the Colonel helping me?

Jim went on. "Look, be careful. Be really careful getting involved with these people. You've got to know their motives, and their motives are never good. Why, just last month, this Zairean friend and I were out in the bush near here. We stopped for some soldiers at a checkpoint. While we were haggling over the bribe we'd have to pay to get by—just to pass you have to cough up some money—one of them bayoneted our rear tires. But we didn't know. We drove on and a minute later the wheel went *bumpety-bump.* I slowed down and said I'd change it. 'Don't stop!' my friend shouted. 'They'll catch up and rob us if we stop!' So we drove another couple of miles on the flat and changed the tire. To gain time. You see, I thought we'd paid the bribe and gotten away but they were thinking ahead of us."

Bob added, "All these generals are buying barges so that they have something to make a living on when Mobutu goes. That makes sense. But what you're supposed to do for *him* doesn't. What's the catch? A colonel doesn't need you for *anything.*"

The lunch dragged on. The son passed more gas. They all laughed and slapped their knees. We got the bill, split it, and went our separate ways. Whether the Zaireans considered it as such or not, the presence of these missionaries in Zaire seemed to me an affront, a holdover from colonial days as humiliating for the country as it was disgusting and embarrassing for me, and I resolved to seek no help from them throughout my trip, whatever the circumstances. But their suspicion of the Colonel's motives matched my own, and I found myself wondering if I wasn't getting deep into something I did not understand.

✦✦✦

One day, before dropping in on Pierre, I found I had to change more money. A walk around the Ville landed me at a South African bank just off Boulevard du 30 Juin. There I was received by the congenial young managers, Marc and George, as a long-lost friend. They changed more dollars for me into zaires and offered me the use of their safe during my journey. In fact, they said that they would do anything they could to help me prepare for my trip. I told them I had to outfit myself for the barge—could they lend me a driver and car? That would be no problem. A driver would come by and get me the next day at the Centre.

It was the dry season in Kinshasa. Every day clouds would mass above the palms, but it would never rain. The next morning broke humid and hot. Opalescent hummingbirds flitted around the crimson and pink blossoms outside my room at the Centre. A shining red Land Rover with tinted windows pulled onto the lot. André, as the driver introduced himself, was in his late twenties, and wore a jeans jacket over his lean build; he had a beard that softened the contours of his V-shaped jaw. He looked tough behind his dark glasses, but when he took them off his eyes were kind.

"Doesn't this Land Rover stand out in all the wrecked cars around here?" I asked him as I climbed aboard. "Don't the soldiers think you're rich and bother you?"

"I carry myself like an undercover cop—see my sunglasses?—so they're afraid of me. It would be a disgrace to be a soldier. The soldiers . . . they are the *disgrace* of Zaire. Every soldier is my enemy. Just *let* one try to mess with the Locomotive."

"The Locomotive?"

"That's what I call the Land Rover here. The Locomotive."

Our mission was to buy everything I would need to survive a two-week ascent of the river. "Or three weeks, or four," André said. "You never know. In any case, *pas de problème*. The Locomotive will get us around. We'll start at Simbazigita Market."

Soon we were gliding through the sunbaked and ashen bidon-villes of the Cité, with the Locomotive turning heads at every corner. Smiling women in floral head wraps sat on their haunches and sold *shikwanga*. Congo Beat blared in salsa melodies from boom boxes at soft drink stands. Always there were children playing. I was beginning to see that Kinshasa was lively, even in the slums. I was starting to look past, or close my eyes to, the poverty.

Along the road to Simbazigita we raised a plume of fine gray dust. The market, a mess of cinder block hovels and wooden stands cobbled together in a field, sat at the end of an airport runway. We parked and a gigantic Russian cargo plane thundered just overhead. The stands shook with the roar of the engines.

As soon as we stepped out a crowd of vendors set upon us, shoving thumb-sized bananas, chunks of manioc root, buckets of palm grubs, and tubs of caterpillars in our faces. Their knees were knobby, and their ribs showed through their T-shirts. I tried to remain impassive behind my dark sunglasses. André protected me like a bodyguard, hustling me through in a dignified way that caused no offense. We bought, among other things, rice, macaroni, onions, canned tomatoes, peas, cutlery, and plastic jerry cans for water.

The pretty women merchants flirted with André. The market was a pickup spot, he said, but he told me that he "feared God" and always left alone. We got back in the Land Rover.

"Now for the *bambula*."

"The *bambula*?"

"The charcoal grill. Most important. You'll need to cook."

In Zaire, where charcoal was often the only fuel to be had, *bambulas* were treasured items. We pulled around another row of stalls but stayed in the car. André rolled down his window. "Ey, we need a *bambula!*" he yelled into the crowd. It was as if someone had fired a pistol to start a race: the crowd scattered into the stalls and came at us running, brandishing *bambulas* and shouting prices. I had six or seven *bambulas* in my face; *bambulas* were clanging on the hood, dancing in the air; men were drumming them with knives. André raised his window, leaving only a crack open at the top.

"Don't talk to the *mondele!* You're dealing with me here, not the *mondele!*" Another cargo plane took off, shaking the air. André shouted above the roar. "No, fifteen thousand zaires, not fifty thousand! Look at me"—he pointed to his eyes—"not at the *mondele!*"

The crowd pressed in and rocked the Locomotive. André opened his window to look at one *bambula* and three or four were hurled inside. We hurled them back out and closed the windows. Every inch of window was covered by the faces of the merchants and the steel of *bambulas*.

"Fifteen thousand!" he shouted. "Thirty!" they shouted back, their bony hands and faces mashed against the glass.

"Ah, you are not serious men!" André put the Locomotive in reverse and started backing out. We got no more than a yard away and prices came down to fifteen thousand. I had my pick and took the one I wanted.

André tossed the money at the merchant and backed on out. "As you see, the people of Zaire are warm-spirited," he said, smiling. "You must be polite to them and understand they are hungry. They won't eat if they don't sell."

The next day the Colonel and his brother picked me up at the Centre in the silver Mercedes. We drove around Gombe—a posh district of mowed lawns and white-walled colonial homes—with the Colonel often taking calls in Lingala on his cell phone. His voice had a distinct nasal tone that contrasted with the booming notes of most Lingala speakers, and I wondered if this might not have something to do with his native dialect (he was from the province of Equateur). We pulled up to the gate of a villa and a middle-aged European appeared—a disheveled, gouty sort in a silk bathrobe whose nose was bulbous and red with drink. The Colonel got out and they went inside.

"A Belgian," the brother said. He patted his hair and checked his reflection in the mirror. "You know, you're going to need a motorized pirogue on the river."

"Why?"

"To get away from the whirlpools."

"The locals don't have motorized pirogues, do they?"

"And what about the snakes? And the lions? And the leopards? And the hippos? Have you thought about them? The hippos are worst of all. They'll bite through your pirogue to get to you."

The Colonel sauntered out of the gate and opened the car door. He turned to me, his eyes slit. "Diamonds!" he exclaimed. "I deal in diamonds! Ha-haa!"

We drove around on more of the Colonel's errands. When I spoke to him he did not respond, or he would interrupt me in the middle of one of my sentences and ask his brother something. This was jarring. More than just outlandishly rude, it was an utter denial of my existence. But I was coming to see that his were the manners of royalty, of an African chief in whose presence one should never speak unless addressed. I, a commoner, should not take offense, but had simply to conform.

Back at his office the supplicants were many. The Colonel sat down under Mobutu's portrait and crossed his arms. His brother took up position behind him. The phone rang. The Colonel spoke a roughshod English with the caller—"*un Arabe*," he said to me, covering the mouthpiece—and discussed payment schedules and the delivery of palm oil.

As soon as he hung up, the phone rang again. He answered. "The General," he whispered to me. "*Oui, oui.*" He snapped his fingers for my passport. I handed it to him, and he read the number into the receiver. "*D'accord, mon Général.*" He hung up.

The electricity failed; the ceiling fan slowed and creaked to a halt. Within seconds a damp heat and tense silence fell over the room. The Colonel locked his eyes on mine, and the others saw this and watched. He stared so intently that I found I could not speak; it was as though he held me in some sort of hypnotic thrall; a bead of sweat worked its way down my left temple.

He stared, I sweat.

Finally he broke the silence with his nasal, high-pitched voice. "You are embarking on a grand adventure! You will be the first to descend the Congo in a pirogue! You are taking a great risk—but so is the soldier who will accompany you. He won't see his family.

He will shoot at crocodiles. He will fight off bandits. His life will be in danger. What will be his reward?"

I wasn't sure I would hire a soldier—I had not met a candidate and had no feel for the subject, and, in any case, I had not considered what a suitable fee should be. But before I could reply, the Colonel turned back to a supplicant and fired a question at him. As the man answered, the Colonel drummed the oak table with his gold ring and closed his eyes. Then he opened his eyes and again fixed them on me. "What will the soldier receive for his risk?

I didn't know what to say, so to stall for time I decided to orate. I stood up.

"The soldier, if I hire one, must not be out for money. He must have the courage—yes, the *courage!*—to risk the river! If he has any doubts, let him remain at home. If he is out for money alone, let him stay home. If he fears, he must stay home!"

"Yes!" shouted the Colonel, pounding the desk. "He must be prepared for adventure! But so must you!" His voice rose to a nasal zenith. "Are you ready for the trip on my boat?"

"I am ready."

"There will be much diarrhea and malaria. Are you strong?"

"I am strong."

"You must have medicine. You must eat well and take your pills. For fifteen days—twelve if I can push them—we will travel up the wildest river in Africa. You must have, yes, the *courage,* the courage to endure it all! The river is dangerous for everyone, white or black, even on a boat!"

"I'm ready!"

Without warning he stopped talking and turned toward the window, as if seized by a totally unrelated but engrossing thought. My audience was over. I hesitated for a moment, then walked out.

✴✴✴

The night before departure I lay awake in my mosquito net, anxious and sweating, listening to lizards scamper scratchily up and down the walls of my room and mosquitoes whine outside my window. During my two-week stay I had grown accustomed to

Kinshasa, and it now felt like home. I had developed a routine of visits—to the Colonel, to Pierre, to André at the bank. Marc and George would often invite me to the Surcouf, a bar near their home in the Ville, and we would spend the evenings there having dinner and a beer or two. The staff at the Centre had started to trust me, and I now enjoyed chatting with them.

But this was all to end. I was, after all, in Kinshasa only to leave it for the river. Yet I was as much afraid of the river as I was excited by it—or was fear the only thing I now felt? I tended to discount the opinions of the missionaries, but Kinshasans told me that the tribes along the river were dangerous ("cannibals," some said), and that the animals were as fierce as they were numerous. Still, none save two of the Kinshasans I had met had actually been on the river; their fears could easily have been those of urbanites with stereotyped notions about an unfamiliar wilderness. And I still wondered about the Colonel and why he should care to help me.

The heat was suffocating. I unzipped the door and inhaled, mosquitoes danced their way inside, I zipped up. I had only my musings in the dark, and I returned to the one truth, the truth of time and finitude: we each see a finite number of dawns and dusks, then it is all over. We fill our days with comforting fictions—with religions and customs, with conventions and goals and hopes and hobbies and plans—that help us pass the time and give us the illusion of achievement and order, but the purpose of these fictions is to hide the Truth. I was about to abandon these fictions, to cast off from their shore. But I did not sense liberation at hand. No, I sensed an abyss, as a blindfolded man walking a gangplank perceives the void beneath his feet.

In the morning I wrote a long letter to Tatyana. My eyes flooded with tears—I could not stop them—and I was rent and exhausted by the time I finished it. Why couldn't I pull out of my journey, admit that I had made a mistake? There was no way back now, I told myself. I had left everything to come here, and the only way out was to stay the course, to exercise my will, and provide my own direction. Having come this far, I *had* to go on to the end. This was the fiction I had created for myself.

Shoving Off

THE RIVER WAS A SHEET OF STEEL IN THE HARSH MORNING SUN, pockmarked by migrating clumps of water hyacinth; the barge creaked and listed in the hot currents; in the lank grass along the bank rats and lizards lazily sniffed and scavenged. There was no breeze, and the sweltering air weighed heavy on the skin; an odor of rot and waste invaded the nostrils. The hour of our departure had come, but the heat nullified thoughts of action, inclining one only to seek shade and doze away the day.

A pickup truck from the Centre had brought me down to the dock. I sat under an awning on the barge and watched porters—barefoot youths in tattered shorts—balance my gear and provisions on their towel-turbaned heads and tread their way down the wobbly gangplank to the deck. As before, I had climbed down the ladder, this time holding a bulging paper bag in my free hand. The previous day I had visited Marc and George at the bank and exchanged four hundred dollars for a bushel of zaires in small denominations. The Zaireans among the bank staff told me that upriver big bills (which meant anything over five thousand zaires, or about one dollar) weren't generally trusted, so I asked them to give me zaires in denominations of a hundred and two hundred (the equivalent of a penny or two apiece), which made for a hefty bundle of cash.

I pulled out one of the notes and examined it. BANQUE DU ZAÏRE—CENT NOUVEAUX ZAÏRES. Although it had been printed only the year before as part of Mobutu's currency reform (inflation had reduced the old zaires to a million to a dollar), the bill had already acquired a less-than-venerable patina of *shikwanga* grease and *commerçant* thumbprints. Its obverse bore a portrait of a blasé Mobutu next to an artlessly executed image of a leaping leopard; on the reverse there was a picture of an unnamed bridge, along with the warning: "Counterfeiters will be punished by penal servitude." At the bottom was the name of the private company in Munich that had printed the bill. It was a tired-looking piece of currency whose design hinted at no imagination, no pride, no guiding sense of national mission.

The porters laid the last of my gear at my feet. I sank my hand into the paper bag and paid them with a fistful of bills.

Onshore people were gathering, standing arms akimbo and staring at the barge and waiting—but for what? Most watched the porters, who were now lugging aboard hundred-pound sacks of sugar, salt, and flour. Everything went in the hold, sack after sack after sack.

I rose and decided to set up house. The scullery cabin with the plank bunks was filled with someone's gear, so I placed my bag in the main cabin on the deck, behind the awning. The main cabin was a capacious, orange-painted steel chamber with a pit toilet, a metallic cubicle for showering, and three sturdy wooden bed frames. On one of them I unrolled my foam mattress.

While I was unpacking, a slight, green-eyed man with a notebook walked in carrying a duffel bag. He wore brand-new aquamarine sweatpants and a fresh white shirt; he looked pleasantly cool, though there was a tad of acerbity in his efficient demeanor. He raised his chin and spoke. "I am Jean, the accountant, and you are in my cabin." Keeping his eyes on me, he staked out a bunk and plunked his bag on it. "There's an empty cabin around the side. You can move now, please."

I apologized and packed up. I lugged my bags around to the scullery and found it had been emptied of the gear I had just seen. I stepped inside. Roaches scuttled over my feet and moths fluttered in my face; I spat and swatted and stamped around, brushing bugs out of my hair. Then the door creaked shut and left me standing in damp blackness—there were no windows and no lights, only a tiny vent high on one wall. The cabin was oven-hot, and stirring with insects in every corner.

There was a rap on the door. I opened up. A man in his late twenties stood before me in khakis and a polyester shirt printed with a vomitlike hash of browns, yellows, and oranges. His face was spotted and greasy. He cleared his throat and spoke in English. "I am pasTOOR." He shook my hand. "I teach God."

"Nice to meet you." I was too preoccupied with my cabin to say more.

"You are a *Belge?*"

"No. I'm not Belgian."

I asked him to excuse me for a few minutes while I settled in, but he started talking in what sounded like pidgin English and waved a pamphlet around, which was, along with God, apparently the subject of his discourse. I couldn't understand him, but he failed to understand me when I asked him to repeat, so I switched to French, but he refused to speak that. I gave up telling him I was busy and stepped outside. He followed me around to the accountant's cabin, asking me more questions in broken English, and became frustrated at my incomprehensible answers.

Jean stepped out on deck. I asked him when the Colonel was due to arrive. The pastor gabbled and interrupted his answer. Jean threw him a nasty look and repeated himself: he didn't know, but when the Colonel did arrive, he would certainly settle the matter of my accommodations.

Feeling queasy from nerves and the heat, I returned to my cabin with the pastor still at my heels, still flapping his tongue. "Please," I said to him in English, then in French, "I need some time to myself to settle in. Can we talk later?"

He raised his voice. "I talk you *now*. About Jimmy Swaggart." He shoved the pamphlet in my face: it was about the once-disgraced American evangelist.

I pushed the pamphlet away and he shoved it at me again. With bile rising in my throat, with the asphyxiating heat, with the pervasive odor of rat dung and the rankness of the river, and with the idea taking shape in my mind that I was going to have to spend two weeks in a stifling steel box, riding upriver in the company of this tongue-wagging pastor, I excused myself from him rather less than politely, closed the door on him rather less than softly, grabbed my flashlight, and started to unpack.

✦✦✦

All day the porters loaded the barge, and the Colonel was nowhere to be seen. Senior crew members hammered away in the cabins of the *pousseur,* putting finishing touches on their accommodations. Deckhands, a sinewy turbaned lot, set up their quarters down in the hold, where they would stretch out on plank bunks above the sloshing water. A tall, angular fellow named Jilly with a clipboard and invoices was to be the freight manager. With a towel around his neck and his declamatory manner, Jilly seemed perpetually under siege and responded with outrage to clients attempting to slip past him an unpaid kilo of sugar or quart of oil. A third man, a pot-bellied retired postal employee called Papa Jacques, would not be working on the barge (although he brought along a sack of sugar that he hoped to sell along the way), but because he was old and jolly and known to the crew, he was allowed to sit by Jean's cabin on the business bench, next to the refreshment stand (a cooler filled with Primus beer and Cokes). Jean's cabin would serve as the *Bureau de batelier*—the office of the barge—and the unofficial head-quarters of life on deck.

Around four-thirty the sun had nearly completed its searing arc above our heads. The sky started to redden in the west, and a commotion arose on shore. *"Yaka! Yaka!"* A dozen men were dragging bundles down to the dock, trailed by womenfolk crying, pulling at their clothes, flailing their arms. The pastor showed up at my side and launched into a full-volume psalm in Lingala, adding his own strident note of religious hysteria to the clamor. The women slapped their thighs and stamped their feet, wailing as if frenzied with grief, and their loved ones clambered down the gangplank with their bundles and shouted their good-byes.

A corpulent man in a baseball cap strode aboard humming a Congo Beat tune. The captain. He had an easy air, a floppy belly, a broad smile; he looked like he loved his beer at the end of the day. Belly first, he turned and strolled around the *pousseur*. Next thing, a chugging rumble resounded from the engines, the ship's horn blasted, the crewmen cast off the mooring ropes, and the barge lurched to life on the restless currents.

We pulled out ponderously, churning the blue waters, with the skyscrapers and dock cranes circling around us as we maneuvered into the channel. The engines roared hard. Soon Kinshasa was receding into the humid gray haze of dusk behind us. Ahead, toward the equator, the sky and water dissolved into a mist of luminous azure. We were on our way.

I thought of the missionaries and their descriptions of crowded barges and peeing passengers and cholera. Of course they had been wrong—what did they know? I was almost alone on board, except for the crew, the pastor, and a few merchants. I would be able to study the river at my leisure, to absorb information at my own pace.

I walked to the bow to savor my luck. The pastor jogged out from the barge office, pamphlet in hand.

He spoke in French. "Please, I'm reading this. It's about Jimmy Swaggart. I love him." He stood there picking at a bump on his chin. "He is from your country. You love him, too, don't you?"

"Love isn't the word."

"*Comment?*"

"I don't think you need to know my opinion of him. We should change the subject."

"*Comment?* But I'm asking you a question."

"Okay. To put it charitably, I don't love him. Or respect him."

My words appeared to sink in only gradually. When they did he backed off, regarding me with suspicion, then turned and walked away.

A little while later a gunboat apparition appeared in the mists ahead of us. As we drew closer, its hazy outlines defined themselves into those of a sturdy, three-storied vessel teeming with armed soldiers on its many green-and-white decks. The pastor came out and stared at it. The *Kamanyola,* he said. Mobutu's yacht.

It was dangerous to sail close to the *Kamanyola*—we could be taken for attackers and fired upon—so we gave it wide berth and headed around it up the river. The mists soon closed back over the yacht and hid it from our view, but the flag Mobutu had created for Zaire—a black fist clutching a flaming torch—stayed with us, fluttering above our bridge.

I walked the deck. The pastor shadowed me, mumbling lines from his pamphlet, apparently as disgruntled with me as he was determined to set me straight. But within half an hour we were veering back to shore, drawing toward the port at Selza, a suburb of Kinshasa, where a crowd was scrimmaging on the pier. When we were three or four feet from the dock, people began casting aboard foam mattresses and baskets and bales of cloth, leaping over the watery divide onto our deck, clutching straw mats and dangling *bambulas*. Gendarmes thrashed at the crowd with rope whips, but in vain: by the time we moored, every free square inch was occupied.

The sun died a vivid death in a violet sky. Jean opened his refreshment stand, and the beer started to flow. Congo Beat blared forth from the barge's loudspeakers; men fell in with the tunes, dancing loose and rocking, smiling, swinging their hips; women busily unrolled blankets on the deck and set up house. The pastor climbed upon a crate and shouted a homily to a widening circle of devotees.

It was a jubilant scene, but the utter dearth of free space, the closeness of the crowd, the racket, and the notion that I would know nothing else for two weeks hit me hard. To distract myself, I sat down on the bench by the barge office and treated Jean, Jilly, and Papa Jacques to a round of beers. The reasons for the crowd were simple, they told me. Onatra, the national shipping company, had gone bankrupt and only rarely sent a boat upriver. As a result, merchants had turned to private barges for transport and as a means of conducting trade with the interior, where most Zaireans lived. None of our four hundred passengers would see the inside of a cabin for the duration of the trip. They would even bathe on deck: the secluded bow and stern, at different times, would serve as bathing platforms for men and women. There were two toilets on the barge, but most people simply lowered their rears or raised their privates over the edge to take care of their needs. I asked about fresh water and how they would get it: when the passengers needed a drink, they would drop their buckets (a bucket on a rope was standard travel gear) into the river and scoop. Yes, dysentery, typhoid, and other waterborne diseases might afflict some. Only the Colonel, the senior crew, and I would have clean water.

Jean sipped his beer and looked at the dancers. "Despite all this, they're happy. This trip can mean good money. It's tough, but they'll make the best of it."

I felt less optimistic; in fact, I felt as if I was going to throw up. I wished them happy beers, and, exhausted from the day of heat and deafening music, reeling from the animated and sweaty gyrations of the mob, I picked my way through the babies and dancers and cooking women to my bug-infested scullery to see what I could make for dinner. I would force myself to eat, no matter how I felt.

≈≈≈

"You're in my cabin!" said a bearded man peering in my door. He was small, with a sort of menacing arrogance about him, and he stroked his beard with disdain. "I'm the manager here. What are my wife and I supposed to do? Sleep on deck?"

"No problem. I'll move." I had no idea of where I would go, but I would never be able to stand the cabin anyway.

He looked at me and scratched his head. "Well, okay, you can have until morning."

Outside the cabin I set up my kitchen: *bambula*, charcoal, pot of water, rice, and canned meat. The pastor was soon at my side. He thrust his nose toward the bubbling pot and greedily sniffed up the vapors. Then he swung open the cabin door and gawked at my provisions. "You have all this food? All for yourself?" He rifled through it, examining every item, and said I would be eating well on this trip, and what about him?

I concentrated on my cooking. When my meal was ready I had to force-feed myself, spooning rice into my mouth, chewing it a predetermined number of times, swallowing and chasing it with water. Clutching his Swaggart tract, standing only a foot or so from my face, the pastor peered at me, peered at my food, back and forth.

Finally he whipped a small bowl out of his back pocket. "Give me some!"

I dished him out some rice and meat. He gobbled it up.

I finished and politely excused myself. I walked into my cabin and shut the door, and lay down on the plank bed.

///

The music blasted from a loudspeaker right over my door; the knotty planks and scuttling roaches made comfort elusive. Still suffering from nausea, I gathered up my mosquito net and sheets and crossed over to the *pousseur,* where I ran into the chief mechanic, who introduced himself as Nze.

"The deck is too noisy for you, isn't it? Come, I'll show you a quiet place." Nze looked to be in his fifties. His voice was intelligent and gentle, and I responded to his avuncular warmth immediately. He led me around the back of the craft and up a ladder to a place on the roof above the bridge. "How's this?"

It was perfect. A yard-high bulwark rose between us and the barge, which would afford me some privacy and cut down the noise. Most important, up here I would be alone, I would have a retreat.

Nze told me that years ago he had worked in Germany, and he understood how "we" lived. The conditions on the barge would be tough for me to handle, he warned; they were tough on everyone.

"Thanks for your concern," I said. "I hadn't expected this to be so difficult."

"Anytime you need help, just ask me. I'll do whatever I can. Tomorrow I'll arrange for you to take a proper shower; you'll need that." He helped me set up my mosquito net.

"Where is the Colonel?"

"The Colonel has a villa in Selza; that's why we've stopped here. He'll join us in the morning. Good night for now."

I climbed inside the net, lay down on my foam mattress, and watched the stars until sleep came.

At dawn we were coursing past grassy savanna marked here and there by trees whose majestic canopies spread like giant green mushrooms against the bare sky. It was gray and cool, and I had slept well. I climbed down the ladder.

Jean was sitting on the stern of the *pousseur*. "Would you like to bathe?"

He led me around the *pousseur* and through his quarters to his bathroom, and called a deckhand, whom he ordered to draw my bath. Soon I was handed a bucket slopping with unctuous green water, warm with a frothy head, scooped straight from the Congo. As I scrubbed and rinsed with it, I had the sensation that it was an organic fluid. It felt viscous, sebaceous; I seemed to be bathing in plasma. It stung my eyes. But somehow I finished my ablutions feeling clean and refreshed.

When I emerged from his cabin the other passengers were settling into the rhythms of river life. Everywhere on deck straw mats lay strewn with bolts of cloth, piles of underwear, plastic cups, colorful beads, sacks of sugar and salt, Ayu soap, malaria pills in white boxes, batteries, needles and threads and scissors, cookie tins, Bic pens and school notebooks with green covers marked "L'Éléphant," and more. The merchants laughed and bantered among themselves in Lingala, interrupting their talk to shout, *"Ey, mondele! Bonjour!"* as I walked by. Mothers scrubbed down two-year-olds; skillets sizzled with onions and chunks of fish and balls of dough; *thump-thump-thump* resounded as women in rainbow robes pounded plantains into mash with carved mallets; flat-footed old men padded by with armloads of bananas. A congregation led by the pastor chanted Lingala spirituals at the stern. Just behind them a pirogue was moored; on rattling chains it trailed five yard-long boka, or Congo catfish, along with a couple of carp, oily-looking and brown, each five or six feet long and a couple of feet thick.

There was no space left on deck, but the crowd was still growing. Pirogues with three and four passengers apiece were cutting across the river, swerving through our wake. Once they were within a couple of feet of us, the men at the bow would jump onto our deck, clutching a rope tied to the gunwale, then affix their pirogues to our railings. Thus moored, they and their families would come aboard, with bundles of belongings tied around their shoulders. When they saw me they did double takes, but most smiled and hailed me as *mondele! Ey, mondele!*

Still a bit sick to my stomach, I felt less than sociable, but for the first time in my life, with the crowd, the heat, the journey ahead, and the sheer strangeness and newness of everything I was experiencing, I found myself so shaky and unsure of whether I would make it from one day to the next that I had to rely on the conversation and kindness of others to keep my spirits high enough to eat, bathe, and sleep. It was either move and socialize or rest and be overwhelmed with nausea and anxiety. I toured the boat and made friends.

The manager never moved into my cabin. Instead, he assigned the lower of the two bunks to Bopembe, a kindly deckhand who was very concerned about the security of our belongings. He attached a padlock to our door and gave me a key. "We must be careful. As we head upriver, we will have many fishermen and villagers coming aboard. Many are Bangala, so thieving comes naturally to them."

I sat down next to Papa Jacques by the office. The skies were cloudy, the breeze tepid, the currents strong. Jacques patted his sack of sugar. "Want to buy some?"

"How much?"

"A hundred pounds."

"I don't think I can eat so much sugar."

"Well, I've got to sell this sugar. I'm a pensioner, you see. I'm riding for free, but if I can sell this sack I'll make some money to buy fish with, and they love fish at home."

I told him that if I found a customer I would alert him. We sat back and watched the river.

Later I was in my cabin eating macaroni. The pastor stuck his head in the door. "I invite you to my sermon. I will talk about God."

"Thanks."

"I'm starting now."

"I'm eating right now, but thanks for the invitation."

"I am inviting you *right now*. Don't turn away from God." He lifted the lid off the pot and looked at my macaroni. "I'm hungry. I need to eat before the sermon." He whipped out his bowl.

I stopped chewing. I hesitated, then ladled him a serving. He did not thank me, but rather started asking me how I felt about Jesus. I swallowed and told him, please, I would see him later.

As he got up it occurred to me to ask him a question. "Wait. Didn't you bring any food?"

"No."

"*No?* How far away is your village?"

"Four days away."

"You came on a four-day trip without food?"

"Not only without food, but without water. I'm a pastor. People give me everything. They think it's the same as giving to God."

A few minutes later, just the other side of my cabin wall, he delivered his sermon, and it was well attended. It was in Lingala, but it was peppered with the French words for salvation, resurrection, damnation, and eternal life—European concepts for which Lingala had no words. Or maybe it had, but from the pastor's point of view it made sense to use the French. The French, for Congo River dwellers, would have retained the incantatory ring of the mysterious, the dimly understood, the magical, and demand elucidation only he could provide.

⁓⁓⁓

"Tay-ler!"

The Colonel was standing on the bridge. It was the first time I had seen him since we cast off. When I looked up he turned away.

"You should go see the Colonel," Bopembe said.

It was getting dark. I walked around the *pousseur* and climbed the ladder. The Colonel had retreated to the living room in his cabin. His television was on full-bast, showing a Zairean dance program. Smiling, round-bottomed, barefoot women in floral wraps, their ankles narrowly spaced and their knees spread bow-legged, as if they were riding invisible horses, were flapping their elbows and making subtle thrusts of their hips to a Zairean pop tune. The camera closed in on their jiggling behinds and pulled back, closed in and pulled back. The song went on and on; they jiggled and flapped and thrust, smiling vapidly as if entranced.

The Colonel was barefoot and in baggy striped shorts. His belly bulged over the waist cord. Leaning against the wall was an M-16.

"Tayler!" He pulled me to the couch and put his arm on my shoulder. "How are you doing? How do you like my boat?"

"I'm fine. Your boat is excellent."

"Any problems?"

"No, none."

On the screen the bottoms were shaking. They were big bottoms.

"You know, I deal in diamonds! And gold! I have traveled to your country and to Belgium. I know your life and how you eat, I know your customs. That Coke Light you were drinking—did you buy it in Zaire? I imported it, just for you! One of my businesses is importing food from Europe."

He jumped off the sofa and rifled through some papers on the shelf. The women on-screen, with their elbows extended and rears wiggling, suddenly looked like ducks. The song ended, but it was immediately replayed from the start.

"These are my businesses. I've used a computer to draw up my staff list. I have three companies and employ sixty people. I spent three hundred thousand dollars building this *pousseur*. See?"

All sorts of occupations, from watchman to accountant to manager, were listed on spreadsheets soggy with the humidity. Next to duties were names and salaries. He had a number of residences and a large personal staff.

There was a knock on the door. In walked a seven-foot-tall man with a club in one hand and a belly to match his brawn.

"Colonel!"

The Colonel grabbed his M-16 and walked out.

We were slowing down. Our spotlight played on the islands, bounced off the trees, illuminated the marshes and the floes of water hyacinth drifting at us out of the blackness ahead. There were soldiers on the bow. The captain shouted through the loud-speaker, "Everyone, turn off your lights!"

The barge went dark. There was the sound of the engine, the flashing of the searchlight on the water and forest and backs of the soldiers. We had just passed Maluku, the last settlement in Kin-shasa Province. The Colonel didn't return to his cabin, so I climbed the bridge and readied myself for sleep.

After midnight . . . a huge orange moon . . . a penetrating chill. I awoke shivering so violently that I could hardly pull up my blanket quickly enough. The engines were chugging away, powering our rocking ascent against the onrushing currents of the giant river. Clouds of mist swirled low above the black water. Away from the moon, the sky was a boundless firmament of cobalt scintillating with stars and planets, streaking now and again with meteors that fell behind the low mountains, beyond the horizons.

I watched the stars and the meteors. I felt suddenly alone and remote from everything I had known; it was as if my past now belonged to another, perished world that I would never inhabit again. But as I gazed at the sky more and more became clear to me. The pinpoints of diamond light and splashes of celestial fire drew my thoughts away from myself, toward the ether, and offered me cold but aesthetic comfort among the galaxies, galaxies more clearly visible here near the equator than anywhere, galaxies that I was seeing for the first time with my own eyes, galaxies, constellations, and powdery blue-white nebulae that floated light-years, light-centuries, light-millennia away, so far away that perhaps they had died long ago, leaving only their light to travel out into infinity. Our sun had been born in a fiery explosion five billion years ago, and it would die in a supernova five billion years hence. Pondering these distances, these eons, my personal concerns and dilemmas, the discomfort of the barge—all this vanished.

Thus solaced and gradually warming up under my blanket, I slipped back into sleep.

Day three found us amid whitecapped waters and buffeting winds. The sky was lowering and iron gray; lightning flickered from the equator ahead. We were plowing into rafts of water hyacinth, through the narrow part of the river known as the Chenal. No pirogues came out to meet us, and villages were few. But the first signs of a great jungle were appearing. On ridges stood massive, broad-boughed trees; the underbrush of the savanna was gathering into higher and denser clumps. The wind was showering us with stray dwellers of the forest—thumb-sized termites, beetles, dragonflies.

By my cabin, which I now used only to store my gear, I found squatters: a wan-looking woman with bugs in her hair and her two-year-old son, a floppy baby with oddly loose skin. He cried softly, all the time, and he wore a PARTY NAKED! T-shirt.

The mother turned her eyes to mine. "*Mondele,* give me an onion!"

I found some onions among my provisions and handed them to her. I continued on my way around to the barge office bench, where in the mornings I made it a habit to enjoy a Coke after breakfast.

A young man grabbed my arm. "I want to talk to you, *mondele.*" He had a vigorous handshake and a space between his teeth; he said his name was Patrice. Patrice was twenty-five years old and originally from Bandundu. "I was working as a tailor in Kinshasa, but when the *pillages* began, I lost my business, so I took to the barges. I have a fiancée—she'll leave me if I can't buy her dresses and jewelry. So here I am, risking this voyage. People get diarrhea and dysentery on these trips, and sometimes the boats sink. Man proposes, but God disposes. Now tell me why you, *un blanc,* would ride this barge."

"Well, I'm planning to pirogue my way down from Kisangani."

He told me that was an insane idea, so insane that he would not dignify it with further discussion. Instead, he explained how the barge trip worked for him and the other merchants. Once they got farther away from Kinshasa, they would be selling their merchandise—the manufactured goods that were lying all over the deck—to villagers paddling up in pirogues. They would then immediately use their profits to buy the manioc root, smoked fish, monkey, crocodile, and antelope offered by these same villagers. These foodstuffs would later be hawked in the markets of Kisangani after the ascent. Even crew members would be stockpiling smoked fish or monkey for trade or for their families at home. Everyone aboard became a skilled *débrouillard,* a master at getting by, or he didn't last. Here, before the trading began, the merchants were eating little, and many were hungry. They needed to sell their wares and buy fish, but we were too near Kinshasa—even three days out was still considered near—for the few villagers coming aboard to be interested in manufactured goods, and their pirogues contained little more than very expensive fish, too expensive for most passengers. The best trade was ahead, in the great forest. "Until then, we will be hungry, *mondele.* Remember that! Thank you for your time."

He shook my hand and made his way into the crowd.

The hunger, the forest, the hunters and fishermen, the life measured in meals. I was witnessing something very old, something ancient, even, and true. The rich few here ate well and grew big bellies; the masses were skinny and lived from meal to scant meal. This life was survival; it was something I had never really seen. People like the tailor, people who could maintain their dignity, command respect, and suffer hunger at the same time, knew more than I did, and I wanted to learn from them.

On the office bench sat Papa Jacques, who adjusted the tarp to make sure that rain, if it came, would not spoil his sugar, and Jilly, who patted his brow with his towel and tabulated freight revenues. Seated on straw mats in front of them, facing a brood of children, were two young women. One wore her long hair in a bun and was very pretty, with high cheekbones, a long nose, and eyes with gold-flecked irises, gold that was brought out by gilt embroidery on her dark-green dress. Often she would turn around and hold my gaze, furrow her brow, and then laugh, slapping her knee. When I held her gaze she always looked away. I wanted to talk to her, but I sensed that she and her friend were related to someone on the crew, and it seemed improper even to inquire.

✦✦✦

We chugged on. The next dawn we awoke to a rainy fog. Loaded with pineapples and manioc tubers, pirogues in V-shaped formations of three and four were shooting toward us through the mizzle and docking at our sides. I got up and went out to the deck and stood at the railing, composing shots with my Nikon. Fog blown by a strong head wind rushed over us, parting occasionally to reveal forested mountains on high banks.

"Nina! Nina!" someone shouted. "Nina!" An excited murmur arose on deck. A man forced his way through the crowd and hurled himself overboard, just missing a pirogue. Thirty feet from the barge floated a fish the size of an inner tube, coiled dead and belly-up amidst the gray choppy waters.

"An electric catfish, a nina!" shouted a boy next to me. "What a prize! It will bring him ten dollars. And if it's still alive it will electrocute him!"

The man missed it, it floated past, and then the drama became whether he could catch up with the barge again. He thrashed the water in a strong but sloppy crawl, half-hurling himself out of the water with each stroke. He landed near the *pousseur* at the stern, and hoisted himself aboard. A hero for the entertainment he provided, he raised his arms to general applause.

Just then a voice rang out from the loudspeaker. "Hello, people! You have been enjoying the ride on our boat. But have you all bought your tickets? We don't think so!"

We looked up. Who was this?

"Okay, people, we're coming to get you!"

Stowaways

"CLANDESTIN! FRAUDEUR! CLANDESTIN!"

The shouting came from deep in the crowd. Clothing was being torn, sandals were scuffing the deck, merchants were diving behind their wares.

"Clandestin!" Stowaway!

Augustin, the security chief (a.k.a. the chief), emerged from the melee and stomped down the deck, a truncheon in one hand and a squirming youth, whom he held fast by the collar, in the other. Following him was a wild-eyed and wiry Bangala soldier with DANGER DE MORT tattooed on his arms, a red beret pushed low over his eyes, a dagger in his belt, and a whip in his hands. Behind him was the gloomy manager. The crowd was laughing at the wriggling *clandestin*. This was the closest thing to theater on the barge, and the more he whimpered and resisted, the more they enjoyed it.

The chief brought him around the stern and paused in front of me. "This boy is a *fraudeur* and a liar," he declared. "He didn't pay his way. You would like to take a photo?" He held the stowaway out for me: the poor fellow dangled at the end of Augustin's arm, twitching and jerking like a hanged man, his feet barely touching the ground.

I put down my camera and said no.

Augustin shrugged. *"Bon."* He stripped the youth to his underwear, kicked open the trapdoor to the stern's hold, and tossed him in.

As the barge forded the currents, heading toward a horizon of storm clouds, the chief, the soldier, and the manager, assisted by a couple of young men who had been begging Jean for paid work, launched a ship-wide hunt for stowaways. Suspects were diving into piles of cloth, hiding amid sacks of sugar, burrowing between bushels of corn. A pimply youth who had greeted me each morning with shouts of "Rambo! Terminator! Clin-ton!" got involved and helped wrestle them out, calling my name and shouting "Look! Look, Rambo!" as he practiced punches and kicks on his captives. The chief—constable, judge, and administrator of punishments—took one screaming youth and tossed him into his pirogue and cut the line; he confiscated the merchandise of others. For the next hour, man after man was seized, dragged astern, stripped, and hurled below deck. Little boys had great fun jumping up and down on the trapdoor as the imprisoned cried out for air. Those few who resisted, the chief pummeled with his bare meaty hands.

Soon, the hold was filled, the rear deck was congested, even the *pousseur* railings were crowded, used as impromptu pillories to which the stowaways were handcuffed. Jean and the chief heard each man out. All were given a chance to pay their way, either in goods or in cash. Many had a story to tell, a few pleaded poverty, but most coughed up sufficient zaires for the fare.

Some didn't, though. When the hearings were over, Augustin grabbed one of the deadbeats by the back of the neck and shouted into the crowd, "Does anyone want to pay for this liar's ticket? No?" He pulled out a razor and the man began bucking and twisting and shouting in Lingala. Little girls covered their eyes with their mothers' skirts, women turned away.

The chief forced the man to his knees and stood over him, waving his razor, then he grabbed him by the jaw.

"You still don't have any money?"

"I'm poor! Please, mercy! Have pity on me!"

The chief tightened his grip and began shaving the man's head, stroke after stroke, down to humiliating baldness. He shaved the heads of the rest who wouldn't pay, then let them go. They were allowed to circulate freely on deck, but at the next village they would be handed over to the police.

After it was all over, I cooked a lunch of rice, peas, and frank-furters in front of my cabin. A couple of the shaven stowaways came up and beseeched me for a portion, holding out their bowls, and I obliged. The chief saw this and pushed them away, saying, "Enough! Move on!" He smiled at me, slapping his club in the palm of his hand. "You shouldn't give them anything. They are cheats and liars."

That day, as the barge exited the confines of the Chenal into broader waters, the pastor shook my hand and jumped down into a pirogue. It would take him ashore to his village on the edge of the forest, and I would see him no more.

彡彡彡

The next dawn, dragonflies and fat sluggish moths covered my mosquito net. The heat in Kinshasa Province had been bearable, but the merchants warned me that after Bolobo, which we had just passed, the climate would turn equatorial. I emerged from my net and found the river had become a sheet of glass spreading to in-finity, overhung by a suffocating mist; the air had turned heavy and sour with tropical rot. No banks were visible, except for the occasional island—ragged outcroppings of black tree silhouettes—drifting by in the steam. Noon brought white heat and steely white light; the river became a lifeless, utterly still lake of glare, ten miles across, all colors reduced to black and gray against the white of water and sky. The barge's surfaces became untouchably hot, shade diminished as the sun rose directly overhead. The mer-chants erected tarps up and down the deck and lay prostrate under them, torpid with the heat. The crew reclined in shady corners of the *pousseur*, perspiring, lazily chasing away flies.

I went to Jean's to bathe, but his steel cubicle bathroom was an inferno, and I sweated even as I rinsed off. Afterward, I found a pool of shade on the bridge deck and spread out within it. Bees buzzed around me, flies harried me, but the heat made me sleepy, and soon I found myself drifting into feverish hallucinations, into jarring dreams of falling and collision.

There were shouts. I opened my eyes to see a barge passing by, heading downriver. The flag of the Central African Republic drooped lifeless above its *pousseur.* It was even more crowded than our boat. After hailing us with raised arms, the passengers, and their craft, faded away into the steam.

┉

The wan little woman squatter knocked on my cabin door, holding Party Naked under her arm half-upside down. He whined all the time, never crying, his voice faint, as if coming from somewhere far away. When he peed, he usually did so on his mother's skirt. She would then shift him to her other knee and let the stain dry in the sun. His left big toenail, I noticed, was daubed with hot-pink nail polish.

"*Mondele,* give me an onion!"

I did. She took it, slung Party Naked under her other arm, and went over to her tiny *bambula.* This day, as every day, she was cooking a pot of mush—manioc meal. She often asked me for food, and I always gave her what she wanted, but on the sly. When others saw me do this, they asked for handouts, too, and I didn't have enough to go around.

As I was shutting my door a teenager stopped on his way to the *pousseur* and introduced himself. He lisped, but his French was fluent. "You are different from us," he said, looking me over. "You eat well and this makes you strong. Everything about you shows you are rich and eating well. Your skin, your hair. You don't really have to work. But look at us. We row pirogues and this weakens us. We are a very weak people, weak from hunger."

He said a sullen good-bye to me and continued on his way. I finished locking up. The padlock on my door stared at me and told a truth: I had to lock up my food or it would be stolen by hungry people. I could not even give away food freely for fear of running out myself, such would be the demand. My cabin was full of food and water—amounts of both measured to last till Kisangani—and I carried a sum of money that probably equaled the yearly income of twenty-five Zaireans. I suddenly felt obscene on the barge; I felt an impotence and a weird outrage at myself for being there.

There was nothing to do but seek the shade and wait out the heat.

***

Now the wide steaming basin of the river was starting to produce a bounty that cheered the merchants. More and more fishermen paddled out from clusters of houses on stilts above the water and brought aboard wicker-frame valises of smoked fish; soon, valises were stacked everywhere. There was also more and more fresh fish, and the abundance drove prices down to the affordable. Merchants bought it and set about treating it to last the journey, splitting open the bellies and gutting them, salting the flesh, and laying it to dry in the sun. Flies landed on the fish and deposited eggs, which the merchants flicked away when they wriggled to life as maggots.

***

The fierce heat didn't last long: in its weather the equator is a zone of brief but intense pain as well as relief. When the sun began to go down, the river flooded with purples and reds, and cool air washed over us. We were now ascending watery byways no more than forty or fifty yards wide, floating past island after forested island, where giant solitary trees stood like august elders in dominion over masses of junior seedlings and a myriad of scrapping birds and monkeys.

The music came on. Jilly invited me over to the barge office for a beer—or rather, he invited me to treat him. I accepted. I had been considering asking him to be my guide on the river, if I should decide to hire one. He had run the river a dozen times and knew it well; he appeared hearty and reliable, doing his difficult job for the Colonel with a flamboyant alacrity. By the office we found the manager, saturnine as ever, and genial old Jacques with his sack of sugar. Jacques fretted and scratched his head. "No one wants my sack of sugar. Everyone wants to buy economy-size packets. Can I interest you in a sack of sugar?"

I ordered a round of beers. Babies were nursing at breasts, women were stewing fish and cutting up plantains and sewing, men were dancing to the beat. I sat there and soaked it all in. For the first time I was relaxing, slipping into the easy swing of African life, feeling as though I would do more than survive my trip, as though, indeed, I was heading upriver toward a new beginning, a fresh start.

Jilly sipped his beer. His wife, an amiable woman who wore her short hair in tight knots, was pounding manioc with a pestle, facing away from us. Jilly pointed at her. "See how my wife respects me? She's showing me respect."

"How?"

"By not looking at me and getting in my affairs."

"That's respectful?"

"Yes, she knows her place. Your women don't know the meaning of respect. They don't show you respect. They don't even want to have many babies."

I knew that large families served as support networks for aging parents, but Jilly's combative assertions provoked me to argue from my own vantage point. "Not all women want to have babies. I have women friends who don't want to have children."

"Then why in God's name are they on this earth?" He grew livid. This was a subject he had clearly thought a lot about. "God put them here to multiply. Here we have a lot of children. Some are weak and will die, others are strong and will live. But it's God's will that women have a lot of babies, as many babies as possible."

"Why not have one or two children and try to give them everything, instead of having seven or eight and hoping the strong will make it?"

"Because we are on this earth to have children, I'm telling you! It's God's command! Your friends are wrong, and you should tell them so. They are breaking God's command. I don't break his command. I will have a lot of children because that's what God wants."

"Tay-ler!"

The Colonel came over. The crew sat up straight. "Have you

told them your mission? This American," he said, pointing to me, "is going to try to come down the river in a pirogue."

Jilly's wife turned and gave me a wide-eyed stare. "You're going to die, young man!" She shook her head and went back to her manioc.

"We Africans don't like adventure," said the Colonel in his intense nasal voice. "We don't understand it. Part of your problem will be that no one will believe why you are on the river. They will be suspicious and afraid of you."

He stopped talking. The music had died and Jilly was silent. We all looked toward the river. The forest was blackening with night.

***

Our captain liked to talk, and he welcomed my presence on the bridge, so I often went up to visit him. He would show me his old map, tracing our route through the islands. The river was low and navigation difficult—shifting sandbars threatened the barge.

The next afternoon he and I were checking our progress—we had covered about four hundred kilometers—when ahead of us, on the roof of the barge office, a Zairean in long white robes and skullcap was prostrating himself on a prayer mat, clicking prayer beads.

The captain gestured at him. "We don't like the Arabs, even the black Arabs, like that one. They came here and sold us to the whites. Now they come to buy diamonds. They are in collusion with our rulers. Our rulers let the Arabs take suitcases of diamonds out of our country for a few zaires' *matabiche*. The Arabs make so much money from us, and they don't invest a cent here. Unlike the Indians and Pakistanis, who do, who have their own businesses."

While we were talking, boulders of black cloud filled the sky and tumbled toward us, fulminating with thunder and exploding in lightning. At first slowly, then frantically, the merchants began covering their wares.

The Colonel shouted to the captain from the barge deck below. "A typhoon! Pull over, fast!"

The captain turned the wheel hard. The barge swung starboard and drew up to the bank. I raced up to the roof and grabbed my gear. As I was climbing down the ladder, mosquito net under my arm, a curtain of rain hit us, followed by a blast of hot wind that rocked the barge and tossed up a churning surf, bending trees double on the bank. The sagging tarps above the deck filled with water, then tore free, dumping their load of rain over the merchants and their wares. It was an insane scene of meteorological mayhem, an orgy of sudden violence wrought by the skies.

A merchant in a baseball cap danced on the roof of the barge office, holding his mouth open to the rain.

By nightfall the sky cleared, and we continued our ascent through winding aquatic alleys. The Milky Way stretched a wash of stardust above the water; the river was spreading and dark under a shroud of mist.

"Mayeee! Mayeee!"

An old deckhand was thrusting a pole painted with alternating red and white meter-long segments into the water, shouting *"Mayeee! Mayeee!"* (Water! Water!) His wail reminded us that we could never be sure of the river. But of the surrounding forest, now a jagged blackness jutting up into the stars, we could be even less sure.

Dancing on the Equator

IN AN OVERGROWN CLEARING ALONG THE SHORE STOOD A majestic assemblage of rotting walls and vine-covered Roman columns: Mobutu's half-built equatorial palace. As we floated by, the merchants gathered at the edge of the barge and gawked. "The palace of the *Grand Voleur*," they called it. The Great Thief, however, had been forced to abandon it and his other residences on land for his yacht when the *pillages* hit. It was easy to discern in the stately ruins Mobutu's stillborn desire to show his affinity for the region: Equateur, where we now were, was his native province, as it was the native province of the Colonel and most of the country's elite.

Soon after passing the palace we drew upon the town of Mbandaka, which straddles the equator, amid an enervating heat. The sun hung, a glareless orb of molten silver that glowed through ashen mist above an ashen river; the air was waterlogged, and I found myself sweating through my clothes, almost gasping for breath. The forest was consuming the town, smothering with luxuriant creepers and sagging palms the decaying white stucco houses and straw umbrella huts on the clearing above the dock.

To signal our arrival the captain switched on the music. Danger de Mort rose and took up position near the gangplank, snapping taut his rope whip, but the heat quickly discouraged him and he sat down again. When the gangplank was tossed ashore a few locals lazed aboard to see what our merchants had to sell; a few passengers, including the Colonel, got off to check out the food stands in the clearing. It was almost too hot to move, and Mbandaka promised little, so I stayed put on the roof.

Two men in dark sunglasses and pressed white shirts marched

down the clearing, heading our way. The crew looked at them, then at me. Even here, in this remote settlement, the state had its agents, and they were hungry for *matabiches*, bribes.

"Don't give them anything," said the deckhand next to me. "They're coming for you. They'll make problems, and problems mean money. They're from the Bangala tribe, you see; they're the biggest thieves. Mbandaka is the first town of the Bangala homeland." I looked at Danger de Mort, who was a Bangala; I could perceive the same bony lineaments and half-demented jumpiness in the swaggering gait of the security men.

When they started up the gangplank, everyone cleared out of their way. Once aboard, the senior officer turned his dark glasses my way and stabbed a forefinger at me, then stabbed at the deck by his feet: *Get down here NOW!* I grabbed my passport and climbed down.

We met outside the Colonel's cabin. Two sets of dark glasses regarded me, reflecting my glistening, sunburned visage in quadrupled miniature; above the glasses two frowning foreheads dribbled copious sweat.

"We are from SNIP. Show us your papers."

"I'm the guest of the Colonel."

"Yeah, yeah, let's see your papers, and fast. We need information. We need to talk in private. Come around here."

On the bridge they leafed through my passport and snorted at the various stamps, which by all appearances they found highly unsatisfactory. The senior one shook his head. "You are going to have to see our commander in town."

"Why?"

"Why is not a question for you to ask. You're going to have to explain yourself and your mission to the commander. He will decide your case."

I was not getting off the barge without the Colonel. "With all due respect, my papers are in order," I asserted. "I'm the guest of the Colonel. If you have a problem, please see the Colonel. He's in town at the moment. You do know the Colonel, don't you?"

He tilted his head up and stared down his nose at me. I stared back, feeling perspiration trickle off my forehead into my eyes. It burned. I turned away and wiped it off.

He patted his brow and sat down in the captain's seat, as did his aide. "Well, okay then. We'll wait right here until this Colonel comes back."

"Fine."

I took out J. D. Salinger's *Nine Stories* and opened it to "De Daumier-Smith's Blue Period," and started reading. The senior officer snatched it out of my hands and scrutinized it as though it were a packet of high-grade heroin, then, disappointed, gave it back to me. But in truth I could not concentrate enough to read: I felt exposed and nervous. How was I going to handle such a situation when I was sailing downriver alone? A *lettre de recommandation* from a general might mean little to officials who needed to feed their families.

Soon, however, the heat overcame us all, and we dozed off, slumped in the bridge chairs. One hour passed, then two . . .

The Colonel ascended the gangplank and came around the stern. I hurried to meet him at the ladder. "Hello. SNIP has come for me."

He paused, without looking at me, then quickened his pace toward the bridge.

A few minutes later the SNIP men emerged from the bridge, smiled, and wished me "good travels, my friend!"

⚞

We had spent a week on the barge and Mbandaka was the closest thing to a city we had seen. True, it no longer had electricity or running water—with Mobutu's misrule those amenities had long since disappeared—but Jilly and his wife, Mama Tété, over a dinner of stewed eel and mashed bananas, told me about a discotheque with a generator and suggested we pay it a visit. So, with lightning flaring up in silence to illuminate the nighttime mists, we climbed down the gangplank, and Jilly used my flashlight to lead the way.

As we walked along, vines hanging from unseen trees tickled our faces, crickets chirped in palmy black glades; the impression took hold that we were somewhere deep in the jungle. But then we heard music: the Latin sounds of Zairean pop.

"That's it," said Jilly. "That's Chez Tatine. The club."

On the path near Chez Tatine there were people squatting around feebly glowing kerosene lanterns, selling *shikwanga,* palm grubs, beetles, and caterpillars. Jilly stopped and shone the light on them. "Mind if we have some hors d'oeuvres first?"

"Go ahead." Then I understood he was asking me for money. He bargained and I paid the sum required. Jilly took a leaf-full of slithering treats from the merchant and popped them into his mouth one by one, chewing with his mouth open. Some of the bugs made a crisp crunching sound; others, perhaps the soft-bodied caterpillars, went down with a squish.

Up ahead a generator was chugging. A blue-green-red neon sign announced Chez Tatine—a few white tables under straw umbrellas scattered around a plank dance floor, a bar stocked with Primus beer. Jilly began to shimmy and bop even before we entered. Mama Tété kept her purse to her side and held her nose prudishly high. The dancers were mainly men and prostitutes. Of the latter there appeared to be quite a few, judging by the appraising eyes that followed us.

"Our leaders decided to build a beer factory here instead of a hospital," said Jilly. "So instead of a place for the sick in Mbandaka we have beer. And we do love our beer." We ordered three bottles.

Outside, the mists were igniting with luminous zigzags of lightning; here, under the straw umbrellas, the music was all lilting Zairean melodies, tunes that matched the heat and mood and required little more than sways and cadenced nods from the perspiring dancers.

We sipped our beers. Jilly leaned toward me. "Look, I want you to bring a boat engine next time you come from the States."

"A what?"

"An engine like the one on the *pousseur.*"

"But . . . the *pousseur*'s engine is the size of a Mac truck."

"So? That's not a problem for you. Just ship it over here. You could build a boat to go with it and I could work on that boat. You can afford it."

"What gave you the idea I had that much money? I don't."

"But you *will* have the money. You'll make millions with this expedition. Tell me, what are you really looking for? Diamonds? Gold?"

"Jilly, I *have* told you. I'm here to pirogue down the river."

"Well, I don't care whether it's gold or diamonds. Just try and bring a boat engine next time you come."

Setting down his beer, he jumped up and trotted out among the hookers and started gyrating, but in their midst he danced by himself, enjoying the tunes, his eyes half closed. The hookers were dressed in loose skirts, in half-buttoned blouses that flapped open at times and revealed their breasts. They moved with an entranced rhythm of heat and languor; they smiled and bobbed in the humid air; their faces beamed with pacific self-absorption; there was nothing on this earth except this bar in the jungle, this beery cheer, this salsa beat of Zairean pop in the warm night. I gazed into their faces and thought, Where would they be in ten years? What were their days like? As I pined away in Moscow they had been coming here, to this bar, and dancing till dawn. Could I ever learn to take life so easy?

The beer and the heat made me sleepy. To wake myself up I excused myself from Mama Tété; I walked to the edge of the bar, then stepped off the platform onto the grass and moved out of range of the speakers, into the night. I stood for a minute and strained to listen. In filtered the chirping of crickets, the shrieks of monkeys, the hooting of owls, the erratic menacing buzz of insects cries of life heralding another world, a world at my feet and above me, but hidden, going on stealthily, existing secretly under cover of leaf and branch and mist and dark.

The mosquitoes drove me back to the bar. An hour later the barge's horn sounded, and we hurried out of Chez Tatine and down the jungle lane, heading for the river. The lightning now appeared to be flashing a warning, but about what I could not say.

Into the Great Forest

A BRIMSTONE DAWN WAS BREAKING AS WE WERE PREPARING TO leave Mbandaka. There was no rain, but from every tree-crenellated horizon lightning bolts tore to earth, splitting goblins of mist. Delayed claps of thunder drowned out the captain's commands, shouted over the loudspeaker, to fishermen to pull their pirogues away from the barge, or else. Mbandakans who had come aboard were jostling by the gangplank to get off, and passengers who had gone ashore were thronging on the bank to climb aboard. Lightning flashed across the deck, catching Danger de Mort in manic poses as he thrashed the crowd with his rope whip, trying to keep a passage clear for the security chief, who hacked at the liana moorings of pirogues with a machete. From behind the forest to the east an infernal red glow was stealing up the sky, suffusing the mists over the river.

The gangplank was finally drawn up. The *pousseur* shook with the ignition of the engines, and we began pulling away from shore, the barge swinging backward, the forest, lit now and again with lightning, revolving around us.

Suddenly there were shouts from the water, then screams. The bridge spotlight swiveled and cast its searching beam through mists and moths and fell on an upturned pirogue, on people splashing amid floating boxes and valises of fish and bamboo mats, all being swept downstream. There was nothing to be done about it now. The engines roared and we started upriver.

Thinking I might try and catch an hour's sleep, I retreated to my spot above the bridge. But I ended up sweating, wide awake, with the mosquitoes clustering thick and noisy on the gauze walls, the sun rapidly becoming a presence of pure heat behind the

93

clouds. Finally, when it was thoroughly light, I gave up and began taking down my net.

∕∕∕

"Monsieur Jeff!"

Roger, one of the mechanics, hauled himself up the ladder and stepped onto the roof. I knew why he had come. He had several times offered me women from the barge, mounting my ladder rung by rung, followed by candidates large and small, light and dark. He was polite, if rather formulaic, in his introductions, and I always politely refused. This time, the girl with him was fifteen or so, her hair done up in corn rows, her wraparound skirt fastened in a knot on her hip. She had a demure, endearing smile. But she had little reason to be demure: every day at sunup I had seen her emerging from the cabin of a different crew member.

The two of them walked slowly across the roof. Roger halted and motioned to the girl. He cleared his throat. "I present this young girl to you."

She smiled bashfully.

"Thank you, Roger, but as I've told you, I already have a wife. I'm faithful to her." This seemed the easiest way to turn him down without causing offense.

He cocked his head and cleared his throat again. "I said, I present this young girl to you." He made the same gesture. "She can be your wife on the barge. She is young."

"Yes, she is. But I don't need a new wife. I'm happy with the one I have."

"We all have wives at home. This young girl is just for the barge. We all need women while we are away from our wives. For our health. Feed her and she'll be your wife for the trip. That is all. There is no problem."

Her bashful smile became an impish grin. I smiled and put together the words in Lingala for "I'm sorry, but I already have a wife," and she shrugged and walked back to the ladder. Roger, dropping his gaze, made as if to leave too, but he then paused and turned back to me. He regarded me, his brow starting to furrow, his eyes suddenly growing hard. I asked him if he had something he wanted to say.

He did. "You don't like our women. You write in a book and take pictures. What are you doing here?"

"I'm learning about the river. I'm going to pirogue from Kisangani to—"

"I think you're here for something else." His gaze narrowed. "I think you're looking for something. Our country is rich. *Mondeles* come here for our diamonds. Maybe you're looking for diamonds."

"I'm not looking for diamonds. I'm here to travel the river, as I've told you."

I recalled him following me with his eyes on the barge. His questioning made me feel guilty of something, and I wondered if he wasn't offering me women to test me in some way. But I suppressed the notion: to what end would he be testing me?

"Roger, as I've told you, I'm here to travel the river."

"Why?"

"Because it's fascinating." I didn't feel inclined to go deep into my motives for undertaking the trip. We were passing houses on stilts. "To see houses like that. We don't have houses like that in America."

"You have better houses. I think you have another reason for coming here. You will leave a rich man. How much does the plane ticket from your country cost?"

I did not want to answer this. My London-Brazzaville-London ticket, bought at a discount from a bucket shop on Earls Court Road, still had cost me five times what he would probably make in a year. "Look, wouldn't you like to see America?"

"Yes."

"Then why can't you understand why I want to see Zaire?"

"You are not telling me your true purpose in coming to Zaire." At that, he turned away abruptly and climbed down the ladder.

It began to drizzle. Oddly shaken by his suspicion, I gathered my gear and retreated to my cabin.

All day we rocked and pitched on the choppy river under a sky of gunmetal clouds that lashed us with brief showers of hot whipping rain. The forest was low here, mostly squat palms rising out of dense swamp. Pirogues tossed on the waves as they paddled up from stilt villages, often missing their moors and nearly capsizing in our wake. Yet life on the barge was not unhappy: women cooked and sewed and tended their babies; merchants sold their wares to villagers, who came aboard in greater and greater numbers; children played and ran about, or dozed under tarps or in their pirogues. The rain, when it came, doused us in a warm, soothing wet and was preferable to the tiring humidity that had dogged us since we left the cool, windy Chenal.

For hours that day I sat up in the bridge with the captain, watching the river lanes unwind ahead of us and draw us deeper and deeper into the jungle; I followed the green clumps of water hyacinth rushing past us down the rippled sheets of iron-gray water.

The Colonel stepped in. "Tay-ler! Ha-ha-haa!" He grabbed my shoulder. "No diarrhea? No malaria?"

"No."

"We're in the homeland of the Bangala now. You need to eat, eat!"

"Why?"

"The Bangala like the flesh of the *mondele*. They say it's like sugar!"

He laughed, throwing his head back. We all laughed. It was getting easier and easier to talk to him, and I thought I might mention Roger's suspicion, to find out what he made of it. I told him about the incident on the roof.

"Yes, I know they're wondering about you," he said. "You have to understand. We think of white people as intelligent, as people who know how to build airplanes. We think such intelligent people wouldn't possibly come to our country just to pirogue on a river. We think they must be looking for something. Like diamonds. So there's some suspicion about you."

The Colonel didn't seem to include himself among the suspicious. Perhaps with his wealth he had enough leisure to sympathize with my more or less existential motives for making the trip. I had never gone into them with him, though, preferring to say I was out for adventure, and he had never asked. As for others, like Roger and the merchants struggling to get by day to day, I now understood such motives had to be foreign, even unbelievable to them.

After a while I caught sight of his watch. I noticed that it was Russian-made.

"Like my watch?" he said. "It's good for the rain. It has writing in Russian on it."

I looked down and without thinking read aloud the writing on the face: *"Vodonepronitsayemyye."* Waterproof.

His smile disappeared. "You can read this language?"

"Yes. I live in Russia. I told you that."

"But the letters aren't the same as ours."

"I know. I had to study them."

He scrutinized me, peering into my eyes in a stunned, vaguely hostile way that made me look away. Saying nothing more, he turned and walked out of the bridge. The captain also was staring at me; the same sort of dull suspicion Roger's eyes had conveyed I perceived in his. Inexplicably, I grew anxious and felt almost guilty. I sat back in my seat, trying to look unaffected, and watched the horizon. Why should *they* be suspicious of me? And if they were, why should it bother me?

Lightning was rippling through the clouds and reflecting off the river; the clouds were lowering over the trees, pressing in on the forest.

✧✧✧

The next morning Nze wiped his muscled hands on a rag and exited the engine room. "My wife has just cooked a musumbu for you. It's a special fish. Very tasty."

A few minutes later his wife, her head wrapped in a scarf and her plump face beaming with a motherly smile, brought me a steak-sized filet of the freshest, most succulent and crisply fried fish that I had tasted on the barge, or even in my life. It was garnished with mayonnaise and onions. I devoured it. Pleased, Nze watched me eat.

"Nze, thank you," I said, wiping my lips. "I've been feeling low lately."

"I know. And I know why. Don't take the suspicion personally. You see, life here is tough. We Zaireans are good people, but we've had a bad history, and it's left its mark. That's all."

I was wrestling with feelings new to me. I was white and sojourning in Zaire, a land despoiled by whites. Yet Zaireans by and large had treated me with an eager and disarming respect, hailing me everywhere and unabashedly as *mondele*—a friendly, if racial salutation—but in equal measure, I was coming to see that I was mistrusted on account of my color, perhaps now mistrusted even by the Colonel, on whose charity my safe passage depended. Nze believed me—or at least I thought he believed me. I felt a connection with him, whereas the suspicion of others put me off, and I did not know how to respond to it.

✧✧✧

The ninth day found us hugging the bank under a tangled mass of green lucent in its nearest reaches with sunlight pouring in from above, but dark and gloomy farther in. *La grande forêt,* they called it. Occasionally a monkey would scream and bound branch to branch back into the trees, or parrots would squawk and take flight. Huge, gangly kulokoko birds screeched at the sight of us, like pterodactyls horrified to discover men trespassing in their prehistoric domain, and wuff-wuffed away in heavy-winged flight. Once I caught sight of a cobra, some fifteen feet long and black, swimming through the water hyacinth, its curved emblematic head and neck slicing the coffee-brown water.

Trading on the barge was intense. We now trailed dozens of pirogues, and the fishermen, brawny Bangala with bass voices, were thick on board, their vigor and physique distinguishing them immediately from the merchants, who were mostly Kinshasans stunted to one degree or another by malnutrition. Many times Bangala youths dove from the banks and swam out to us, their arms thrashing out powerful crawl strokes. But most arrived on pirogues, bringing five-foot-long eels, bamboo-and-liana crates of manioc root, valises of smoked fish, football-sized chunks of smoked forest elephant, tethered antelopes, and squealing pigs. Sugar cane now abounded—it was bought by the stalk, peeled, and sucked as a sweet.

Watching life on deck relieved my anxiety about not being accepted: it was like theater, with elements comic and tragic both. A villager paddled up with a five-foot-long live crocodile, its jaws roped shut, in the bottom of his pirogue. After a bout of furious bargaining, during which the villager struggled to keep his balance despite the energetic contortions of his catch, which he held down by keeping his bare foot on its prickly head, a merchant from Kinshasa tossed him fifty dollars' worth of zaires. He assented, and the two of them struggled to get the angry black reptile out of the pirogue without receiving a blow from its tail or dropping it into the water; bystanders helped, but the croc still whacked one boy in the face with its tail. When they had dragged it away from the edge of the deck, the merchant took to pounding in its skull with the handle of a machete until it ceased struggling, its emerald eyes slit with black and staring fiercely, even in death.

Papa Jacques was still fretting over his sugar, but he managed to sell some of it at a discount. He counted his profits and called over a fisherman who was perusing medicine at a stand. "Show me that fish of yours. I'm hungry and now I have some cash!"

The fisherman, dressed in shreds of green shorts, walked over with what looked like a burnt garden hose slung over his shoulder.

"How much for that smoked eel?" Papa Jacques demanded.

"*Vingt-cinq milles,*" the man answered. Numbers were always expressed in French, with the rest of the negotiation carried out in Lingala.

"*Te. Cinq milles.*"

The fisherman made a face of pure disgust. *"Vingt milles."*
"Te. Huit milles."

On and on they bargained, but the ritual ended without a sale. Papa Jacques was angry. "These fishermen think they're big men. They are very rich and mean. They only wear rags to make us feel sorry for them. But what can you expect? They're Bangala, and they are only good for thieving and warring."

Dusk came and the weather calmed. We were a spearhead slicing into an azure river-and-sky mélange, seemingly released from the bounds of earth, floating in a blue domain. Astern, to the west, the river was bankless, tinctured lilac, bleeding red, running into cool purple with the sun's descent.

Having recovered from the day's heat, I sat under the light behind the Colonel's cabin trying to read V. S. Naipaul, a futile endeavor with the moths and cicadas swirling around me. Then something the size of a golfball slammed into my temple. I looked down and saw a huge armored beetle writhing at my feet. Jilly came over and picked it up. "We eat these beetles, you know. Come with me and answer a few questions."

He led me to a circle of palm wine drinkers on the bow. Now that we were in the great forest, palm wine was a big seller on deck, brought aboard from villages where it was made by allowing palm sap to ferment for a few days in gourds. The talk of the men in the circle was easy and calm, nothing like the boisterous, money-related rap one generally heard up and down the barge. They said hello, and poured me a wooden cup of wine from a distended calabash. A couple were smoking marijuana, *mbangi* in Lingala, and its pungently sweet aroma perfumed the air. "Have a smoke," they urged, their eyes reptilian slits.

I declined.

"Oh, come on, *mondele!* You're missing a lot! Bob Marley would never have made his music without *mbangi*."

"That might be. But I've never smoked anything in my life."

One of the drinkers adjusted his baseball cap. "So how are Zaireans regarded in your country?"

"That's hard to say. Not many people in the States know any Zaireans."

"You are kind. I think we're famous as thieves. In some languages saying 'Zairean' is the same as saying 'thief.' It's on account of our ruler. He gives us a bad name the world over."

The drinkers were chasing their wine with some sort of crunchy-chewy snacks that they were drawing from a bowl at their feet, popping into their mouths one at a time, and chomping on. I looked down: the snacks were fat white fried palm grubs.

Jilly chose that instant to shatter the *mbangi*-induced calm. "Listen"—here he picked a thumb-sized, curled-up grub, white-carapaced and black-legged, from the bowl and used it as a pointer. "Listen, your country is supposed to stand for human rights, but what about the rights of a man?" He bit off the head of the grub and chewed it lustily a few inches from my face. "What about the rights of a man? Huh? Here, have a grub." He shoved the bowl under my nose. "Now I hear that your government would forbid me to have more than one wife. I should be able to have as many wives as I choose—that's my right as a man. But your government would forbid it. That's unfair."

My fingers remained suspended over the grubs. Jilly grabbed one and pushed it into my hand. It was heavy, and its shell was smooth and hard as shellac.

"That's unfair! Well, what are you waiting for. Eat your grub!"

The circle looked at me. I raised it to my lips and . . . and . . . bit through its shell. It squirted something—maybe palm oil, or perhaps its innards burst. I don't know. Whatever, I found it chewy; if not exactly tasty, it was at least tolerable.

"So, isn't that unfair?"

I muttered something about polygamy being un-Christian. Then it hit me. *I am eating a larva,* I thought, as I worked the grub from cheek to jowl, chewing the crunchy bug, sensing tiny scratchy legs on my tongue, fighting back a gag reflex.

"Un-Christian?" Jilly was relentless. "Polygamy goes back to Jesus' day! It's your government that's un-Christian, allowing pornography in the streets and forbidding me my basic rights as a man! If I could afford it, I would have five wives, and they would be happy with each other, they could all help each other. Here, try a caterpillar." He held out another bowl: its contents were not fried but very much alive, brown and squirming. Still inwardly reeling from the grub, I had to refuse, but a little girl, seated next to one of the *mbangi* smokers, looked at me wide-eyed, took one of the wriggling creatures, put it to her mouth, chomped through its length, and swallowed with a gulp.

"Now listen," Jilly went on, "your country is famous for human rights, but it's a place where people are exploited. I have heard of caves in America where women dance naked for a dollar. You go inside this cave and put down a dollar. And your government would forbid me to have that woman if I gave her a few more dollars. It's all so unfair. Showing me a woman and then forbidding her. And then there's that joint nudism your families practice. In Africa a woman must be covered from ankle to neck."

"Ankle to neck!" he ranted as he urged grub after grub on me. I bit into them, grub after grub, I chewed apart carapace after carapace. There had to be far worse comestibles on this earth, my palate told me—though if pressed at that moment, still in shock at the thought of *what* I was eating, I could probably not have named one.

Night fell and the mosquitoes drove us off the bow. I wanted to get away from Jilly, from his strident ranting, from his rancorous and grubby hospitality, but he followed me back to the barge office. "Look," he said, "my wife has been saying to me all day, 'When is Jeff going to give me money for fish?'"

She had been offering to cook a fish meal for me if I gave her the money. I had wanted to do this but had not got around to it. "Well, maybe tomorrow. I've eaten already."

"Not for you—for her! She's hungry and she wants you to buy her fish. 'Monsieur Jeff has a lot of money—a *lot*—but he's starving me,' she says. So when are you buying her some fish?"

With the grubfest and his rant and with mosquitoes chewing up my exposed ankles, I snapped. "What are you saying, Jilly? She's *your* wife! *You* buy her fish! I buy you Cokes and beers and now you want me to feed your wife?"

"Look, tell me," he went on, unfazed. "How much money do you have on you? You have a lot, I know it. But how much exactly?"

I said nothing.

"You'll make millions on this expedition of yours. You're after something big out here. We know it, we all know it!"

"I told you why I'm here! And I'm not a bank. Only a lunatic would bring a lot of money on a trip like this. Think about it."

"But you can always get more dollars in America!" He stomped his foot. "You're from *America!*"

I stormed back to my cabin, leaving him standing there in a huff. I shut the door and sat down in the black. For ten days Jilly and I had been sitting together in the evenings drinking Cokes and beers, and still all I was for him was a source of cash, a *mondele* on a mission, a *mondele* deceiving everyone aboard with a ridiculous lie about a pirogue trip. Who trusted me here? And whom could *I* trust?

In the dark I saw Tatyana and drifted in thought back to other times, to comforting times, to long easy drives on weekends into Moscow down the birch-lined road from the cathedral-rich, onion-domed town of Sergiyev Posad, with Tatyana at my side in the front seat, reaching down to kiss my fingers on the gearshift, her soft black hair brushing my forearm; I recalled the rustle of poplar leaves on autumn mornings in our courtyard; I conjured up long winter nights when we escaped the musty apartment and went for strolls outside in the freshly falling, scintillating snow. Most of all, I thought back to the lingering lavender twilight of our last meeting in early June, by the river in Pushkino. I thought of all this and where I belonged, but where was I now? And where was Tatyana? Would she wait for me, or decide that if I was insane enough to leave her for Zaire she would find somebody else?

A sting, a spark. Something slimy and stinging swatted my calf. I jumped up, nearly braining myself on the upper bunk. Bopembe opened the door, and the deck light fell on a yard-long electric cat-fish squirming under my bunk.

"I bought that nina today," he said. "Please be careful not to get electrocuted."

⟡

That night the specters of great trees loomed black against the Milky Way's lustrous wash of stardust. With our spotlight prob-ing the waters in front of us, searching for shoals, illuminating swirling beetles and crow-sized bats, with mosquitoes showing like a fine mist in their millions, we threaded our way through a dark labyrinth of isles. Drumbeats announcing our arrival re-sounded from villages ahead, and we were beset by pirogues, many carrying stacks of blackened monkey carcasses, their eyes and mouths wide open as if they had been smoked alive in stark terror. Some paddlers were bare-breasted women; others, men in loincloths. All night there were shouts, drumbeats, armadas of canoes laden with bush meat streaming toward us.

The Bangala soldiers—besides Danger de Mort there were several aboard now—kept watch all night, stalking the decks, their rifles at the ready, their eyes on the darkness ahead. From the jungle we heard wails, drawn-out screams, and wavering laments; they echoed up and down the river, from the right bank, then from the left, issuing out of watery lanes that led like tunnels into pitch-black woods. The cries made my blood curdle. Fishermen hailing the barge, the crew told me.

⟡

"Tay-ler! Charles Tay-lor! *Le guérillero libérien!* Ha-ha-haa!"

The Colonel. When I looked up to the bridge, he turned away, as was his habit.

I found him in his cabin with his attractive cook-servant, a deli-cately featured young woman in a blue blouse and loose skirt, snuggled on the couch next to him.

"Want to watch a movie with us? Sit!"

I took a seat. They were watching a horror flick in which the protagonists were tormented by an evil magician and his team of loyal zombies. Every time the protagonists fell asleep graves opened up and half-decayed skeletons leapt out. The servant recoiled at the beheadings, the exploding guts and splashing gore, but the Colonel loved it, leaning forward, his belly over his belt, shouting encouragement to the monsters, laughing at the hapless victims. My nerves already frayed, I couldn't watch and took to examining his cabin. On a shelf over the VCR there stood a row of hardcover books. I was curious: what would the Colonel read in his spare time?

"May I?" I asked him, picking a book off the shelf.

"Certainement!"

It was a comic book. In hardcover. They were all comic books. A few were more elaborate than cartoons, actually, containing photographs of white people with bouffant hairdos and wide-lapelled polyester clothes professing love and nursing jealousy for each other. The dialogue was in French; they were comic-book soap operas of some sort. I put them back on the shelf.

Heads were flying on-screen, maidens were being raped. The servant averted her eyes. The Colonel gulped his beer and leaned forward, shouting, "Ha-ha-haa!" Having nothing else to do, I sat down on the couch and watched, and waited for it to end.

≈≈≈

Up on my rooftop sanctum I read a lot during the day. Salinger's *Nine Stories,* Naipaul's *In a Free State* and *One out of Many,* Updike's *Brazil.* I wrote letters to Tatyana (which I hoped to mail in Kisangani), but I covered them when visitors came by; after seeing the Colonel's suspicion on seeing me read Russian, I thought it best to be discreet.

The next afternoon a diffident and lanky twenty-eight-year-old merchant from Lokutu came up to the roof and joined me. I put down my book. He introduced himself as Desi.

We were keeping close to the bank. We passed a village where children were playing in a clearing. When they espied me, all but one took off running for the forest. The boy who remained made a motion with his arms as if machine-gunning me, and soon all his little pals imitated him, firing on me from the bushes. Desi said, "You see, they fear you, the *mondele*. White people to them are murderers and villains. The children hear how the Belgians used to eat little boys and girls, and they think you, or any white, is a Belgian. For them to kill you would be an act of self-defense."

I looked at Desi, impressed by his frank and articulate explanation. He was tall, loose-boned, with a small head and an engaging smile. There was something soft in his manner. I had earlier learned that he was a distant relative of the Colonel's, and that he came from upriver, from a tribe known as the Lokele, who were raised in pirogues and fished for a living.

Desi took the reaction of the little boys in stride: "These are Bangala. Of course they're *méchants*. That's their nature. They want your money. You're white, so they think you're rich."

His words put me in mind of Stanley's description of the Bangala. Stanley had called them a "very superior tribe" who entertained a "singular antipathy . . . toward strangers," in whom the presence of non-Africans "excited the most furious passions of hate and murder"—and that was *before* the Belgians had enslaved, maimed, and massacred them.

Desi and I spent the next hours together watching the jungles and villages go by. Much more than Jilly, Desi seemed like a worthy candidate for river guide. Watching the increasingly hostile reaction of villagers on the banks, I was more and more inclined to think I should not attempt the descent alone.

▰▰

On our eleventh day the boat rocked with the wind. The clouds were thick and suffocating, promising rain. I went around to visit the Colonel, but found his servant seated on his couch and looking solemn. "The Colonel is aggrieved," she announced. "His little sister has died."

I walked on to his room. He was lying on his bed, his hands behind his head, staring up at the ceiling through his sunglasses. From behind his sunglasses tears streamed out and rolled into his ears. I sat down. I was very sorry, I said. I touched his arm.

His breath caught on a stifled sob. *"Merci,"* he said, not moving his head.

I sat with him a while longer, saying nothing more. Since we met he had allowed me to ask nothing about him, and I knew nothing about him aside from what he told me in his jovial outbursts, or what the crew had related to me with hushed breath (that he had gained Mobutu's favor, and thus his rank and fortune, said to be $7 million, by exposing a traitor in the dictator's inner circle). My suspicions about his motives had dissipated; I now saw that he had brought me along for his own amusement, for the novelty I provided him, and that was fine with me. Without knowing more about him, I could not truly call him my friend, but he had helped me a lot, and I felt sorry for him.

I got up and went out to the living room. Nze was there. "It is the will of God," he said, and walked on to see the Colonel and pay his condolences.

I stayed outside his cabin all afternoon, feeling I should not leave him. On the banks, the villages had become disorderly and ill kept, messes of scraggly huts and laundry under high cliffs of forest, and their inhabitants, dirty and dressed in rags, shouted curses at me, but the Colonel's grief awakened dormant remembrances of recent deaths in my own family, and I paid no attention.

Just before the sun set, the Colonel came out on deck. We were passing a village. At the sight of me, women and children ran for the forest, but the youths stepped up to the bank and swaggered and shouted.

The Colonel walked over to the railing. On his belt was a thirty-eight-caliber pistol.

"Look at these people! They are unregistered in any book, they are uncounted and without papers. You have heard them howl in the night! They are savages! Zaire is wild! Wild!"

He sat down in the chair next to me and said no more.

∎∎∎

A thunderstorm broke that night. The rain pounded us in warm drenching torrents, while the wind swept down and rocked the barge on the wide river. I sat under the roof of the *pousseur*. Between thunderbolts howls resounded from the jungle, bloodcurdling cries that rent the rainy air: the crew's assertions that these were the salutations of Bangala fishermen seemed absurd; rather, it sounded as if the Bangala were taunting the barge, taunting the skies. I couldn't stand it anymore and retreated into the Colonel's cabin, where the bugs were thick—moths, termites, slow-fluttering flies—and stretched out on his couch until morning.

☞☞☞

On the twelfth day we docked in Lisala, the first town since Mbandaka. Porters came running down the banks to unload the sugar and grain we had in our hold. In exchange, we acquired chickens and pigs. We also had a pig of our own to deliver, a huge black sow that had come aboard a few days earlier. It squealed and bucked and refused to walk the plank to the shore. Her owner simply pushed her over the side; she crashed into the mud, and her front legs snapped like twigs.

The commander of SNIP in Lisala walked crisply down the deck, flanked by two aides. He was dressed in pressed khakis, as were his men. He and the Colonel embraced and talked. After a while the Colonel introduced me.

"This is Tayler. He wants to pirogue down the river."

After all we had seen on the barge, the idea, stated flat-out, now sounded insane, like the concoction of a lunatic.

"Well, it's a real abattoir from Lisala to Mbandaka," the commander responded in a matter-of-fact way. "This is the homeland of the Bangala and the Ngombe. You might have heard about the two Belgians. In eighty-eight or eighty-nine, they took off from Kisangani in a French amphibious Phoebe Jeep. They reached a village near here. They landed and set up a video camera to film their welcome by the villagers. The tribesmen came out. While one was shaking their hands the others came up from behind and hacked them down with machetes. They cut them to pieces, smoked their meat, and ate them. This was on the video we found. The tribes around here are *méchants*. Truly *méchants*."

Ngombe tribesmen had killed and eaten both foreigners and Zaireans alike there, he said. In the past, they would sneak up on barges and, using gaffs, drag people sleeping on deck into the water, drown them, then paddle away into the blackness with their mangled human booty, which they would smoke and consume later. This was no longer common, but it did happen.

The commander went on: "Many people around here in the villages have never seen a white man. If you're alone they will take you for a mercenary. In their eyes, either you're a mercenary or in search of diamonds. No white has ever reached Kinshasa after starting out from Kisangani. Not one."

The Colonel pointed to the M-16 leaning on the wall and said that it and the guns carried by his security men were for protection from bandits who attacked barges, setting upon them and carrying away money and women; for this reason, barges traveled fast through this part of the river and preferred to take on few pirogues. The SNIP commander confirmed this. "Yes, it's bad here. If you seriously plan to travel through here by pirogue, you will have to be armed and ready to risk your life, or you won't make it."

✦✦✦

Late the next afternoon we left Lisala. The sun fell behind the horizon, splashing the west with crimson and orange.

I remained on the Colonel's deck. The Colonel was still visibly shaken by his sister's death, and I didn't want to leave him yet. Pirogues were streaming toward us bearing young men. The Colonel arose and grabbed his rifle.

"No docking! *Voleurs! Voleurs!*" He fired a battery of rounds into the air. The pirogues dropped back. The Colonel returned to his seat next to me.

An armored beetle slammed into the side of my face. The Colonel laughed. "He's saying, *Bonjour, mondele!* Ha-ha-*haa!*"

I laughed, too. After a minute I thought to ask him how he was.

I turned to him. He was looking into the sinking sun, and tears were pouring out from behind his sunglasses.

✐✐✐

All night the soldiers made their rounds, forbidding the villagers to dock. Some of the merchants complained: they needed customers. The spotlight over the bridge ceaselessly swept the forest and waters ahead.

I was seated at the stern with the Colonel. Two shadows, black splotches amid the glitter of the moon on the water, became clear as paddlers. The Colonel took off his sunglasses and watched them. They were paddling hard, plunging their oars into the water, dragging the pirogue closer to us in bounds. We both now leaned forward. The boat was traveling full speed, yet they were catching up. The Colonel grabbed his gun. They reached the stern and began lashing the liana to the railing. The Colonel shouted at them; they laughed; he fired a burst of rounds toward the sky from his automatic. The security chief came running and tossed a log at them. With something like a war cry, a rippling howl, the piroguists cast off, still balancing on the waves, and berated us till the blackness enveloped them.

"This is a terrible wilderness," the Colonel said, and went back to his seat.

Later, after he had gone to bed, I felt sick to my stomach. A fierce wind drove me off the roof to a spot on the walkway to the bridge, where I set up my mosquito net. Then the rain came. I lay on my side, watching the rain strike the river, cramps wrenching my gut, with the gentlest pellets of water blown sideways into my face. The talk with the SNIP commander convinced me that my plan of traveling solo downriver would not work, and I decided I would hire a guide.

✐✐✐

Sometime after midnight a cry from the water awakened me, the cry of a child. A woman's scream followed. I sat up. The sky was black, moonless, filled with clouds; lightning was flashing over the water. A woman came running along the deck, jumping from the barge onto the *pousseur,* her eyes searching the dark currents. Her son had fallen overboard, she shouted, and he was somewhere out there, struggling and crying out. Up and down the barge men leapt into pirogues.

We slowed and begin turning around. The spotlight searched the brown water and rushing rafts of water hyacinth, but the cry was growing fainter and farther away. The mother flailed her arms; her screams cut the air and echoed off the forest walls. Pirogues cast off, their paddlers working furiously to keep their crafts clear of the rotating barge.

The captain cut the engines. The forest hung above us, high and black and layered with mists, echoing with yelps and screams, whether animal or human I could not say.

A half hour later, the pirogues came paddling back. They had found the boy, and he was alive. The engines roared back to life, and we surged ahead.

Upriver

"YOU THINK YOU'LL DOMINATE ME? I'LL DOMINATE YOU!"

The Colonel thumped his index finger into the bony chest of the SNIP officer who had come aboard at Bumba, sixty miles upriver from Lisala, and tried to take me away. The officer, a spindly fellow whose oily sweat gave his skin the sheen of an eel, had been telling me that my passport was marked with "a stamp from Ngobila Beach and not *specifically* from SNIP," which meant I was "in Zaire illegally" and would "have to see his commander in town *tout de suite*."

At that moment the Colonel came striding down the deck, his shoulders hunched, his arms dangling half-bent, his eyes leveled at the eel. The confrontation ended with the officer backing away and threatening to bring the mayor.

"Bring the mayor!" the Colonel said. "Now get off my boat!"

A little while later a tall man of coal-black complexion, dressed in a Hawaiian shirt and suede loafers, with the barrel-bellied, cologned hauteur of a Bumba grandee, arrived and embraced the Colonel. The three of us spent the afternoon talking over my expedition. The eel stood on shore, waving to me plaintively, performing a penitent pantomime that told of hunger and penury, of an empty wallet and an empty belly—mightn't I take pity on him and toss him a few zaires?

This was an officer I would likely run into on my way downriver, and he had to know I was not to be messed with. I would not show him pity, which might be interpreted as weakness. I turned to the Colonel and the mayor, and gave them my full attention.

✦✦✦

Bumba, an outpost of white stucco storefronts and ruined colonial-
era villas set at the edge of the jungle, was the last town before Kisangani. The crew said that pirogues would be expensive in Kisangani
and advised me to find one here; Bumba also seemed like a good
place to decide on a guide. Desi had impressed me, but I wanted to
interview other candidates as well.

During our chat with the mayor, there was a knock on the cabin
door. A wiry man in his forties, with a balding pate and long thin
nose, walked in.

"*Mbote. Mondele,* I am François. I know the river. I have been a
boat captain for ten years. Come, let's talk about our expedition."

"You could have a worse guide than François," the Colonel
said. "Talk to him."

François carried himself in a way that expressed as much con-
ceit as confidence. He moved and spoke slowly, following his own
private rhythms, answering questions when he was ready. But who
was this François, and why should he possess such manners? He
invited me to his home in Bumba, so we set off into the town.

Trees and tall grass shot up in Bumba's lots and yards. We made
our way through sun-splashed alleys of orange dust, stepping over
runnels of sewage, traipsing between middens of ash, and came
to a huddle of mud-plastered stone and straw-roofed rooms set
around a courtyard of packed earth, where a white girl of six or
seven was playing. She was entrancingly beautiful, this girl, her
skin bronzed, her chestnut hair streaked with gold. She spoke a
boisterous Lingala with her Zairean playmates; she was indistin-
guishable from them in language and bearing—the nonchalant
bearing of an urchin at ease with adults as well as those her own
age. Slumped in the shade nearby sat her mother, a slovenly and
buxom Latina matron with a ponytail of thick black hair, dressed
in an African skirt.

"You *fled* the children, didn't you?" François said, noticing my
surprise at the girl.

"How is that?"

"You whites. You came for the diamonds and made your families, then you *fled* them when you got what you wanted. This girl here and her mother are Portuguese. So was the father. He abandoned them. And you whites leave black women with babies, too. You just take what you want and *flee*. You flee even your own children." He shook his head.

We stepped inside one of the rooms and sat down on stools on the earthen floor. François called over a boy passing by the courtyard gate with a wooden bowl on his head. The bowl was filled with cola nuts. With fulsome aplomb, François ran his tongue over his front teeth, then squeezed, sniffed, and bit the tips of each nut before picking one and handing the boy a few zaires. He popped the nut in his mouth and started sucking on it, rolling it from cheek to cheek. It was a natural amphetamine and quickened his speech.

"Look, I'll do your trip," he said. "But I guide only, understand? You must have other paddlers and a soldier. My price is fifteen hundred dollars. Half in advance." He squirted nut juice through the gap in his teeth. "Got that?"

"I think that's too expensive."

He squirted more juice. "I know my river. That's my last price."

He might have known the river, but he was older than I would have preferred, too expensive, and, I thought, on the arrogant side. Ideally, my guide would paddle as much as I did, and I told him this. No way, he would not touch a paddle. We could not agree.

He took my rejection with a shrug, and we spent the torrid morning watching the little girl play in the dust with her friends, then, after the sun passed its zenith, headed back to the barge.

On the way down to the river, François said he wanted to help me anyway, so he told the children we encountered on the street to spread the word that a *mondele* wanted to buy a pirogue.

Then we stood on the stern of the *pousseur* and waited. Soon fishermen came paddling up the rushing current; others came slipping swiftly downstream. A veritable logjam of pirogues developed, with gumwood dugouts bouncing off each other, their owners waving and shouting at me in Lingala. A contingent of naked tots showed up, rowing scows no bigger than ironing boards; they shouted for my attention, too.

There was one pirogue I liked: a sturdy craft about thirty feet long, big enough for three or four people but not so heavy as to make rowing a chore for two. The owner asked for six hundred thousand zaires. Too much, whispered François. I began examining others. Right away the owner dropped fifty thousand. But this was still too much. Finally, the price came down to four hundred thousand, or about sixty-five dollars, including three paddles—the correct price, according to François. We shook on it. I handed the owner a brick of hundred-zaire notes; he gave me the bow chain and padlock and key. François and I fastened it to the railing on the *pousseur*.

I had a pirogue.

ırı

The sun dropped in a skywide flush of crimson and violet. I came down to the stern of the *pousseur* and marveled at my pirogue, then jumped aboard it. The river churned alive beneath the flat-bottomed hull, its power surged through the wood. The pirogue had been hacked from a healthy tree and looked fit to take me downriver. It was sturdy and I could stand in it with relative ease; I climbed up on the side and tried to overturn it by rocking, but I couldn't.

Nze saw me and came over. I asked him to jump aboard, and he joined me in my experiment: even two people couldn't overturn this craft. "This pirogue will do the trick. May God help you!" he said, climbing back onto the *pousseur*.

I sat down on the stern. Coffin-sized rafts of water hyacinth were racing toward me, catching on the pirogue and whooshing on past. Fishermen paddled by me upriver, throwing their weight into every oar stroke, their back muscles rippled and defined like shiny, well-molded porcelain. They stared perplexed at me as they approached, and they turned to stare some more after they passed. By getting into a pirogue I felt I had entered their world, and they seemed to perceive the same.

It was time to go make dinner.

␣␣␣

The next afternoon I noticed Desi talking to the Colonel. I began mulling over his qualifications as a guide. He had grown up paddling a pirogue and had made the Kisangani-Kinshasa trip a dozen times on barge runs. He was soft-mannered and companionable; with a forty-five-day trip ahead, that would be no small consideration. He prayed on deck and enjoyed the respect of the crew and other passengers. His French was fluent enough—he had finished sixth grade, which was as high as one could go in the villages here—so communication would not pose a problem. All in all, he impressed me.

Finished with his talk, Desi walked over to the stern and looked down at my pirogue. He said it was a good pirogue, suitable for the voyage to Kinshasa. He knew I was looking for a guide, but he appeared too shy to suggest himself.

I asked him to show me his piroguing skills. We hopped down into the craft and I unfastened it. Once free of the barge the pirogue suddenly came alive, sovereign in its own domain. Leaning into his paddle strokes, Desi directed us out and away into the hyacinth-studded blue water. For twenty minutes or so he paddled me up- and downriver, directing the craft with practiced ease. We pulled back to the *pousseur*.

In Desi I saw a person of integrity, someone I could trust with my life, if need be. He asked for much less than half of what François had demanded, with 50 percent in advance. That seemed reasonable and I could afford it. I would provide all his food and pay for medical care, if such care were necessary, and buy him the clothing and gear he needed (which would be his at the end of the trip). If we succeeded in reaching Kinshasa, I would give him a sizable bonus as well. And I would cover his return fare on the barge.

I drew up a contract that stated these conditions, writing out the document in French on a piece of paper torn from my Lingala notebook. Desi sounded out the words, took my pen, and signed his name; then I signed.

I had a guide.

After two days in Bumba we were on our way again.

⁄⁄⁄

The next night Paul, the first mate, spread out his maps in the bridge and shone a flashlight on them, and we talked over my descent. Barges followed the navigation route, which was, essentially, the channel. In places it was marked with white boards nailed to trees along the bank, but mostly it had to be divined by signs recognizable only to seasoned captains. There would be no need for Desi and me to stick to it, for our pirogue could travel in water as shallow as a foot or two. Paul pointed out danger areas on the map: the Ngombe-Bangala region between Lisala and Mbandaka, and within it the area around Île Sumba and the village of Bongela, which he described as "*méchant* and filled with robbers." Especially perilous was what he called the *rivière*—a sort of byway creek that diverged from the Congo by Bongela and ran behind Île Sumba, then reentered the river thirty-five miles later at the island's base.

I thought back on the hours and hours I had spent listening to advice about the river from Zaireans, starting with Pierre in Kinshasa. Don't camp on the islands or travel in the shallows—crocodiles and hippos lurk in both. Don't camp on the banks—leopards haunt the banks. Always sleep in villages, where there is fire. Never sleep in villages—the people there are poor, and the risk of robbery is high. (The Colonel said this. I usually found his words the most rational and consonant with my own thoughts.) Avoid sailing in the middle of the river—storms can strike suddenly, leaving no time to make shore. Stay away from the banks, where everyone would recognize me as a *mondele*.

So much contradictory advice, but no one among those who dispensed it had traveled the river in the way I intended to.

⁓⁓

The next day we pulled into the village of Yambinga, where we were to stock up on palm oil. Yambinga looked deserted, but porters in loin cloths showed up in throngs and vied for the task of carrying barrels of palm oil aboard our barge. They labored hard as hell under those barrels, which must have weighed a hundred pounds or more, carrying them on their backs up the gangplank and walking taut steps to the hold, then slowly, with great precision, setting them down.

How many porters we had seen on this trip! In every village they were the same—muscular, purple-black from the sun, with shaved heads, speaking only Lingala or their dialects, so poor that they had neither shoes nor shirts nor belts for their shorts. They leapt into action without being hired; they fought among each other over customers. They never slipped off the ramp or dropped their loads. They never complained. They just did their job, then addressed the foreman, who doled out to them a few zaires—the equivalent of *pennies*—for an hour's work in the brutal heat.

At every port there were always crowds of them. I wondered what their life was like. What did they hope for? What did they talk about among themselves? What were their concerns? They lived now as their forefathers had, illiterate, without knowing more of the past than what could be handed down to them by word of mouth. How would such people regard the world?

I was tired of this barge, fatigued by this heat, and sick of this food; but these porters were never tired, or never looked tired, and the bank of this equatorial river, this remote village at the edge of the great forest, was all they would ever know. I pondered the genuine and unadorned life they seemed to lead, a life revolving around food, drink, and family obligations and village duties, and considered whether I could ever adapt to it, replace my messy and anguished existence with it, and be saved by it. Perhaps I would get a taste of it during my descent by pirogue.

✐

Desi told me he was a good cook, so I asked him to show me what he could do. On my *bambula* he prepared a tasty lunch of fresh fish and macaroni, and we ate it on the roof above the bridge. The sun was hot, in a way that extinguished the desire to move and inclined one to close the eyes and sleep, but it was too hot to sleep. We decided, after a while, to go ashore in the glare and have a look around.

From the barge, Yambinga appeared to be a flat mud clearing, surrounded by huge rusted cisterns and dotted with a few dilapidated brick buildings; the actual village, it turned out, was off down a trail, a short way into the forest. The clearing stank in an acrid and cloying, even nauseating, way. Desi said the stench came from the local palm oil plant, but it seemed to originate with the palm nuts that lay on the ground everywhere—maybe they were rotting. We bought some tiny bananas from a village girl, but peeled they had a foul scent, and their bitter taste churned my stomach.

We took a path that led us through the forest and wound round again to the bank, and sat down on a sandy clearing, looking out over the river, the clumps of water hyacinth floating by—*Kongo esika,* in Lingala, said Desi. Tsetse flies buzzed around us. They had followed us from the *pousseur,* where they reposed in the shade and waited for victims. Tsetses were clever in their tactics of attack; it was as if they knew people despised and feared them for the trypanosome they often carried that caused sleeping sickness—a common malady upriver. They would land a yard away, wait, circle and buzz a little closer, land again, wait, then alight on a secluded spot, such as behind the knees. They were maddeningly persistent, and soon they had bitten me, painfully, several times.

I was wearing shorts and so kept a sharp eye out for tsetses. Desi stared at the hairs on my legs, then poked them.

"Why do you have this hair?"

"I have Italian blood in me."

"And why is your skin red here?"

"Well, I'm white, so I get burned in the sun."

Neither answer explained anything to him. No matter. He told me about his wife and newborn daughter, who were now staying in Bumba; he hoped we could stop to visit them on the way downriver. His life was a series of barge trips up and down the Congo, a tiresome routine of uncertain weeks on deck, but the money, if the trading went well, sufficed to live well on.

A girl paddled by with a small live crocodile in her pirogue, on her way to sell it on the barge. The breeze changed and brought the stench of the palm oil down upon us, and the barge horn honked, calling us back.

And now it was the yield of the forest we were seeing for sale, the fish having diminished and gone up in price as a result. During our stopover in Mombongo, men brought aboard monkeys red and gray, carrying them (dead) by their tails, which had been tied around their necks; pirogues paddled up with wild pigs and antelope. A herd of domestic pigs and a flock of goats now occupied the bow; cages of chickens littered the walkways. Boys circulated with porcupines in cages; they could be dequilled and fried nicely. Old Jacques bought a piece of smoked boar (it resembled a chunk of coal), and he kept a four-foot crocodile (with its jaws roped shut) tied up near the barge office, to be killed and eaten when the time was right.

I stood admiring the crocodile when a rain of squirming, half-inch-long maggots sprinkled over me. Above me, on the roof, merchants were shaking the maggots out of the fish they had salted. Maggots were dropping into the barge office through the cracks in the roof, falling onto Jean's bed; he scrapped them off and stomped on them, squishing them into white-green sludge. He was not disgusted; he just wanted to keep his bed free of clutter.

Party Naked and his mother had gotten off somewhere around Bumba. Where they had been squatting by my door there was now a five-foot-high stack of fish valises—and a corresponding puddle of wriggling maggots.

░░

"Mayee! Trois mètres septante-cinq! Mayee! Trois mètres cinquante!"

The next night the old depth sounder on the *pousseur* was working his pole all the time, thrusting it into ever more shallow water, grabbing his straw hat each time his stooping labor threatened to dislodge it from his gray-haired head. His shrill cry wailed above the thunderous rhythmic chug of the engines.

The merchants had been complaining all day. They were hungry, having bought little fresh fish since Bumba (they would not eat the smoked fish in their valises, which was for resale only). To distract themselves from their empty bellies, many played checkers, scratching out boards on the rusted deck with their knives and using Primus beer caps for pieces—upturned for red, downturned for white.

Desi came to see me by my cabin, moping. "There is nothing to eat. No fisherman are coming aboard now." I gave him food from my stock to cook a meal for us both.

"Mayee! Deux mètres septante-cinq! Mayee! Deux mètres cinquante! Hooa! Un mètre vingt-cinq! Hooa! Un mètre—"

The depth sounder's pole caught and bent and tossed him back against the wall. The barge lurched, rocked, and lurched again. I grabbed the rail, others fell flailing into their merchandise. The engine roared and sputtered, crew members raced toward the *pousseur,* jumping over cooking pots and sacks of salt. The spotlight at the stern dropped onto fulminating clouds of sand in the water behind the propellers.

We had run aground so violently that one of our two rudders had been severed and an engine incapacitated.

I was exhausted. Almost three weeks of heat and crowd and hassle on the barge seemed to have drained the life out of me. Nze said this was a serious accident that could delay us by three days at least. We were already a week late; the Colonel's declaration that our journey would last two weeks had been forgotten long ago. For the first time, I wanted to scream.

To the south over the forest, lightning flared silently at first, then with rumbles of thunder. The Congo's warm fluids rushed past our motionless bow in a rippling V. There was nothing to be done now, said Nze.

The Colonel called a crew conference behind his cabin. The captain was there, as were Nze and Roger and the other mechanics. Desi and I attended also. The Colonel began by scolding them for an extra day we had spent unloading cargo en route. Heads dropped in shame.

Then the Colonel's voice hissed with the nasality I had heard first in his office back in Kinshasa. "Now, I want to hear from you, Nze, what you propose doing about the broken rudder."

Although his subject was rudders, chains, and severed steel, Nze stood up and spoke with passion, concluding with: "Only a thorough, three-day repair stop in Lokutu will save us. Only there can we find a solution to this disaster."

The captain seconded his suggestion: three days in Lokutu would solve everything. It seemed an open-and-shut case: the rudder was broken, and a new rudder could be purchased and attached in Lokutu.

The Colonel leaned back in his chair, saying nothing, and looked at the crew, who leaned forward. Then heads lowered all around; the Colonel's silence suggested that Nze had uttered inanities unworthy of response.

Nze raised his head. "Umm, if we just went to Lokutu to get a new rud—"

"I have spent a small fortune—thirty-six thousand dollars, to be exact—on the merchandise aboard my boat," interrupted the Colonel. "I'll not risk thirty-six thousand dollars for a thousand-dollar rudder. The purpose of this voyage is to make money. I am here with you to see how you operate and to see who among you makes decisions. Now I see no one is able to make the correct decision. I'll decide in Kinshasa who among you stays with my company and who among you goes. Your job, I tell you, and as I told you before we set out, is to get the merchandise from Kinshasa up this river to Kisangani, one rudder or two, no matter what it takes. Excuses and explanations don't put money in my bank account."

He paused. Heads remained lowered.

Nze opened his mouth, but the Colonel cut him off. "At least one of you should have understood the purpose of this journey." He got up and went back to his cabin, having announced no decision about repairing the rudder. Moths and cicadas and giant beetles swirled violently around the halogen light, and bats dipped among them and feasted.

In despair I retired to my spot above the bridge. A full moon shone out from among the clouds, hanging over the silhouettes of trees on the distant bank and dappling the waters below with orange. Nevertheless, rain came that night, soft and slight in the beginning, then hot, copious, and pummeling. I gathered up my net and retreated to the awning under the bridge. Until dawn I watched the lightning flare up and show the river around us as wide as the sea, I shuddered at the crash of thunderbolts that seemed aimed at our craft on the open water.

The next morning the *pousseur* detached itself from the barge and chugged a wide arc across the river, which was glass-smooth and hued with mother-of-pearl in the still cool air. It backed up to a sandbar and halted. It transpired that one of the crew members was going to have to dive underwater and haul the dangling rudder to the surface. An altercation erupted in Lingala among the crew as to who might be chosen to do this, and Desi translated for me. The prevailing fear was that "enemies" of the man underwater— and they all now declared they had enemies—might assume the form of a crocodile and, while he was at work, attack and kill him. No one would take that risk.

I asked Desi if he believed this.

"It is true. A sorcerer with the right fetish can send a crocodile

or a hippo to kill any man he chooses. Men whose wives are preg-
nant are especially vulnerable."

The arguing continued.

Desi stepped forward. "I'll do it!"

A stunned silence followed. Desi stripped off his shirt, and the
crew made way. He leapt into the green, waist-deep water, inhaled,
and plunged beneath the surface.

Ten seconds ticked by. Twenty. Thirty. There was no sign of
him. At forty-five seconds we heard a scraping from under the
deck. At fifty-five seconds bubbles blipped on the water. In a
splashing explosion of breath and brown shoulder and dripping
kinky hair, Desi popped his head above the water, but the rest of
him stayed beneath. Two more crew members jumped in; they
pulled the damaged orange rudder out of the water. An hour later,
the good rudder had been placed behind the engine that worked.

Desi climbed back aboard. "This is a brave boy," the Colonel
said, slapping his hand down hard on Desi's wet shoulder. Desi
looked at his feet. "No one would risk the crocodiles but this boy.
Brave."

We returned to the barge and reattached it, then swung round
and started up again, moving on toward a black-clouded horizon,
past five-story broad-canopied trees guarding the entrance to the
jungle like jealous sentinels. The river here was narrow, the banks
high. The palms on shore had given way to stately gum trees, to
towering teaks and tamarinds; the forest had become, in a way,
more solid than anything we had seen during the preceding thousand miles.

~~

We were drawing near a stretch of sandy shore. Villagers, mainly
young men in rags, came whooping and hollering out of their huts.
They leapt into their pirogues and paddled furiously toward us.
The security chief whistled in alarm. The Colonel emerged onto
the bridge platform bearing his M-16. The villagers let loose what

sounded like a war cry, and the chief yelled to them not to dock, but some tried anyway. At this, the Colonel brandished his rifle and began firing shots into the air, and the villagers abandoned the barge, with one pirogue capsizing in our violent, single-engine wake.

"It is dangerous here," the Colonel said. "These people are cannibals. They will see you and say, 'Ah, the flesh of the *mondele* is like sugar!'" He laughed uproariously, as he always did at this remark. Then his voice steadied. "This is a dangerous area for robbers and murderers. The deep jungle is wild in people as well as beasts. You must have one soldier with you, or maybe two. Or else they will cut you to pieces and smoke you like a monkey. Ha-ha-*haa!*"

✂✂✂

The next noon, one thousand and eighty-four miles and twenty-one days after leaving Kinshasa, with smoke billowing out of our engine room, we docked at Kisangani. Ahead, just beyond the bend, was Boyoma Falls, which prevented further navigation on the river.

The merchants, though they complained that business had been bad on this run and that they would barely break even, laughed and shouted jokes to one another as they hauled their smoked fish and bush meat down the gangplank.

With Desi at my side I stepped ashore, dazed with fatigue, disoriented. We followed the merchants off the barge and began making our way up toward Avenue Mobutu, with its placarded hotels and diamond traders, with the bells of the city's broad white cathedral chiming over the din of the crowds.

One journey was over, and another was about to begin.

Kisangani

JUST THIRTY MILES NORTH OF THE EQUATOR, KISANGANI, LONG AN entrepôt where diamonds, gold, timber, and coffee were traded, had suffered the *pillages* of the early 1990s and in places had acquired the burnt-out and desolate look of much of Kinshasa: dock cranes rusted along the waterfront; storefronts gaped smashed and abandoned in the center; piles of rubbish smoldered in the outskirts. But the city had another side: a stately cathedral, white-walled and roofed in red tile, greeted arriving riverboats; its former colonial quarters retained an unmistakably European ambience; and many of its people were genial Swahili-speakers, descended from dwellers of the forests that spread over volcanic mountain ranges to the Great Lakes region on Zaire's eastern border. Yet there was something brooding about Kisangani, lost deep in the jungle at the point on the river where boats could go no farther, something that whispered of tradition and tragedy both. If it was here that the first hints of the old civilizations and cultures of East Africa could be detected, it was also here that Arabs, having marched in from the Indian Ocean coast, established a major slaving depot, and here that the Eastern Rebellion had bloodied the land at the time of independence.

To me, however, after having ascended the Congo River through the Bangala homeland, Kisangani felt like a safe haven, a comfortable refuge (it had running water and electricity, at least most of the time) in which to rest and recover my strength. Once off the barge, I took a suite at the Zaire Palace and slept for fourteen hours straight, lost to the soft bed and whirring air conditioner. But when I awoke, my newfound comfort created a vacuum inside me that was filled by a rush of trepidation and nervous energy: I had to get ready for the descent.

In a way, preparations had begun when we docked—with deceit. Because the Colonel, Desi, and I judged the risk high that we might be followed out of Kisangani on the river and robbed, we agreed that no one should know exactly when we were planning to depart. Desi also asked that no one be told he was guiding me; he feared a jealous rival might put a hex on him, so that he would fall ill and I would have to hire someone else. Thus I informed Papa Jacques, Jilly, Jean, and the others that I had yet to choose a guide, and that I was staying a week or ten days in Kisangani, when in truth we would leave after five days. This meant no good-byes or words of thanks to the people who had helped me through the most taxing journey of my life.

To keep an eye on our pirogue, Desi now slept in my old cabin on the barge (which would remain in Kisangani for at least ten more days). The next morning he showed up at the Zaire Palace in a fresh white shirt, a thin black tie, and black trousers, and we set out on our first of many shopping excursions, the aim of which was to turn our pirogue into a floating cornucopia. Over the next few days we bought provisions, stocking up on salt, sugar, soap, rice, spaghetti, cooking oil, tomato paste, coffee, tea, and canned frankfurters, sardine-like pilchards, peas, and carrots. We also bought the additional gear we would need: tin cutlery, pots and pans, machetes, flashlights and batteries, charcoal, a UNHCR tarp, blankets, an extra paddle, and a mosquito net and foam mattress for Desi. He asked me for a tracksuit—we bought that. When I suggested we buy him mosquito repellent (I had my own measured supply from the States), he objected—he had never used it—and requested instead skin softening lotion, a king-sized bottle of Revlon body lotion, to be exact. We bought that, too. Desi proved an able and loyal negotiator who not only bargained down prices and double-checked everything sold him, but who also hired and kept close track of the half-dozen porters who lugged our acquisitions back to my suite.

At lunch in the hotel restaurant, I broached the subject of health on our expedition. I told Desi that I was unaccustomed to the tropics and thus more likely than he to fall ill, and that water from the river might prove more dangerous for me than for him (on the barge I had seen him drink it straight), since his immune system had already received considerable exposure. It would therefore be necessary that he prepare our food with sterile water, which we would bring with us in jerry cans, and that we eat off plates rinsed in sterile water: this would keep us both healthy. I also told him that I would buy whatever medicines he needed, arrange for him to see a doctor before departure if he wanted to. These measures would benefit him as much as me, for his health was my safety.

"Very good," he said, clearing his throat. "And what about . . . medicine . . . for worms."

"You have worms?"

"No . . . but . . . medicine for worms would be a good idea. Just in case. There are many worms on the river."

"No problem."

We visited the pharmacy and I bought worm pills, as well as an additional supply of Fansidar, a last-ditch malaria medication. Like most people along the Congo, Desi had suffered attacks of malaria in the past, and once in a while they recurred. The Fansidar might come in handy for him as well as me. It also turned out that he needed a toothbrush, toothpaste, soap, and a towel—he had been borrowing these things from a "sister" on the barge. We picked up these items, too.

But our most important health-preserving resource would be clean water. We went down to the hotel kitchen and hired a cook's assistant to boil enough vats of tap water to fill our seven jerry cans (a supply that would last us until Mbandaka).

While the assistant was boiling water, we returned to my suite to lay down other ground rules for our trip. We would travel during the daylight hours to avoid hippos, crocodiles, and snags, covering twenty-five to thirty miles between sunup and sundown. At that rate, allowing for sufficient rest stops, our descent would take forty-five days (it had taken Stanley forty-four); we had food supplies for two months. To avoid falling prey to robbers, we would camp in secluded spots out of sight of villages.

I then produced the navigation charts and tried to involve Desi in a discussion of our route, but he couldn't read them, and anyway, the exercise seemed superfluous to him. "*Le bon Dieu* will decide our fate. We will face the Congo alone," he said flatly. "If He wills us to die on this trip, we will die." He had grown up in a pirogue and never dared approach the water with anything less than the respect due a jealous god; rather, he was wont to make obeisance, afraid of the hubris that resolution implied. Planning would be my domain. Guiding would be his: he knew the river by sight and feel, and had no use for my charts.

Desi arose to go downstairs—he had to finish monitoring the kitchen personnel. As he was about to walk out I stood up. "Desi, while you're down there I'm going to go to the satellite phone"—there was an Indian in town who rented out his satellite phone—"and call the American Embassy. I'm just going to let them know you're with me, and tell them to expect us in Kinshasa."

He paused.

"You see, Desi, the embassy must know who I'm traveling with. In case something happens."

He nodded and walked out.

The notion to tell him this entered my thoughts spontaneously. I was not going to make such a call: the last people I expected to come to the rescue on the Congo were coddled diplomats from Kinshasa. But I wanted Desi to think he was registered somewhere, just in case; I wanted him to believe that in addition to the Colonel, there were others, people connected to the feared powers of embassies and secret services, who knew he was to answer for my safety.

Still, I went to the satellite office—to call Tatyana. For an hour the Indian operator dialed and dialed Moscow, to no avail. Out of patience, he insisted that I had the wrong number, which was not so; rather, it seemed that somehow the phone systems were incompatible, or that the satellite required some code or other number be dialed that I did not know. I left dispirited that I would not be able to speak to her before setting out.

✦✦✦

The next day, as promised, the Colonel presented me with a *lettre de recommandation* from the Chief of Staff of Military Intelligence of the Office of President Mobutu. Typed on embossed stationery bearing the letterhead *REPUBLIQUE DU ZAIRE—PRESIDENCE DE LA REPUBLIQUE* over the image of a scowling leopard framed by a pair of crossed spears, it demanded all relevant authorities grant me *libre passage* during my descent of the river from Kisangani to Kinshasa *par pirogue,* and accorded me the right to a military escort. Nevertheless, I decided against hiring a soldier in Kisangani. If I did so, the soldier could advise others of our departure, but the stretch to Lisala was not dangerous enough to make him necessary (it was mainly Lokele land and thus, Desi asserted, perfectly safe)—this amounted to an additional risk early on, for no real purpose. For a soldier we would do better to wait until Lisala, from which point on we would certainly require armed accompaniment to pass through the Bangala-Ngombe homeland on the way to Mbandaka. Until Lisala, we would make do with a gun Desi promised to buy in Lokutu, a few days downriver.

≁

Time passed quickly in Kisangani, but we managed to stock up and get ready on schedule. One day I was walking alone along Avenue Mobutu, having given Desi the rest of the afternoon off. A Zairean grabbed my sleeve. "*Mondele,* you should meet one of your kind here. Inside the shop."

A sign reading DIAMONDS hung outside a storefront. Inside, half a dozen smartly dressed young Zaireans were standing around. A harried-looking white man of forty-five or so emerged from the back room, placed a jeweler's loupe to his eye, and sat down behind the counter. I went up and said hello, and he welcomed me with ebullient enthusiasm. He introduced himself as Roger, a Lebanese American, and asked me to have a seat.

The Zaireans pressed close around the counter. These were middlemen, entrepreneurs who journeyed into the jungle down secret pathways and bought diamonds—industrial-grade stones, mostly—from prospectors mining isolated plots along remote creeks. "I have this stone," one said, drawing a pebble-sized chunk of what could have been broken glass out of his pocket. Roger seized it, peered at it through his loupe, and stated a price. The Zairean smirked and suggested a higher amount. Roger scoffed and said no, but upped his offer. The Zairean laughed, then lowered his. In this way they reached an agreement. Stone and money changed hands. Next!

Roger, who had operated a similar diamond business in Liberia, was doing well here, though he wasn't specific about who his clients were, and I didn't ask him to be. But the business could be rough. A lot of money was changing hands, and the stakes were high; the demands for bribes (occasionally accompanied by physical threats and even assault) from Zairean officials were constant. Later a Zairean entered and held out a stone. Roger ignored it and had the man ejected from the store. Once, he said, this middleman had come in with a stone, received an offer for it, then turned it down, thereby learning its value. "I'm not in the business of providing free information," he said, "and that guy knows it. He's banned from my shop."

That evening Roger showed me a good time, inviting me to dinner at the Hawaii Restaurant, then home to meet his wife. He enjoyed his life in Kisangani, despite the corruption and the ever-present possibility of new *pillages*. The *pillages* worried him least of all: he was originally from a village in Israeli-occupied southern Lebanon and was used to violence.

✦✦✦

On my last night in Kisangani Roger introduced me to other expatriate diamond dealers at a luxurious villa in the suburbs. (Most of the expats left in town were diamond traders and clergymen, plus a dissipated elderly man of dubious nationality who acted as consul for several Western countries.) The dealers heard out my plans to descend the river. They told me of two Englishmen who had tried the trip a couple of years ago. They made it through the storms and down the abattoir between Lisala and Mbandaka, but a barge ran over them one night near the equator—they survived but lost all their gear. Another Englishman had died of malaria on the barge just before reaching Kisangani. With these attempts added to the reports I had heard of the macheteed Belgians and the capsized Peace Corps Americans, I had a newly enriched chronicle of death and failure to ponder during my last hours.

Neither Roger nor the others ventured out onto the river; their business in town was risky enough. "From what I can tell," Roger told me, "disease and the weather are going to be your worst enemies. If anything gets you out there, it'll probably be a storm or malaria. Anyway, I doubt you'll be as unlucky as those Italians."

"What Italians?"

"Eight Italians were just murdered in Goma [a town to the east, on the border with Rwanda]. The BBC just reported it. Could have been Rwandan refugees who killed them, or maybe Zairean soldiers; they still don't know. Pretty gruesome. You're going to have to be really careful if you run into soldiers on the way. They're out of control."

After dinner we stopped by his shop, where he changed four hundred dollars into zaires for me. He even offered to call Tatyana for me, so I wrote out a message in Russian, spelled phonetically in Latin letters, for him to read, telling her that I was okay. After that, he walked me up Avenue Mobutu to the turnoff for my hotel.

He extended his hand. "Well, my friend, good luck. You'll need it."

I shook his hand and he was gone.

It was a casual parting, but it left me alone with my fear, which I had suppressed in his voluble company. Tomorrow it would all begin. Suddenly unsteady on my feet, feeling nauseated (doubtless from nerves), I set out down the dark deserted lane leading back to the Zaire Palace. It had grown unbearably humid and hot, a sign of coming rain and a reminder that here, on the equator, the seasons differed from those in Kinshasa: there was never a dry season. A full moon hung hazy behind mist, frogs piped out a chorus of croaks from the river, moths fluttered in my face, things slithered in the grass at my feet.

Up in my room I made a final check of our gear and provisions. Desi stopped by to tell me that he had arranged with a taxi driver to pick us up at four the next morning. The plan was to disappear from Kisangani under cover of darkness. He wished me *bonne nuit* and left for the barge.

There was another knock on the door. It was the Colonel. He looked grave. "Don't play games with your safety. Hire a soldier." He fixed me with his eyes. He stepped forward and hugged me hard, then wished me *bon voyage* and walked out.

I closed the door and leaned back against the wall, feeling my heart pounding. In fact, I was trembling. Whether he was in league with Mobutu or not, the Colonel had helped and protected me. He had treated me like a son; he had been straightforward with me; he had asked nothing of me, nothing at all. During the long trip up-river I found only he (and Nze) dealt with me without pretense, without discernible ulterior motive; and only he both perceived the risks of my venture and thought in practical terms of how to surmount them. Now I would go on without him.

The air conditioner whirred. Above my bed hung a painting depicting snow-capped Swiss Alps, pines, and a lake the color of the turquoise sky. Lying under the sheets I thought, *That is where I belong!* I suddenly yearned for landscape like that, as if the Alps were my home.

But I banished this thought. Indeed, I feared even entertaining the notion of canceling the descent, lest my will disintegrate or memories of Tatyana intrude and break me down. I left Russia desperate, ready to risk my life to remake myself, and I could not forget that or back out now.

I jumped up and grabbed my maps and spread them out all over the floor. I had just completed a three-week trip up the river, but I thought maybe I could divine something new and comforting from them. The Congo was narrow near Kisangani, but after Baulo it began to widen. By Yangambi islands started to proliferate, and soon there were hundreds of them, forming a fearsome maze. Near

where the Aruwimi River joined the Congo, the Congo widened
again to some ten miles, all islands and claustrophobic waterways,
and river after river, the Mongala, the Lulonga, the Ikelemba, all
poured in, magnifying its might, expanding its volume. Mbandaka
and the equator lay an infinite distance ahead, an infinite series of
daily travails and risks away. From Mbandaka, the banks spread still
farther apart, until they were fourteen miles from each other. After
this they narrowed to the Chenal and the currents rushed in a frenzy
south to Kinshasa. I ran through the whole route on paper, imagin-
ing what I would see, how I would feel as I pirogued by each place,
trying to remember what I *had* seen and felt on the way here. But I
felt a wave of dizzying panic: it was as if I remembered nothing.

Then the electricity failed, killing the lights and the air
conditioner.

I put away the maps and tried to sleep, but I couldn't. I lay
awake in apprehension, staring at the ceiling, sensing the heat seep-
ing in through the windows, listening to the chirruping of crickets
and the bizarre squawks of nocturnal birds outside my window.

I began to sweat. I suffered the overwhelming presentiment
that I was about to confront forces against which my motivation,
maps, and meticulous planning meant nothing. People on the
Congo survived by crowding together, as on the barge or in villages; now Desi and I would face the jungle and the river alone.

The minute hand on my watch ticked slowly round the dial,
drawing closer and closer the predawn hour of departure. I tried
to imagine where I would be a day hence, but I could not.

I grabbed John Updike's novel *Brazil,* which I had been reading
since the barge. I lit upon the line: "Faith is necessary. Otherwise
there are too many decisions and each one seems too important."

But what if one had no faith? What if one believed in nothing?
I fell asleep.

Alone on the River

LIKE A CHIMING VALEDICTORY FROM A WORLD WE WERE LEAVING behind, the bells of Kisangani's cathedral came pealing out to us through the darkness as we slipped away from the bank, the bow of our pirogue cutting a pale gray V in the indigo river. Sweat ran into my eyes, soaked through my shirt, and blanched into expanding blotches on the thighs of my cotton trousers. The bells rang out a fifth time. Their peals lingered and died, leaving us with the swish of our paddles, with our bow silently parting the mists over the Congo's black currents.

We had left the hotel just after four in the morning. The "taxi" Desi had ordered turned out to be a *pousse*—a two-wheeled cart pushed by a withered and wheezing barefoot old man. After half an hour of creaky, torch-lit passage down the red dust road, we reached a deserted clearing on the river below the cathedral and halted.

"I'll go get the pirogue," Desi whispered.

He stole upstream along the bank toward the barge, where our pirogue was moored, ducking low and keeping to the shadows to avoid the dock lights. I waited with the old man, listening to his consumptive lungs crackle above the hiss of the river. Lightning flashed in silence, throwing up the gargoyles of great trees on the other shore, illuminating phantoms of fog wandering over the inky waters.

There was soon the faintest sound of an oar, then, in the mists, backlit by the dock lights, appeared the silhouette of a man paddling a pirogue. Desi. When he neared the bank he stepped out and the pirogue scraped the sand; I grabbed the bow chain and dragged the craft half ashore. Quietly we transferred our belongings from the *pousse* to the pirogue, extinguishing our flashlights when we perceived someone walking along the road above. I paid the old man and he left us, wheezing and straining to push his cart up the embankment.

Desi and I looked at each other, then turned to the river. Eleven hundred miles to Kinshasa . . . my heart was thumping and sweat stung my eyes. Raising his hands, Desi faced the blackness and began muttering a prayer, an invocation in Lingala punctuated with the French for salvation, mercy, the grace of God. I lowered my head—I had never prayed, but now I did, or at least I listened to Desi pray. He finished. We stood for a moment, as if to let the words take effect. Then we grabbed our oars and climbed aboard— I at the bow and Desi astern—and pushed off.

rrr

By the time the cathedral bells died, we were coursing out into midriver. Seated, I plunged the paddle into the water and pulled, plunged and pulled, the paddle weighing heavy in my hands. The pirogue was sluggish and tough to turn, and navigation demanded a skilled pilot—which Desi was. The air was dead-still and thick with humidity, hard to breathe; the mist, rising off the river like steam, bathed us in heat and wet.

Soon Kisangani was lost behind the bend, and the sky was paling with the approach of dawn. We slipped into a channel of fast-moving water, and it hurried us along the bank under the over-arching trees of an island—Île Bertha. Fish bubbled up into the glassy water. The jungle was awakening, ringing with gurgles and caws, echoing with yowls and screams. Monkeys hooted and scampered about unseen, shaking the branches above us. Flamingoes scattered and took flight, fluttering pink against the dark green of the forest; ospreys circled and soared, sharing the lightening sky with egrets. The brush along the bank was coming alive with blue-crested kingfishers that dove into the river and emerged flapping and splashing with minnows in their bills.

We plunged our paddles into the currents and pulled, plunged and pulled, waiting for the sun to rise behind the clouds.

It never did. Later that morning as we were slipping along, carried by the current some fifty yards from the bank, I paused to rest, glancing sternward to see how Desi was coming with the tea he was preparing over the *bambula*. I recoiled. Behind him in the east, the sky roiled with advancing black clouds dragging iron-gray skirts of rain.

"Desi!"

He glanced over his shoulder, then went back to his teapot. "That's not coming our way."

But it was. Minutes later the winds struck, howling down upon us, swinging round our bow and seeking to blow us out into mid-river, pelting us with leaf-and-twig flotsam from the forest, raising a thrashing surf and a blinding spindrift. Waves pounded the pirogue, and we grabbed our oars and paddled. We got within forty feet of shore when the rain hit.

"Jump out!" shouted Desi. "Jump!"

Simultaneously we quit the craft in a bound as the storm descended. I had the bow rope in hand and it jerked my elbow socket as I plunged into the churning brown water, but when I regained my footing I found it was only waist deep. I strained to keep my eyes open in the horizontal rain. Desi pushed from the stern and I dragged, the current and slick clay alluvium keeping our footing tenuous in the shallows. Within ten minutes we were in a narrow-necked cove, struggling to lash our blue tarp over our provisions, which were scantily covered but still dry in plastic sacks. We sat shivering under umbrellas, watching the river boil white and the sky rage black.

Half an hour later the storm passed, leaving low clouds, a silence punctured by the ubiquitous drip-drop-drip of water trickling from leaf to leaf, and the urgent tinkling of new runnels rushing down the bank. The air was clammy and chilled, and the whine of mosquitoes arose. After having folded up his umbrella, Desi took a plastic scoop and began shoveling out the rain sloshing around in the bottom of the pirogue.

"We need bamboo," he said.

We pulled the pirogue back to the river and started out. A bit downstream Desi nodded in the direction of the forest, which here stood high above the water atop a root-covered cliff of ocherous clay. "There!" We pulled ashore. He alighted with his machete and climbed the roots up into the forest. Somewhere behind shields of ferns and drooping loops of vine stood a thicket of bamboo.

Desi returned with five or six hollow and flexible bamboo stalks, each some ten feet long and three inches thick. We took our provisions out of the pirogue and he set to work, hacking the bamboo into yard-long segments that he placed in rows in the middle of the craft. On these segments we put our provisions—this way, they would ride above the water in the bottom. We also repacked things in a way that made sense and was comfortable for us. Desi sat at the stern, with the *bambula,* charcoal, cookware, jerry cans of water, foam mattresses, and other gear and provisions directly in front of him. On top of all this we secured our tarp. Just behind my wicker chair we placed my backpack, and each of us had umbrellas and machetes in buckets by our feet. This arrangement allowed us access to what we needed, kept things dry, and left legroom to spare.

As Desi was hacking apart the last segments of bamboo there reverberated a faint chugging, the faraway murmur of an engine. He paused and we scanned the river. Some minutes later an assortment of ramshackle white barges attached to a *pousseur* appeared and headed upstream toward Kisangani, hugging the distant bank.

"The *Colonel Ebeya!*" said Desi. "It hasn't run in *years.*"

When the *Ebeya* had sailed away behind the forest, we shoved off. As we floated downstream, Desi set about cooking a meal of rice, tomatoes, canned meat, and plantains, stoking the fire in the *bambula.* We kept to midriver; at such a distance the occupants of the occasional pirogue paddling near the bank could hardly have recognized me as a *mondele,* and for now, at least, I wanted to keep it that way. And so we floated, alone on the water, our *bambula* steaming the aromas of our first meal into the moist noon air.

✦✦✦

I found I had almost no extraneous thoughts: my attention was focused solely on the task at hand—paddling and observing the river. The sudden assault of the storm failed to leave a lasting residue of fear; too much was new, and the demands of my labor with the paddle allowed little more to dominate my reflections than the weight of the wood in my hands and the persistent sensation of abrasion in the area between my right thumb and forefinger.

Later the current washed us near the bank, and we came upon children bathing in the shallows. At the sight of me, big brothers grabbed little brothers, big sisters grabbed little sisters, and the lot of them tore splashing and screaming into the forest, shouting *touri! touri!,* leaving one young man dressed in ragged brown shorts and the shreds of a brown shirt, looking up from the fishing net in his hands.

I greeted him cheerfully. *"Mbote! Sango boni?"*

He stared at me, transfixed. It appeared to dawn on him only gradually who I was. When he understood, he dropped his net and started waving his arms. *"Nazalina nzala! Ey, Nazalina nzala! Ey, mondele! Ey, le blanc! J'ai faim! Ey! Venez ici!"*

We paddled on, leaving him gesticulating on-shore.

✦✦✦

By afternoon the skies cleared to an azure soft and pacific, and the lyrical trilling of songbirds rang from hollow to shady hollow. When sunset came we had covered thirty miles. We espied a glade on an island and made for it. In dragging the pirogue ashore I discovered the ground to be a viscous muck that sucked the shoes right off my feet, but farther in it was drier and harder and suitable for camp. Well out of sight of the river, Desi fastened our UNHCR tarp at eye level to a rectangular arrangement of tree trunks, forming a protected area under which he erected his mosquito net on a frame of yard-long branches he had stuck into the ground around his foam mattress. I put up my own tent underneath the tarp, then filled a bucket and went off in the bush to bathe.

The sun went down at six. My head heavy, my clothes damp, I crawled into my tent, zipped up the door, and stretched out, numbed and aching. Our site soon grew raucous with the descent to roost of thousands of grackle-like birds in the foliage just above our heads. When the birds fell silent, mosquitoes beset the glade in swarms that charged the air with the buzzing of thousand-volt wires.

"How do you feel, Desi?"

"Sore. I'm unused to paddling. It's been a while."

Somewhere behind us drums sounded from a village hidden in the forest. Their tempo was urgent, and Desi sat up in his net. "Something has happened," he said pensively, his ears attuned. "They're calling a man back home. Because . . . because . . . someone has died. Those drums are . . . announcing . . . a death."

The drums beat on and on, becoming muffled, and then a chanting began, a haunting dirge, and there were shouts. It unsettled me and I switched around in the tent to face the river through my net door. There was no moon, only a blackness filled with drums and chants and the high-voltage buzz of mosquitoes that screamed and whined thick as fog where my breath exited the gauze. I covered myself with my sheet and, as if drugged, dropped away into a deep sleep.

But later in the night the chanting roused me. From the forest there was coming a wailing, a shrill ululating howl, and Desi was mumbling to himself in low incantatory tones.

"Desi, what is that?"

"They're singing over the body now."

He was singing along with them.

✦✦✦

Just before dawn there were footsteps around our camp, crisp prancing footsteps that cracked branches and rustled leaves. They woke me up, and I strained to see through my net door and rear window, but could discern nothing. Our visitor, whatever it was, pitter-pattered here and there, stopped at our half-filled *bambula,* examined my tent, peered for a while at Desi, then moved on into the forest, leaving not a trace.

Who would have followed us here?

The wan light of dawn crept over us, fog floated above the river and drifted around our camp. The sun edged its way over the ridge opposite and tinctured the fog with pale orange. With the warming color the foliage began dripping dew; everything in the forest was soon dribbling, leaking, spattering. But then the shadow of a man appeared by our pirogue.

Desi was awake. He shouted, *"Mbote!"*

"Mbote!"

It turned out that the man had lost his way in the fog, and the sight of a strange pirogue had confused him even more. He and Desi chatted as we broke camp. Still sore, I ate the remnants of last night's rice and meat, and we pushed off, parting with the villager and allowing the current to take us to the channel, now and then dipping our paddles in and pulling the pirogue ahead when we slowed.

***

There was a cry from across the water, a "hee-hooa! *Mondele!"*

In the fog a few yards in front of us a pirogue materialized bearing a fisherman. With scoops of his paddle he swung his scow toward us across the coffee-colored river.

"Mbote!"

"Mbote!"

The fisherman, a muscular fellow, scraggily bearded, with more than a bit of the rogue in his eyes, reached down and grabbed a chain and dragged a two-foot-long capitaine perch, golden and stout, half out of the river. Desi wanted to buy it but I said no—it had meat enough for days and would surely spoil before we finished it.

The fisherman let the perch slip back into the river and pulled on another chain. "Okay, *mondele*, then what about this?"

The water rippled and splashed. The fisherman wrestled with the chain and nearly lost his balance. Finally he lugged out a flopping yard-long creature that looked more like a sea monster than a fish—it growled, sputtering water out its gills, its mouth bristled with inch-long fangs. "How about this mbenga!"

"No! No!" shouted Desi, brandishing his oar. "Put away that mbenga!"

The fisherman lost his grip on the chain; and the monster crashed back into the river. Desi addressed him in French. "Listen, a satellite is tracking the movement of this *mondele* and it's watching us now. If anything happens to him, you and your whole village will be exposed."

The mbenga thrashed, jerking the pirogue. The fisherman was now astride us. Close up, he did indeed look like a rogue, and as he floated by, he examined me with brazen eyes. "Then you think about who you're traveling with," he said to Desi in French, his gaze fixed on me. "What kind of *mondele* is this? He can be just as dangerous to you as to me!" He chuckled and grabbed his paddle. "You're traveling with *un type,* you know," he said, *"un vrai type!"*

Having said that he faded into the fog.

I looked back at Desi. "What was that all about?"

Desi kept his eyes set on the fog, as though the mbenga rogue might come charging back after us. "That mbenga is a bad fish. If a man makes water in the river, it can leap out and bite off his thing. He should not have shown us a mbenga. It's bad luck to see a mbenga at the start of a voyage."

"But you said a satellite's tracking us. What gave you that idea?"

He laid down his paddle. "You know what the Colonel says about you? He says you're *méchant*. You speak many languages, so you can do people evil."

I looked at Desi, nonplussed. Maybe he had got the idea about the satellite from my making a satellite phone call in Kisangani, but could the Colonel have really called me *méchant?* I remembered his look of suspicion when I read the Russian lettering on his watch. But *méchant* conveyed more than just suspicion: the word echoed with the slaving and mercenary evils of Zaire's past, with the misdeeds of vicious Zairean soldiers. Everywhere I went I was called *mondele,* but I felt not a hint of racism in it—it simply signified the obvious and the unusual: here's a white guy. But I had not been called *méchant,* at least as far as I knew, and it stung if the Colonel really thought that of me.

I resumed paddling, sore from yesterday's labor. The shadows of trees dead and alive rose in the fog around us, like tombstones, peering down, as if watching our progress.

*   *   *

The mist lifted to reveal flocks of cranes and chattering parrots swooping this way and that amid the manifold tiers of branches of massive shoreside trees. The river mirrored the sky and forest with flawless fidelity: vines dangled from treetop to water to treetop again; cumulus clouds sailed above us as well as below us; butterflies flitted black, pink, and red against the turquoise sky, their colors doubled in the riverine glass. The disquietude from our dawn encounter with the mbenga man dissipated. Desi was cheerful and so was I; inklings of the *méchant* now belonged to another, gloomier hour. I found it easiest to paddle sitting down, doing a few strokes on the left, a few strokes on the right; Desi preferred to paddle standing up. We were relaxed, our labors made almost pleasant by the beauty and peace of the jungle tableau through which we were gliding.

A crackling screech like the dragging of broken glass across slate cut through the air, bouncing off the surface of the river and into the forest and back again. I turned sternward.

Desi halted his Lingala spiritual in midverse. He raised his chin as he sunk his paddle into the water. "Do you know that Jesus is coming again?"

"What?"

"I say, Jesus will come again. Are you doing His work on earth?"

"Desi!"

"Well, are you?"

"Are *you?*"

"I am." He threw his head back, filled his lungs, and let out another howl. Kulokoko birds flapped away in fear; terrified egrets sought the shelter of the forest. He stopped. "I follow the teachings of the American prophet William Branam. He comes to Zaire and teaches us about God. Do you follow William Branam?"

"I don't have any idea who you're talking about."

"He's from Jeffersonville but he also teaches in"—here he named American cities that sounded like "Hoojiwilly," "Moosooshootville," and "Soolleekcitee."

"Say those cities again?"

"Jefferson-ville, Hoojiwilly, Moosooshootwilly, Soolleekseety. Do you follow his teachings?"

"I'm not sure you've got those cities right. And I've never heard of your prophet."

"Do you want to hear about him?"

"I'd rather hear about lunch."

"Okay. We're going to buy a fish." He laid down his oar and winced, saying he was sore. "There was a time when the people in Zaire were ignorant, when they didn't know about God. Then you whites came and brought us God."

When a fisherman came by Desi bargained with him and bought a meaty mbuku for ten thousand zaires. He cleaned it and made a succulent mbuku-and-rice meal, grilling the fish over the coals of our *bambula*. But after lunch the temperature rose. By noon the sun was a searing ball hanging directly above us, and we spread out our umbrellas and drifted. Huge trees loomed in statuary repose on the banks, bees roared by in black swarms, flies lent a ringing drone to the heat. It grew too hot to talk of prophets. *La chaleur,* Desi groaned, and dozed off.

Perhaps one test, if not the greatest test, of our mettle on this trip would consist in dealing with one another with tolerance no matter what duress we experienced. We had more than a thousand miles to go, and we had to get along, at the same time that we suffered the fatigue that our routine of paddling would bring on. One reason I chose Desi as a guide was that he spoke of God and prayer and piety—words that, whether I believed their sense or not, I took as signs of his trustworthiness and integrity. So, settling under my umbrella, I tried to console myself with this, I suppressed my urge to say more about his putative prophet, and fell asleep watching the high white clouds part and mate on the glassy water.

Late in the afternoon the soaring cumulus castles of alabaster hunkered down into grim fortresses of lead. Erratic breezes whipped the ferns and foliage hanging above the water. The heat was not only not abating with the close of the day, it was intensifying, and the humidity, a malevolent weight in the air, was building.

I sat up. "Desi, we should camp. It's late and the weather seems ready to spoil."

He was already on his feet, peering into the clearings—miniature plateaus three or four feet above the water atop sheer banks laddered with roots—on the island we were skirting. The clearings looked perfect for camping. "I see tomatoes, maize, and peppers," he said, craning his neck. "And over there are more tomatoes. But over there . . . over there there are fetishes."

"Fetishes?"

"Fetishes to keep people away. The villagers put fetishes there to say, 'Keep away from my crops or you'll die!' They don't want people coming here and stealing."

I could see crops but nothing resembling fetishes, which I took to be figurines of some sort. "I don't see them. What do these fetishes look like?"

"I . . . I don't want to talk about fetishes."

Somewhere ahead was the village of Yalrufi, and I did not want to pitch tent in front of a populated area. Each arbor on the bank held a new cultivated clearing and more fetishes. Four-thirty passed, then five. In an hour the sun would go down and we would be caught out. Over the jungle to the south lightning sparked, zigzagging up and down the faces of clouds, clouds black and fulminating like the smoky embodiment of divine wrath.

"It's not safe here," Desi said. "But now we must camp. There will be rain tonight."

We berthed in a spot a mile across the water from Yalrufi's straw huts and scrambled up a tangle of roots to a clearing. A light wind fluttered down and rippled the river into corrugated pewter. We trotted back and forth from the pirogue to camp, hurrying our belongings ashore, stepping carefully around crop shoots, and set up our tarp and tents beneath a giant, wide-boughed tree, a sturdy colossus of the forest.

I grabbed my bucket and soap and rushed through a bath in a secluded recess behind the campsite, sweating as the breeze died. The sun dropped behind the trees, and all at once the mosquitoes attacked, roaring forth in clouds, covering my legs and arms. I rinsed off and went running back to the tents. Desi had finished his bath, which he always took Zairean-style, standing in the shallows, and had just closed his net.

Once inside, I turned on my radio and tried to find a station. It crackled with startlingly fierce static, so I turned it off. Weirdly tense, exhausted from the day's labor, we fell asleep.

At midnight I lurched awake, suddenly uneasy. The mosquitoes were droning away, the air clung to my face like damp gauze. I sweat in the close heat, an asphyxiating, maddening heat that made me want to jump up and tear open my tent door. Thunder rumbled, lightning danced over the treetops. Something screeched from the forest, as if in alarm. Grunts followed, then a crashing in the bush and a snapping of branches, then a heavy breathing, as if through clogged nostrils.

"Desi!" I whispered. "Desi, what is that?"

There was no answer.

"Desi! Desi, are you there?"

I peered through my door. His net bed was empty. Ahead a flashlight shone, showing clouds of mosquitoes in its wandering yellow beam. It was Desi coming up from the bank. "I wanted to check the pirogue," he said, swinging open his net and jumping inside. The grunting sounded again. "That's a gorilla. There're a lot of gorillas around here."

I listened for a while and then went back to sleep.

A couple of hours later a cannonade of thunder exploded above us. White lightning fissured the black sky; the river flashed a horrid negative of itself in the violent light. A sudden wind belted through the forest and lashed the water. But amid the chaos there was a pause, a instant of suspense, a moment measurable on no watch—then an explosion, a prolonged, brilliant blast directly overhead that ended with sparks and the descent of a bough through the corner of our tarp. Rain poured in through my netted flaps. Desi bounded awake, I shot from my tent, and we reattached the tarp; high above us, the crest of the tree glowed with embers, emitting sparks and steam that were whisked away by the storm. A bolt of lightning had struck our tree.

Once inside my tent again, I discovered my bedding a pool of water. As I looked at it I felt pricks of pain on my calves; I had left the netting open, and my tent rang with mosquitoes. I swatted at my legs and withdrew a bloody palm.

Across the water, thunderbolts split the firmament with concussive detonations. Rain pounded the tarp. The wind picked up our pots and pans and hurled them clanking and rattling into the trees. I opened the net and raced out after them. Desi ran past me, ducking, his flashlight a mad bouncing beam in the drenching, swirling torrents. His lanky figure flickered, caught in the strobe of lightning, as he struggled to haul the pirogue higher onto the root mooring, with the river behind him a churning, howling sea of whitecaps. The pirogue secured, he came bounding back and dove through his net door. Thunder and lightning detonated again and again, tree branches cracked and crashed around us, breaking through the foliage, layer by layer, smashing and snapping wood on their way to the ground.

For an hour the storm raged. Then without warning it died. For a long time not even the whine of a mosquito broke the echoing cadences of dripping, pattering, kerplunking drops of water finding their way through the canopy to the forest floor, and to our tarp.

Land without Evenings

AS THE NIGHT WORE ON THE TRICKLING FROM THE TREES DIED away. A hollow silence came to reign. A fog edged in, creeping through the sultry blackness and snuffing out the world. Time was in abeyance, and we slept.

Time remained suspended until light waxed in the east and the fog blushed pink. Then, slowly, the forest began reviving from the assault of fire and water, echoing back to life with branches dripping dew, flies buzzing, parrots squawking. I sat up, my limbs aching, my head smarting with fatigue. My bedding was soaked from the storm, and blood from mosquito bites stained my sheets.

I opened the tent flap. A man in a cloth waist wrap was standing in front of our camp, staring at us, silhouetted against the mist. He had a goitrous neck and nappy hair flecked with gray.

"*Mbote!*" I said, climbing out. I tried to put together the Lingala for "I'm sorry, we had to camp in your field because of the rain," but I failed, and he did not respond to my attempt, but only rubbed his nose and stared harder at me. Desi climbed up from the pirogue. "He's deaf," he said. "He's a fisherman from Yalrufi."

Without our asking, the fisherman helped us load the pirogue. In gratitude I suggested we leave him food. Desi handed him some sugar and soap, and with nods and smiles he accepted them.

We shoved off into a world of white mist, watching our colossal tree shelter, charred at the summit, recede from us; we slipped ahead into a domain of white sky and white river, a watery stage of creamy white without bank or forest, gurgling with the feeding forays of big fish near the surface. The river widened; my map indicated that not so far ahead it would begin breaking into isles, into the first lanes of the jungle labyrinth. Somewhere on the

155

aquatic plain we picked up the current, and it carried us along at a good clip. On course, we put down our paddles and rested.

Desi grabbed his Bible. He thumbed through it, then glanced up. "Are you ready for the coming of Jesus?"

I smiled. "That's a complicated subject. It's hard for me to answer just like that."

"But I want to know if you believe in Jesus, in the Second Coming." He tilted his head back and peered down his nose at me. "You see, we Zaireans are not ignorant. We *were* ignorant. But—"

"But the white men came and brought you God."

He squinted at me as though he suspected something heretical in my remark.

The topic of religion put me in a quandary. Although I was not a believer, I had no problem with those who were; it was rather the history of Christianity in Africa and the selfish motives of its proselytizers that disturbed me. Christianity had functioned in the interests of the colonial powers as the destroyer of traditional beliefs and identity, as the pacifier of legitimate African outrage at colonial exploitation. The European and American missionaries who brought it here spread a dogma whose overarching tenets held that Africans were inferior; white men superior, enlightened beings. All over Africa, missionaries had opposed African independence movements; they had countenanced venal and murderous dictators; they had turned a blind eye to the massacre of hundreds of thousands of innocent people in tribal and ethnic conflicts.

But as I mulled over all this I recognized the sincerity of Desi's faith and felt I should not tamper with it, and certainly not as we sailed down this river. I did not want to alienate him by telling him my views: I needed him on my side.

His eyes weighed on me. "Well, do you believe in the Second Coming?"

"Desi, I want to eat lunch. Pass the *bambula*."

He did, eyeing me suspiciously, then he returned to his Holy Book.

▰▰▰

But not for long. I scented smoke; there were women's voices and children's cries. We found ourselves drifting through dozens of bobbing chunks of wood with fishing lines attached.

Desi pointed at the wood. "Fishermen set these buoys here in the evening. In the morning they paddle out and pick up their catch."

"What fishermen?"

We broke through the fog into view of a sandy clearing and a scattering of wattle huts with gabled roofs of straw. Beneath the huts, pirogues were strewn willy-nilly along a landing. People were bathing and milling about. The village of Isangi, Desi said. When the children saw us they stampeded away from the bank screaming *touri! touri!* The women regarded me with vague alarm: they did not run, but they turned and followed their children up to the bank, looking back at me.

Our bow rope snagged a buoy. I stood up and started to untangle it.

A young man approached the water. "Ey, *mondele!* Don't steal my fish!" he shouted in French. "Ey, *mondele,* leave my fish alone!" Some twenty feet away, he kept up with us, walking along the bank, shaking his fists. Desi thrust his paddle into the water to slow the pirogue, and I pulled at the fishing line, trying to untangle it, but it appeared to be attached to others, and all around floats started bobbing, as if sucked along with us by an invisible force. The man grew irate: "I said leave my fish alone, *mondele!*" He exploded into vituperative Lingala. Standing, I tried to keep my balance, pointing to the tangle and miming an explanation of what I was doing.

More men came running out to the bank, all wearing the shorts and grime-brown T-shirts of fishermen. Soon, ten or twelve people were shouting at me, the *mondele* fish thief, and I couldn't undo the tangle.

"Desi, explain to them what's happened!"

The buoy snapped free. The man picked up a branch and hurled it at me; it plunked into the water a few feet away.

Isangi and the shouts of its inhabitants vanished into the fog. I looked back: no one was following us.

"Touri! Touri!" the children had screamed as they took flight. The word sounded like a corruption of "tourist," but given the way it was used, it had to mean more. I asked Desi about it.

"A *touri* is a *mondele* on an evil mission," he said. "The *touri* has special things, like syringes and Motorolas, which he uses to bewitch people and kill them. A *touri* is always unbathed. And he might have a gun, but he certainly has a Motorola."

"A *Motorola?*"

"The Motorola is a very dangerous thing that the *touri* uses to search out victims and kill them. You see, the Belgians ate a lot of people here and the people are afraid of *mondeles*."

"What do you mean by 'ate'?"

"I mean *ate*. The Belgians were cannibals. The Belgians used to eat people. They especially liked to eat young boys. The Belgians built houses in the forest, and if you went near them, they would lure you inside. This is history. They've found the houses with cellars filled with bones. You see, if you're alone, the people will think you're a Belgian, maybe you're a mercenary on a special mission. You may lure people close with friendly words, then stab at them with a big syringe. This has happened with whites around here. This is history. We know this. Everyone here knows it. The people in the villages know, and they never even go to school. The old tell the young."

"But what about white men bringing religion? Hasn't that changed people's image of Europeans?"

"Yes, for the educated. But many believe what the elders say. Out here, away from the schools, people think whites are dangerous, whites are *méchants*. Whites come to Zaire to take our riches and to kill. This is history."

"So in the eyes of everyone on the river I'm a murderer?"

"If you were alone, yes. But as long as they see you're with me, you're safe. They'll think you're a preacher."

When the fog lifted a headwind began blowing steadily from the east, relentless and fatiguing, canceling out the brisk westward current. We were trying to follow the route, hoping to stay with the current, but as it led across broad pools and wide stretches, we found ourselves more and more prey to the wind. The wind forced us to work the paddles hard, to throw our backs into every stroke, to strain to maintain a decent speed, or any speed at all. Following the route, Desi steered us out to midriver, where we were but specks amid a windswept bay of leaden water under a leaden sky. No matter how hard we paddled, we could not appreciably gain on the dark green band of forest—actually the beginning of the laby-rinth of isles—that was the horizon ahead. Now and then rain would splatter us, falling in heavy warm drops, drops that felt like sweat from the sky.

In the middle of this sea the headwind turned from steady to gusting. When we rested it pushed us upriver. We sank the oars into the water over and over, for one hour, then two. At the head of the third hour we gave up, a mile from either bank.

Desi put down his oar. "My joints are aching."

"So are mine."

Lightning flashed. Over the forest to the south a storm was brewing. Across the horizon ahead, small white clouds were racing past the gray thunderheads like yachts in a regatta. It was too risky to stay our course. I turned back to Desi. "We better get off the river."

We abandoned the route and cut diagonally across the bay, drawing up to a hut on shore—a Lokele hut with smoke pouring out the door. When Desi shouted a greeting in Lokele, a smoky little fisherman came out—an old man with splayed toes and a salt-and-pepper beard. He and Desi spoke amiably—being of the same tribe, there were grounds for immediate trust—and he set about carrying our things inside his hut, taking mincing steps and smiling at me.

Inside he was smoking fish on a bamboo grill. I walked in, but the fumes repelled me and I sat near the door. Swatting zebra-legged mosquitoes I waited for the storm to hit.

It never did. By three or so the sky cleared and it was time to move on. We thanked the fisherman and I left him a small wad of zaires as a present. We loaded up and set off, soon finding ourselves at the mouth of a dark and narrow watery tunnel. Tired of the wind on the wide river, we veered into it, slipping into a dim domain of giant trees.

₰₰₰

There is no evening on the equator. The sun falls promptly at six and rises at six: every equatorial night is the obverse in time of every equatorial day, a coin flipping now light, now dark, with a band of fifteen minutes of resplendent dawn or lustrous dusk in between. The sunsets in particular have no equal elsewhere on the planet: in their sudden meltdown of molten hues, in their drama and Götterdämmerung magnificence, they conjure up ancient feelings, making us tremble at the demise of the day as if it were the death of our world.

The absence of evening, the dearth of a transitional spell in which to set up camp and prepare for the night, made keeping close track of time necessary, and we developed a timepiece-based routine. Around four in the afternoon we began looking for a campground—a glade, a clearing, a high and dry spot with bushes or trees that would hide us from the water. By four-thirty we were ashore. By five we would have set up our tents and camouflaged the pirogue with branches. It would then be time to bathe. Because of the mosquitoes, it was possible to bathe only while the sun was up, but even then there were problems, or at least there were for me, who preferred the privacy of foliage to the breezy public shallows Desi enjoyed using: the jungle was filled with thorns that could tear a shirt or puncture the skin; the underbrush bustled with snakes and hummed with wasps. Still, I frequently managed to locate a closet-sized clearing with protuberant branches for towel racks. After bathing, it was back to camp to eat the cold but still fresh remnants of our midday meal, which was mainly fish (bought for a dollar or two from passing villagers) and rice, or fish and pasta. Then the sun would go down and the mosquitoes would swarm forth, driving us into our tents for the next twelve hours. I often listened to my shortwave radio, finding solace in the BBC and *Golos Rossii* (the Voice of Russia) until I fell asleep.

That night we were camped on the south bank in a hollow sheltered by tall trees whose interlacing boughs stretched high and dense above, leaving us in inky darkness below, while just ahead a hoary starlight bathed the river. Somewhere, a kulokoko honked and yelped and wuffed from branch to branch, its wingbeats heavy and resonant in the damp air. I turned off the radio and listened to the forest, hoping to fall asleep.

But Desi lit his kerosene lamp, rustled about in his mosquito net, and cleared his throat. He began mumbling, first softly, then louder and louder.

"What are you reading, Desi?"

"*Moi?*"

"Yes, *toi*. What are you reading?"

"*Le Code du Travail du Zaire*. It's very interesting. *Veeery* interesting [*Très trrrès intéressant!*]."

"Why?"

"Because it teaches me about my rights, that's why."

He cleared his throat again and resumed his mumbling, but then raised his volume and clarified his diction, trilling his *r*'s and flattening the Gallic nasal vowels, declaiming legislation in French until the jungle rang with the codicils and clauses pertaining to laborers in Zaire and the surrounding glades reverberated with the whys and wherefores pursuant to law after law that protected the inalienable rights of the Zairean proletariat.

Why the reading aloud? Was he simply showing me that he could read and read well, or did he mean to warn me that he or his legal heirs would take court action against me should our voyage down the Congo result in his death or dismemberment?

By nine he had ceased his peroration, and the racket of the wilds arose in the tomblike blackness of the forest to our rear.

rrr

The next dawn, after we had decamped and set out, I found my-self retching over the gunwale, having breakfasted insufficiently to tolerate the prophylactic malaria pill with which I started every day. But still I paddled. Desi had complained of sore muscles and a cough, and it seemed better to show him that nothing was going to weaken me or slow our pace. Before noon we left the river alley and sailed out onto broad water again, with the wind now at our backs. The sky cleared, and the air, saturated with the blue-gold light of morning, smelled fresh, redolent in a way of spring in northern latitudes.

We fell in with the current and drifted, our bow and stern gradually trading places as we looped our way downriver.

Desi was lathering his cheeks with white goo so thick it hardly resembled shaving cream. I asked him what brand of shaving cream he was using.

"It's not shaving cream." After poking around in his bag he took out a Gillette disposable razor and a shard of mirror and began pursing his lips.

"It's not?"

He dragged the razor through the goo. It gummed up and he thwacked it against the stern. "You said we had to keep up appear-ances on the river. I'm doing that."

"Okay. But what kind of cream is that?" I grabbed the tube and read the inscription. "Desi, this is toothpaste!"

"It is also for shaving and pimples."

"No, it isn't. Read the label. It says *dentifrice*." A wave of nau-sea hit me and I leaned over the river to retch.

"You're wrong, *monsieur*. It is cream for shaving and against pimples." Desi thwacked his gummed-up razor against the stern several times, for the paste would not dissolve in water, and exam-ined his reflection in the glass. "I'm healthy using this cream. So I'll keep on using it."

I retched again. "Okay, okay."

We were coursing along beneath the high rift of the right bank, carried by the current, taking advantage of our unexpected leisure to wash our clothes in buckets. Desi's broken tenor wavered above the still river. "Amazing Grace." I loved that song in English, but I felt differently about Desi's French rendition. The trees revolved overhead as we floated downriver, bow-stern, stern-bow, spinning verses of Grace into the jungle.

Desi stopped in midverse and leapt to his feet, grabbing his paddle. *"Tourbillon!"*

The current hurled us past a jagged outcropping of bank, then into the outer circle of a swirling, bubbling pool twenty yards wide. On one side a stout snag cut the water, and we were swinging our way toward it. If we hit it, it could overturn us.

We plunged our paddles into the river without effect: the whirlpool allowed no traction. Our bow shot past the snag and we reversed direction; we were now speeding upriver in a broad twirling arc. At the top we spun round, bounced off the bank cliff, and again plummeted toward the snag.

"Paddle to the left!" Desi shouted. Paddle left we did, and we broke free of the whirlpool, swinging out into stagnant water that felt, now reassuringly, like molasses against our paddles.

Later Desi took out his hand mirror and began preening before his reflection. "I would like to borrow your Polaroid camera. I have something to do in a village ahead."

"What?"

"Well, years ago I had a fiancée. We had a baby. I've never visited her since then, I've never seen my daughter. I would like to see my daughter now. With your permission."

"Of course."

Desi took out his new tracksuit, a slick baby-blue number that gave his bony shoulders a touch of trapezoidal flair, shook the dust out of it, and put it on. He pulled a ten-gallon cowboy hat out of his bag and creased it down the middle. He donned it and examined his reflection again in his mirror.

"Oh. And may I please have ten thousand zaires?"

I gave him the money, and we swerved toward the forested ridges of the right bank. Trees dangled rope-thick vines that brushed over us as we paddled our way to a tiny sandy landing. The children playing on it saw me and froze, then stampeded for the bush. By the time our bow slid ashore the landing was deserted.

"I won't be long." Desi stuffed the zaires in his pocket, draped the Polaroid around his neck, and hopped out.

He wasn't gone long. Within ten minutes there was a hubbub of stern and querulous voices. Desi came skittering down the path, pursued by an unkempt bearded villager and an assortment of rambunctious children, youths, limping elders, and local live-stock. The man paused and bugged out his eyes when he saw me; then with renewed vigor he grabbed the sleeve of Desi's tracksuit and switched from Lingala to a high-pitched French. "You're with a *mondele* and ten thousand is all you're leaving me? How can you treat your uncle this way? Look at all the things this *mondele* has. Give me some of them!" He started rooting around in our gear. Desi gently pushed him back. "We have just enough to make our trip. I can't give you more."

"This is a disgrace," the uncle said. "*You* are a disgrace."

The children were snickering. A boy picked up a twig and hurled it at Desi. It bounced off his cowboy hat, but he paid it no notice. Desi pulled out one of the bolts of cloth he had brought along to sell. "Well, here, take this cloth."

The man snatched it and handed it to one of the children. "So let me get this straight. You're traveling with a *mondele* and you leave me a bolt of cloth and ten thousand zaires? Is that right? Tell me!"

We shoved off. Desi wished the man good health.

"Good health? Come back here and I'll good-health you, you bum! Come back here, you!"

Desi paddled standing up, a bit unsteady on his feet now, look-ing resolutely into the distance despite the hail of insults launched by his uncle and the laughing taunts of the children. Now and then he reached up and clutched his hat tight to his oblong head.

When we had passed the next bend, he laid down his paddle, took off his tracksuit, folded it up, and put it inside his duffel bag. He then solemnly put away his ten-gallon hat and gave me back the Polaroid. He kept his eyes on the water ahead, and paddled.

I felt awful for him. "So what happened?"

"They were not happy to see me."

"No?"

He rowed a bit more. "No. They received me terribly. They said I had no right to visit after all these years. They wouldn't even let me see my fiancée, let alone take a photo of my daughter—they said to do that I'd have to pay them five hundred thousand zaires and give them two pigs. I thought you might not want to give me five hundred thousand zaires, and I knew you had no pigs. So I left without seeing them."

His voice was calm, betraying no grief, but he was shaken.

He said nothing for a while, then, "We can make Lokutu by nightfall. Let's try to make Lokutu."

"Okay."

※ ※ ※

It was late afternoon and a breeze was rustling the forest, caressing the river. The sky, from jade green horizon to jade green horizon, was a vault of glorious azure. The north bank loomed high, the jungle tumbled down to the water in a profusion of tall palms and doom palms, gum trees and tamarinds, their pale boles and dark trunks obscured by sweeping ferns, hanging vines, by hydra-headed roots and blue-red-magenta-blossomed bushes. An endless raft of stationary water hyacinth, narrow mats of chartreuse with lank white flowers trembling in the breeze, bobbed out from the shore on the coffee-brown river.

We paddled, the breeze at our backs, Desi having left behind the memories of his reception at the village, I having lost myself to the beauty of the wilderness. Often as we rounded bends we heard splashing and noticed bushes shaking—beasts were taking flight—but we saw nothing. From taller trees kulokokos and eagles launched themselves into the drafts and soared away, their brown plumage glinting white in the sun; at oar's reach, kingfishers and snipes darted from sandy bank to bush to sandy bank.

The sun began to set; the breeze died away.

"*Mbote,* Desi!"

"*Hooa! Mbote na bino!*"

Two turbaned Lokele youths rowing a pirogue with a woman and child in the middle were overtaking us, cutting across water from an island nearby.

They sidled up to us. Desi held their pirogue to ours, and we all greeted one another. The youths were school friends of Desi's. They launched into an animated parley in baritone Lokele. They were fine-featured, with lean sculptured limbs and long faces; their turbans gave them an Arab aspect.

But everyone stopped paddling—and the sun was going down. Recalling the mosquitoes, I didn't want to get caught out after dark.

"Desi, let's get going!"

The youths laughed and grabbed their oars. We would race. I jumped to my feet and so did the others; Desi loosed their pirogue and we drifted apart.

"*Allons!*"

We plunged our paddles into the glassy river. Our pirogues shot ahead, lurching forward yard by surging yard with our lusty strokes. The river widened into a basin, and Lokutu lay at the far end of it, a dapple of straw yellow against the dark mass of the wooded hill. Above Lokutu the sun was melting down, falling behind manifold ridges of clouds, clouds as peaked and valleyed as earthly mountains, clouds whose formations, floating deep purple and royal blue against the reddening sky, resembled a fairy-tale land of coral castles and moats and writhing dragons, filtering the vermilion rays of the expiring sun through their layers.

Desi and I gained the advantage, skittering over the sheen of the water as over oil.

"*Whooo-haa! Whooa!*"

Our cries rang out across the river, up the valleys and into the jungle. We rowed hard, and egrets took flight from the shallows, their white feathers tinctured with the violet hues of the sun's final effusion, and we rowed harder and harder, sailing out amid the egrets, crossing the courses of storks and solitary parrots.

Winded and glistening with perspiration, the youths gave up, and we slowed, we coasted, slipping across the surface, trying to catch our breath. The red-hot tip of the sun dropped behind the trees on the rise above Lokutu, and the sky washed from lavender to cobalt.

Night. I took out my mosquito repellent, and began lathering it over my arms, and I put on my long pants. I offered repellent to my companions, but they refused.

The clouds of mosquitoes roared down from the trees. My repellent worked, and I reclined at ease. Desi and his friends ceased chatting and picked up their oars, stomping to shake the bugs off their legs, gamboling in place. As the bites multiplied they worked harder, stomping a tap dance on their unsteady pirogues.

The luminous arch of the Milky Way surmounted the sky. The moon rose, silvering the drooping palms, silvering the wide, wide basin, turning the water into liquid silver. Lokutu winked at us, now a sprinkling of yellow lanterns set in the black band of the forest.

Just before we reached Lokutu, we hugged the bank and surprised three teenage girls bathing naked in knee-deep water, the moon dusting their peach breasts and buttocks with light. They laughed and called out *"Mbote! Mbote!"*

We responded, but the current by the landing was fierce and demanded all our attention. We circled into it, we fought it and maneuvered, we pulled near to the sandy beach. At last, our bows slipped ashore with a hiss.

The Woes of SNIP

DESI'S HOUSE WAS AN IMPRESSIVE EDIFICE OF SOLID, WATTLE-laced beams and well-matted straw roof set on clean sandy earth and surrounded by a thatched fence. When we arrived, having made our way up the bank, trailing a half-dozen porters stumbling under the weight of our gear, his mother was tending fire in the courtyard. She welcomed us in. As his brothers and cousins were storing our belongings in a vacant room, I asked Desi to take special care of our water—we could give away food but not our boiled water, on which our health depended. He said okay.

Our belongings stored, we treated the family to a feast of spaghetti, vegetables, plantains, and mbuku, to which they contributed dates, bananas, and fiery pili-pili sauce. Afterward, while we were all reclining on chaises longues stretched out in the moonlit courtyard, and I was thinking how much the scene around me resembled the painted African idylls back in the Hôtel Les Bougainvillées, there was a knock on the door. A little boy had a message for Desi, and it was urgent.

After a while Desi came up to me and whispered, "There is a small problem."

***

In Zaire, most problems that didn't crawl, bite, sting, or cause dysentery had to do, of course, with the police or military. The little boy reported that the local SNIP officer had got wind of my arrival and made a big scene, stomping around the waterfront and demanding to know who had brought me to the village and why the very first thing I did in Lokutu wasn't visit him at SNIP headquarters and ask for his permission to stay. "Just who does this *mondele* think he is?!" he had shouted.

So, on the torrid morning that followed, Desi and I set out for SNIP headquarters up the road. The theatrical remonstrations of the officer sounded like the usual tactics of intimidation—I remembered the SNIP man at Ngobila Beach and his foot-stomping assertions that I was a spy—and I wondered if I would be hit up for a bribe. I had never confronted officialdom on the river without the Colonel; I had the letter from Military Intelligence, but this would be the first time I would rely on it, and I was apprehensive.

SNIP "headquarters" turned out to be an insufferably hot fly-blown hut with a straw roof and dirt floor and straw partitions for walls. Inside, several villagers sat sweating around a table in the "waiting room." They had the resigned look of peons going before an all-powerful magistrate to plead their miserable and unworthy cases. The secretary motioned us into the office ahead of them. I heard the SNIP officer's squeaky voice in Lingala, and I pulled out my letter and walked in, with Desi behind me.

The officer was wearing a sweat-stained sleeveless T-shirt, tan sweat-stained slacks, and sandals. A scar cut across the left side of his perspiring face. He looked away when we walked in, not deigning to acknowledge me. He addressed Desi in high-pitched French.

"What business does this *mondele* have arriving in my town without coming *dirECTement* to see me?"

"You can speak to me," I said.

He took a deep breath and slowly—*slowly*— turned his head in my direction and closed his eyes. He would try to be civil. "Every foreigner must present himself to SNIP when he arrives in my village. We keep close surveillance on all the foreigners in Zaire. And *all* foreigners must follow our laws. They are not at home in Zaire, and they cannot do as they please. They must report to SNIP. We in SNIP know immediately if a foreigner has left, say, Lokutu for Bumba, because we are in constant contact with the CIA, the FBI, and Interpol. If the CIA calls me and asks where the American is,

I can say the American was here at nine hundred hours and he left at ten hundred hours. I can give precise information. However, if the American *doesn't* present himself to me . . . well, that's evidence of his evil intent. He may well be a spy."

I took out my *lettre de recommandation,* unfolded it, tossed it onto his desk, and looked away. A plastic globe was hanging from the ceiling. I spun it and began examining the Amazon.

For a moment he did nothing. Then he patted the sweat from his brow and picked up the paper. He sounded out the words. "*Bon.* Ah, ha," he said in a lowered voice. "Why didn't you show this to me right away?"

"You didn't ask. I assumed you had been informed."

"Well, I *have* been informed but, well, *bon* . . ." He leaned back, massaged his chin, and stared at me. It was rude to stare this way, so I stared back.

He dropped his eyes to the paper and took to scrutinizing it again, then put it down. "*Bon.* No problem. But I do need to register you." He pulled a ledger out of a drawer, licked the tip of a pen. "*Bon* . . ."

He opened my passport and started thumbing through the pages. He came to my Zairean visa. "What is this number here?" he asked himself in a suddenly petulant voice. "What is this—a 'W' or two 'U's? Those Zaireans out in the embassies write like children." The dunces abroad made his work so tough, he griped, yet the security of their country depended on him and his colleagues in SNIP. His voice steadied. "Listen, you've heard about the Italians who disappeared in Goma?"

"The ones who were shot?"

"Yes. You see, it's SNIP who's handling their case, SNIP. I thought it might have been the Rwandan refugees who killed them, but it looks like . . . well, it looks like it was our own soldiers who killed them. See how it is here? You need SNIP. You're not safe unless SNIP is looking out for you. Unfortunately, that's the way it is here."

A black fly buzzed around his office. It landed on his nose, and he swatted at it. No one in Zaire needed SNIP, except, of course, for Mobutu. Everyone hated SNIP. The Zairean equivalent of the KGB, all SNIP did was spy on people, scribble details into ledgers, and demand bribes. SNIP would never protect me if, for example, soldiers went on a rampage, or if we were attacked on the river by robbers. For three decades Mobutu had kept himself in power by relying on a pervasive, corrupt, and brutal internal security apparatus, of which SNIP was a part. But it wasn't just SNIP that was corrupt. The whole Zairean government had devolved into a sham institution, a facade of buildings with brass placards, doors with nameplates, people with titles, and nothing behind them. It built nothing, performed no services, represented no one. It probably no longer paid the pettifogging SNIP officer sitting in front of me his salary.

But as he copied information from my passport and *lettre de recommandation,* swatting angrily at the persistent and somehow humiliating black fly that circled his head determined to extract its lunch of blood, I studied him and extrapolated. From his French, which was well enunciated and correct, it was clear that he was educated. He had decorated his office, straw hut though it may have been, with a globe—he was trying to show he was aware of the world. His talk about the CIA and FBI was no doubt balderdash, but a note of regret, even shame, sounded in his suspicion that his own army might have killed the Italians. He was about forty-five, which meant that he came of age during the economic boom that had once led Zaireans to believe that their country was the hope of Africa. In his youth he probably had taken that hope to heart. Now here he was, middle-aged, in a remote river village, most likely unpaid, probably hated and certainly feared by everyone around him, his hopes dashed. It was a shame, a waste of a life and talent, and I almost felt that I would like to sit down and talk to this man.

But I had to get through my trip—the less time spent with these officials, the better. He finished with my passport. With an imperious mien—I felt like a ham actor—I took back my passport and letter and, with Desi in tow, walked out.

≈≈≈

Lokutu, with its well-tended straw huts sloping down to the river, was a pleasant place. Behind it, in the forest, were coffee, banana, and rubber plantations, many of which had been abandoned after the *pillages*. One could see that under normal conditions the village could prosper as a port for the plantations. But these were not normal conditions.

On the way back to his house, where I would wait while Desi bought a gun, which he would have to do in secret, since we had no permit, Desi stopped me. "Can we buy some worm medicine?"

"We have a lot of worm medicine."

"Not any more."

"Desi, have you taken it all?"

"Worm medicine is cheap here, that's all. It's always good to stock up."

We bought more worm medicine in a pharmacy hut. When we got back to his house we found his brother, an unemployed nurse with long yellowed toenails, inside the storage room going through our things. He said he was just curious to see what I had brought with me. But some of our food was gone. This I didn't mind—it might be considered as compensation for their hospitality.

Then I noticed our jerry cans of water were missing. "Desi, where is our water?"

At that moment I heard the sound of water splashing in a tub and the hollow retort of an empty jerry can banging the ground. I raced out into the yard. Our jerry cans, upended, were strewn in a rough circle around a tub of laundry. One of his brother's two wives was washing clothes using our boiled water. She was pouring it out, shaking the last drops from the last of seven jerry cans. She tossed it aside and sloughed away. More than forty gallons of safe water had been wasted.

"Desi!" I was speechless with anger, apoplectic at his negligence—he had given his word to look out for our water. He came around from the back and I led him into the side room. "Desi, your family has used the water we spent hours boiling back in Kisangani—all our water, clean water enough to last us to Mbandaka—to do the laundry!"

He lowered his head. "It's hard to carry water from the well, so they used it."

"Desi, I've stressed that our health depends on that water. Your health as well as mine. If we get sick out on the river, who will help us?"

He raised his head. "Villagers are strong because they drink the water from the river. Villagers—"

"Desi, I don't want to discuss this. Watching that water was your responsibility, part of your work for me. We will now have to boil more—seven jerry cans more—before we set out. That will take hours. *Hours!*"

Moping, he began gathering up the cans. I sat down and seethed. If there was one thing I couldn't compromise on, it was our health. But Desi had another task to do before he could start boiling water: he had to procure a gun. Like a true martinet, still red with anger, I called him back into the side room. "Look, are you forgetting why we came here? We need a gun. You're going to have to take care of that first. I can help you boil the water tonight." I handed him three hundred dollars (the gun would cost this much, he had said). He took it and, his head lowered, moped out the door and slunk through the gate.

Around eight in the evening Desi returned with a long object wrapped in rags. It was a twelve-gauge shotgun. He had also bought twenty-five shells.

"Good," I said. "Now we have to start boiling water."

In the Zaire Palace the staff had used multiburner kitchen stoves and vats to do the job, and it had taken them all evening. Here, we had only a fire and one vat; it was going to take much longer. Lokutu had a well of sediment-free water, so Desi and I used that as a source. The boiling lasted for hours: each gallon had to be boiled for ten to twenty minutes, then poured into our sterile jerry cans. I sat with Desi, stoking the embers, in the moonlit yard, with the kerosene lanterns flickering in the corners. As he stoked, he flipped the pages of a book in the orange light.

He looked at me, his face burnt sienna in the glow of the fire. "You know, if God wills and we reach Kinshasa—"

"Why do you always say 'if God wills?'"

"Well, from Kisangani to here are people of my tribe. But from here on—do you believe in God's will?"

"We have a gun, a *lettre de recommandation*, and we'll hire a soldier in Lisala. From all accounts, the dangerous stretch will be Lisala to Mbandaka. Isn't that right?"

"Well, yes, but . . . God will decide our fate."

"We'll make it. God will be with us. One thing's for sure: once we start out, the only way out is down the river."

He looked at me, then at the fire. He stood up. "I need some medicine." He turned and went into the storage room.

He didn't come back.

I finished boiling water around two in the morning. I lined up all the jerry cans next to my tent; I would sleep next to them, just in case.

Omens

WE PUSHED OFF FROM LOKUTU DURING THE DREAR HOUR BE-
tween the end of night and the break of day. The kerosene lanterns in the courtyards had long been extinguished, and the village
was black, but behind the ridge above it lightning flickered, charging the sky with a platinum effulgence that backlit the skeletons of
gargantuan trees, and I imagined how we would look from the
summits of those trees: two small beings in a tiny wooden craft
paddling down a broad river. It wouldn't take much to do us in: a
bolt of lightning, a hungry croc, even the microscopic malaria
protozoan carried by a single anopheles mosquito could kill us.
These dismal thoughts beset me as I paddled, leaning into my
strokes, feeling my muscles ache with fatigue.

The current soon swept us away from Lokutu into the widening
labyrinth of jungled islands and gloomy aquatic byways spreading
downriver to the west; it rushed us over the surface of water stirring
with the gurglings of unseen fish and frogs. Keeping near the bank,
we slipped under overhanging boughs, pushing aside creepers dangling invisible in the dark. Twice we collided with giant ferns that
reached out into our course, and the thorns on their thumb-thick
fronds torn open the skin on our forearms as we shielded our eyes.
At times when we rounded a bend we heard water splashing and
twigs snapping, followed by footsteps crunching the compost of the
forest floor—but we saw nothing. We were feared, we were shunned
and fled from, but by what we could not see.

Still, we sailed at a rapid clip—the current, forced here between
narrow island banks, was strong—and the notion that we were
again on our way and moving in the direction of Kinshasa comforted me. After the sun came up we laid down our paddles and

177

reclined, tired from our fireside night of boiling water. I watched the clouds blanch into day; enjoying the cool, I closed my eyes and wondered if Roger had managed to get through to Tatyana on the satellite phone in Kisangani. It was mid-August now. In Russia the nights would be chilling with the first hints of autumn; soon the rains would begin and the northern land would slip from long days of luxuriant warmth and light into the hibernal sleep of darkness and smothering snow, and Tatyana would be without me, and I missed her.

Something pricked my face. Then my forearms. I sat up. We had glided into swampy jungle down a byway hardly twenty feet wide. A swarm of black flies was enveloping us and no amount of swatting scared them away. The bloodsuckers stabbed their proboscises through our clothes, into our eyelids, into our exposed necks and forearms. We swatted and stamped and tried to paddle, to paddle and swat; we went astray, our bow bumping the bank, brush scraping our faces, thorns snagging our clothes. I dropped my oar in the water and Desi, smacking and shaking, grabbed it and handed it back to me. The forest canopy blotted out the sun, we were cruising through mucky dim swamp roofed by foliage dripping with dew.

There was light. We floated out of the forest into a baylet and the flies relented. A carnage of bloodied insect carcasses covered our arms and faces.

∕∕∕

The sun came out. Desi sat sullen at the stern, picking at his umbrella. I asked him what was wrong.

He shifted in his seat. "It's my brothers. They could be working, but they're not. They rely on me. Yesterday they all begged money from me. But I have responsibilities. I have my own family. I have to give money to my wife and daughter, don't I? I also have to give to the church. They get very angry about that. Even Mama complained about the church."

"You give the church money? You didn't even have a tooth-brush on the barge."

"Jesus said we must be generous and give. Giving to the pas-tors is the same as giving to God. So I give all I can. But anyway, I'm now afraid to leave my house for long. I'm afraid my brothers might sell it for the money, and I built it for them, for my whole family, but who can tell what they'll do? They don't want to work. I gave them a sack of rice yesterday but they said, 'Oh, we don't want it! Do you think we want to sit in the hot sun and sell it?' They said, 'Desi, just give us money.' I shouted, 'I should be de-voting myself to my wife and daughter, not to you!' But they said, 'Desi, you're our only hope.' What can I say? I try to live up to that. I ride the barges and make what money I can, and I give them what I can. They are my family. But I have many people to support. It makes me tired."

A tinge of pallor coming to his cheeks, he turned away from me. He took out his worm tablets and chewed one. With fish hawks circling above us, we drifted in the glare and heat, skirting rafts of hyacinth abuzz with bees. For the rest of the morning he paddled listlessly, pausing and looking down, paddling and paus-ing and looking down.

┛┛┛

By early afternoon, storm clouds were gathering, but we decided to risk it and keep going. To camp now, six or seven hours out of Lokutu, would mean wasting the day. But around three the sky blackened and left us no choice. We found a site in which to bivouac—a flat glade on an island of runty, half-leafless trees, on some of which the bark had been eaten away—and put up camp.

I took my bucket and towel and set off to find a hidden spot for a quick bath. The underbrush was sparse here, so for privacy I had to walk quite a way, but as it thickened I discovered the bush leaves were covered with what looked like ash, and they dusted me in gray powder. When I found a suitable thicket I stripped, hung my clothes on branches, and began ladling the water over myself and soaping up. The water was khaki-colored in the bucket, but it was warm and soothing.

Tick. Tick. Flutter. Rustles. Then rustling from everywhere. I froze and looked around. Rain? No. The rustling was coming from the ground. The ground, all dead branches and dry leaves, was alive with fat hopping crickets. They hopped all over my legs, tried to crawl up my shins. I stomped and lathered, stomped and rinsed, stomped and dried off, speculating about the connection between crickets and ash, between crickets and leafless trees . . . had some plague afflicted this island? The bugs were harmless, of course, but maddening.

It never rained. Back at camp I found Desi sound asleep in his net, spread-eagled as if felled by a gunshot, exhausted by our brief day's labor. The usual racket of kulokokos and monkeys was absent here, and I sat down in my chair and pulled out the maps and studied them in silence, flicking off the crickets that infested the site, that hopped up my legs and onto my arms. Since leaving Kisangani six days ago we had covered about a hundred and forty miles. We should now be on an island close to the south bank. But I was not really sure where we were. Many of the place-names on my charts were unknown to Desi, and with a few exceptions they did not correspond to the ones Stanley had described in his journal. We needed to replenish our supply of charcoal in Bumba, a hundred miles away, but with all the islands we might easily miss it. I glanced at Desi and realized how much I needed him to get me down the river. This led to extrapolation about what would happen to me without him, and anxiety at that thought washed over me. This anxiety, the silence of this dead, ashen island, and a growing sense of wilderness isolation prompted me to put away my maps and write a long entry in my journal.

At six the sun set and the mosquitoes drove me to retire. Crickets hopped and scratched their way up and down my tent, covering its white walls with their tiny skittering dark silhouettes.

Now and then there were explosive splashes out on the river, maybe of hippos or crocodiles, and I thought of the gun.

"Desi, you have the gun with you, right?"

No answer. I flashed my light through the rear gauze window and saw it lying next to him.

Distant thunder rumbled through the deserted glades. Listening to it, feeling oddly empty and alone, I slipped into a drowsy well of dark . . .

I was struggling through muddy waters on a sinking barge. The captain came out on the bridge, which was not yet submerged, in crisp dress whites, but he was drunk and staggering and ordered us to abandon ship. A chant was echoing around me: *"Prêtre! Oh, Prêtre! Prêtre! Oh, Prêtre!"* The bow of the barge was rising and the stern was going under.

I fought the swelling muddy water to reach my pirogue, which had been moored somewhere on the side. Salted sharks and crocodiles were strung up on deck, and their carcasses swayed as the barge upended. As I thrashed ahead to my pirogue, which was filling with brown water, I realized that these predators had come from the waters into which we were sinking. The captain shouted, "You've lost your pirogue! We'll see about compensation in the morning!"

Compensation?! Morning?! We were going under! Laws and damages and court cases meant nothing now; words meant nothing; every skill and ruse and tactic I had learned in life before meant nothing to me now. Water was rising around me, flooding into my nostrils and down my trachea, I inhaled and choked and caught glimpses of limbs underwater . . . water and death were real, everything else was false . . . now there was only submersion and open-mouthed gagging terror and river reeds entangling my kicking limbs in brown water and crocodiles and no escape . . .

I cried out and woke myself up. My cry echoed away over the river and came back to me, as if not my own. But outside was a domain of peace: the misty silvered water, the peeping chimes of tree frogs, the gentle burbling of fish. The forest and river were warm and near and fecund and wondrous.

At the snap of tree branches behind me I started.

The deep urgent voice of a man rang out: *"Wapi? Wapi?"* Then a boy's tenor: *"Kuna!"*

A prolonged crashing in the jungle resounded behind us, as of a boulder rolling through brush. Then silence. Minutes later a pirogue with two people in it went gliding past, a few feet from the bank, riding the current, slowing by our campsite. Then . . . nothing, only the moon on the empty river,and the chiming of tree frogs in the inky-black glade.

✦✦✦

The next morning dew was dropping from the trees on the south bank and plopping into the river. We had been traveling since dawn and had pulled ashore, lured by the hooting of monkeys. Craning his neck and looking up, Desi took the gun and sneaked away, leaving me in the pirogue next to the bank. The ridge was steep. He took big steps up the rise, his bare feet sinking back into the mud, and was soon gone behind the forest wall.

Just after we had decamped, Desi told me that the lack of meat was making him lightheaded—we had been subsisting (well, I had thought) on canned meat and on the fish we bought from villagers who paddled by in the morning. Monkeys were plentiful, he said, and killing one would be easy and provide meat enough for several days. We drifted until we heard the telltale hoots. There, Desi steered the pirogue ashore and got out. "I'll return with a monkey. I must eat monkey to regain my strength," he said.

I sat back and waited, keeping my eyes on the treetops, expecting a gunshot to explode the silence and a monkey to come tumbling out of the canopy.

I swatted a flying ant. Then another. There were all at once dozens of them swarming around me. I swatted again. They were wasps, not ants. They dug into my hair and stung me over and over on the scalp; they slipped down my shirt and stung me on my back and stomach. I jumped up and lost my balance in the pirogue and nearly fell overboard; I closed my eyes to the onslaught and fumbled for my poncho, rummaging about in the mess of belongings ahead of me like a blind man, swatting at every crawling on my skin and getting stung.

The poncho was in my hand. I tore it out of my pack and flung it over my head, smacking myself, trying to kill the wasps, whacking at my legs and torso, stomping the wasps falling to the bottom of the pirogue. I sat huddling in the dark under the poncho. To keep out the wasps I smoothed its edges against the bottom of the pirogue and caught my breath, shivering and burning with the stings.

Completely covered by my poncho, I don't know how much time passed before I became aware of a paddling sound, then the clear ring of Lingala over the water, one voice deep, the other less so. A man and a boy were rowing a pirogue toward me, coming from upriver. Falling silent, they veered away from me at the last moment, then, once downstream, started talking and paddling again.

Did I recognize their voices from last night?

A while later Desi returned—with no monkey. "I couldn't see them. The forest was too thick," he said. "But what are you doing with that poncho on your head?"

ırı

A pirogue was drawing near. In it was a family. Father steered, mother paddled, the son waved, and they all smiled at me. They were discussing whether I was a *touri* or a priest. A priest, they concluded—the father said there was no way I could be a *touri*. I asked Desi why.

"You bathe," he said. "And you don't have a Motorola. Or at least I don't think you do."

ırı

Later in the day Desi spotted a kulokoko, stretching out its wings and yawning, perched high atop a dead tree limb. He pulled out the gun. "That will be my meat. That will be my next meal." He put his eye to the barrel and leveled the bead on the bird. We drifted. When we were within range he pulled the trigger.

Nothing happened.

He pulled the trigger again and again with no result, and the kulokoko peered down at us as we floated by. I handed him another cartridge; he loaded and tried again. Nothing. We inserted more rounds, we examined the barrel, we checked the trigger. Everything looked fine—but the gun didn't work. When Desi bought it, it did not occur to him (or me) to test-fire it.

We stared into each other's eyes, bereft of our newfound sense of security. Desi's words about unfamiliar tribes and God's will came back to me. He laid the rifle at the bottom of the pirogue and put his head between his hands. We were floating down alleyways of turgid water through a mango grove, which surrounded island cemeteries of palms and other low trees, standing and recumbent, many the roosts of eagles, the abodes of ospreys and other hawks. Every bank was mud, every clearing was swamp. The underbrush thickened; it shivered with snakes, hummed with bees, droned with mosquitoes; it swarmed with every kind of flapping bug and painted bird. The sun was going down. Through a tunnel of mango trees we espied a raised bower, beneath which spread a tangle of roots.

"We should stop here," I said, "and camp on that rise."

"But the air is foul. I feel weak from the air here."

"If we get caught out the mosquitoes will eat us alive. You'll feel worse after that."

We maneuvered the pirogue down the tunnel, chained it to the roots, and clambered up the bank. It was indeed a foul spot, dank and clogged with chest-high weeds, home to gnarly beetles that buzzed and whirled through the air like small aircraft. We took out our machetes and commenced hacking. As we did so Desi complained of *faiblesse*. I labored to bring our belongings up the ladder of roots, slipping now and then, my feet clogging in the mud.

✦✦✦

The next day began with Desi still complaining of *faiblesse*. We were riding the current under a soft sun, drawing toward a village—a collection of huts around tall drums that appeared to have been fashioned out of tree trunks. A couple of young women came padding flatfooted out of huts with babies on their hips and waved at us to stop. They were pretty, wearing bright wraps around their slender waists, with balloon breasts that pressed tight against black T-shirts. There were holes in their shirts where their nipples were—maybe for their babies' sake.

"Mbote na bino!"

"Mbote! Mbote!"

"They will buy my cloth," Desi said under his breath, pulling a bolt of red cloth out of his bag. He put on his cowboy hat and leaned back, affecting a debonair pose, and held the bolt over his head, waving it. "Who wants to buy some red cotton?"

The women leaned over the bank. "Do you have medicine for malaria?"

"I'm selling this red cotton."

"What about batteries?"

"Cotton, I tell you! I'm selling cotton!"

"Do you have sewing needles?"

"Women, buy my cloth!"

"Do you have matches?"

We passed by them. Desi put down his cloth and angrily slapped his hat back into his bag. "They were not good customers, those women." He lowered his head. "I need to sell this cloth, you see. It's left over from the barge. I need to have money for my wife and baby. With your permission, I'll see them in Bumba, where they're staying with relatives, but I have nothing to give them."

"I'll give you a present for them."

"Thank you."

I looked at Desi. Our stop at his "fiancée's" village and his suave manner with his cowboy hat, his preening in the mirror as he shaved with toothpaste, and his charm and smooth tongue suggested that, until religion dampened his ardor, he had been a ladies' man. Now he was doing his best to meet his obligations to his family, and having a tough time of it.

As we drifted along he raised his head. "One must have many children. God commands us to do so. I must have many, many children."

"If you want more children, shouldn't you earn more money?"

"No. Why? If they have enough to eat to survive, this is good. God said to multiply."

"I've heard this theory."

"I'm multiplying according to God's will. According to what the Holy Book says. I can read you the part where it says to multiply."

"No need to. No matter what the Bible says, I think you need to earn more money to have more children."

"To be alive is enough. By the grace of Jesus we live, by the grace of Jesus we die. Your prophet Branam says this. We should not complain as long as we have a single grub to eat, a single banana, a single root to chew. We must thank Jesus and multiply. Always we must be thankful and multiply." He was buoyed by his own words and grabbed the Bible and began reading it, moving his lips and mumbling out the words.

※

All the rest of the cool day we came upon only one small village—five or six huts around the usual clearing. We needed to buy fish or monkey. Desi shouted a greeting in Lokele. There was no response.

But then two young men in rags came out, muscular young men with hair flecked with dust. *"Mbote!"* they said, finally, as if they had just woken up. They stared as we gained on them; they thrust out their shoulders and walked our way. *"Ozali kosomba nini?"* What are you buying?

"Nazali kosomba nyama!" Desi answered. *"Makaku!"*

The parley went on. They didn't have *nyama* (meat) to sell; they had no *makaku* (monkey) or even *ngando* (crocodile). But something was wrong with them: their eyes were red slits, and their strutting advance to the water's edge meant palm-wine drunkenness or a *mbangi* debauch. As we poled around to approach their landing I smiled and called out *mbote;* they glowered back at me, saying nothing. One of them produced a valise of scrawny fish, and a little boy wearing a NUFF SAID! T-shirt and no shorts came out, playing with himself. He tossed a rock at me and ran back to the huts.

They demanded a price that was three times that for which a valise sold in the market; we ended up buying an emaciated catfish for five thousand zaires.

As we paddled away drums resounded from the village.

"What was wrong with those people, Desi?"

"I don't know. It is strange, but I have not heard their language before."

✦✦✦

That afternoon we were blessed with a glorious island campsite: an arbor high above the water facing west. Desi ate his fish, then helped me through a large portion of canned meat, rice, and the remains of the plantains. Our stomachs were full, and a breeze was now blowing across the river, arriving scented with dates and mangoes, touching us like a fruity kiss blown by the sun, which all day had shone gently over us, and which, as it dropped, shot feelers of flaming red and lurid orange into the purpling sky. The red and orange rippled across the silver river, and the breeze, for the first time since we started out, turned pleasantly chilly.

We imbibed the scene and our spirits soared. We talked about the trip ahead. The soldier we would hire in Lisala would get us safely to Mbandaka; we would take it easy in the slow-watered, hot region around Bolobo; we would fly with the strong current into the cool of the Chenal, arriving in Kinshasa at the other end refreshed, reborn from our trials and revivified by our success. We *would* succeed—we would succeed or die trying, and our resolve, or at least my resolve, *had* to foreordain success.

We crawled into the shelter of our nets and began settling in. Everything was going to work out, and at last we believed it.

✦✦✦

In the middle of the night I awoke shivering: the clear skies had brought cold. Desi was praying aloud. Between verses from the Bible he was sobbing.

After throwing on my blanket I peeked through the tent door. "Desi, what's wrong?"

He did not answer.

Danger

IN THE COOL OF A SAFFRON DAWN WE BROKE CAMP AND ABAN-
doned our little Eden, paddling hard, energized by the hope of
reaching Bumba by midday. Bumba! What was Bumba to us?
Bumba was not just a town on the river—it was the end of the first
segment of our journey, and reaching it marked incontrovertible
progress toward Kinshasa. For Desi it was more: it was where he
would see his wife and daughter.

But as the day wore on the clear sky became our bane; the razoring rays of the sun wearied us and slowed our advance. The
water lane that had granted us swift passage on robust current de-
bouched into a pool sluggish and choked with algae. The air grew
pungent with the scent of water hyacinth blossoms and marshy
vegetation, with the fetor of swamp weeds. Black swarms of bees
hurled themselves through the harsh light like flying buzz saws,
and we wished for the saving cool of dawn. Yet around noon, on
the distant bend, where the river deflected south toward the equator, we made out the whitewashed walls and red-tiled roofs of
ruined villas. Bumba.

Desi took his shard of mirror in hand and began primping,
combing his hair and examining his teeth, then lathering up with
toothpaste and shaving away his fleecy beard. Finally, he donned
his tracksuit and ten-gallon hat. All in all, he cut a dapper figure.

He checked the ride of his hat in the mirror. "My wife and
baby—I have to look good for them."

"You want the Polaroid?"

"Yes, please."

I gave him the camera plus a pack of zaires as a present for his
family. He accepted the money without thanking me. It was, I now

saw, part of my duties as a (supposedly rich) *mondele* to make such gifts to him.

"Remember," I said, "we have to be out of here by three at the latest. We want to be deep in the islands by nightfall."

"No problem."

Hoping to avoid detection, we landed at a deserted beach at the edge of town, but within minutes a boisterous crowd of raga-muffin children and smiling teens appeared and came slip-sliding down the steep clay bank to gawk at us. Under their curious eyes I gave Desi money for a sack of charcoal, a crate of Cokes, some kerosene, and a few other things we needed; this was, first of all, a supply stop. He draped the Polaroid around his neck and jumped ashore, zipped up his tracksuit, and was gone. I sat down and watched the children cartwheel along the bank and dive somer-saulting off a nearby rise into the river. They were amicable and well-formed youngsters, all laughs, and we often exchanged smiles. Many were Lokele.

Desi stayed away a long time, missing his deadline by an hour. When he returned, he came loping down the bank in a happy-go-lucky mood, accompanied by more children and a porter bent under a load of supplies. Desi said his home visit had gone well, very well, and he was *très, trrrès content.* That was all fine, very fine, I replied, but I looked at my watch. What about our deadline, and (I glanced at his acquisitions)—*sacrebleu!*—had he forgotten the charcoal? Holding his cowboy hat to his head he scampered up the bank and ran back into town.

We ended up pushing off just before sunset. Desi paddled with particular urgency, declaring that we had to move well out of the range of Bumba's thieves, and *fast,* as though this were a risk of which he thought it best to remind me, lest I forget, river-naive *mondele* that his tone implied I was. With the mosquitoes soon to descend and Desi's cheerful tardiness alternating with his oddly didactic exhortations to paddle hard, with the coming inconve-nience of having to pitch camp in the dark, and with the possibil-ity that someone might indeed have followed us (for who had not turned up on the bank to stare?), I felt rancor rising in my throat. Although an hour in Bumba would have sufficed, I had offered Desi three, he had taken five, and now we were at risk.

Yet presently a look of melancholy mixed with fatigue stole over his face. "You know what?" he said, "I'm tired." He put down his oar, and reclined.

I kept rowing, but the pirogue spun lazily out of control, unmanageable with me paddling at the bow alone. I could hold in my irritation no longer and thwacked my paddle down.

"Desi, look here. You're in my employ and you know our security depends on our taking certain precautions. You were late today and now"—I swatted mosquitoes off my cheeks and caught my faltering balance in the wobbling scow—"now, look at us! You're resting and it's almost night and we're nowhere near a campsite and God knows who could be following us!"

My outburst caught him off guard. He looked at me perplexed for a moment, as though attempting to divine the ravings of a lunatic. "Why are you so upset?" he asked. "Jesus is looking out for us. Jesus—"

"Desi, come on! Don't change the subject."

"You don't have faith in Jesus?"

"Faith has nothing to do with this!" I was suddenly sick of this Jesus talk: it was an excuse for sloth and irresponsibility. But I did not want to get into that. "Another thing! You've been so lackadaisical the past couple of days. What's wrong? If you're sick we should find you a doc—"

"I am *not* sick! And I don't go to doctors!" He jumped to his feet. "*I* have faith in Jesus—*Jesus!*—and He's looking out for us! I pray for His help!"

"'*His help!*' Isn't there a line in the Bible about God helping those who help themselves? Just do your job!"

"You are *scolding* me!" he thrust out his shoulders, addressing me for the first time with the informal *tu*. "*Why?!*"

"I want to get to Kinshasa in one piece, that's why!"

We stood glaring at each other in the waning light, the sun

dropping blood-red behind the forest. The sounds of the night-time jungle—the alarm calls of kulokokos, the hoots of owls, the weird buzzings of giant nocturnal beetles—were slowly creeping out onto the river. It was useless to continue this argument. I stomped and shook the mosquitoes off my legs. I ripped open my duffel and threw on my long pants, I splashed repellent over myself. "We need to find a campsite before it's too dark to see."

Glaring at me, Desi slowly picked up his paddle.

We floated toward a cliff about ten feet above the water. In the dark its altitude would make us invisible to passing pirogues. We pulled up to the shore beneath it and I got out, slipping on the root tangles, and clambered up its face. We erected a rudimentary camp—no tarp, no tent, just nets—on the lumpy, root-covered eminence, ground that even with our foam mattresses was going to make for poor sleep. As soon as the nets were set up we climbed inside, assaulted by mosquitoes, hungry and unbathed.

I lay down and gruntingly tried to position myself so that the roots wouldn't poke me. But it was futile. Desi lit his lamp and started reciting a passage from the Bible, then thumbed through his *Code du Travail* and perorated a subclause on a worker's right to advance notice in the event of untimely dismissal. That led him, somehow, back to a verse from Isaiah, and he flipped pages and cross-referenced the two.

As I listened to him read I thought, *How little I understand this guy!* His thoughts never matched my thoughts; I could never foretell his responses. But more than just culture and upbringing separated us: our purposes in traveling the river put us at odds. For me, everything here was new and urgent and unique; for Desi the Congo was a harsh and ancient waterway out of which to wrest a meager living while he battled constant fatigue from worms or fevers or whatever it was that was afflicting him. He would not hurry because, danger or no, this river was his home and he lived by rhythms that allowed him to conserve his strength, enjoy himself when he could, and go on.

It was wrong of me to lose my temper, and I regretted my sharp words.

"Desi, I didn't mean to yell at you. Just let's be more careful next time. Maybe it's the nine days of river travel that are wearing on us. Why don't we rest an extra day in Lisala?"

He halted his reading and sat up in his net. After clearing his throat, he clasped his hands and raised his head. "O Lord Jesus! Watch out for us on this huge river! Great dangers are ahead! And please watch out for Monsieur Jeff's woman in Moscow. O Lord Jesus! Watch out for Monsieur Jeff so that he can go back to Moscow and have many, many children with his woman and be very happy there! Amen!"

No sooner, it seemed, had I suffered my way into a spell of fitful sleep than the sun was beating down through my net. We had overslept by an hour. Without having breakfasted, we decamped, sore and grimy, poked tender by the roots, and poled out into the rushing current. But shortly the river widened from three miles across to six, and the current whisked us into a wild profusion of isles and jungle alleys. I asked Desi if he knew the way to Lisala from here; we didn't want to end up on the wrong side of an island and shoot past the town without realizing it.

He listened to my question and said, in a disoriented voice, "I feel dizzy."

"*Dizzy?* Desi . . . Desi, I'm asking you how well you know the river here. If you have any doubts, we should stick to the north bank, so we'll be sure to see Lisala."

"I know the river. But I'm tired."

The morning wore on, growing overcast and humid. We skirted a finger of land and startled a villager in a cove: a stubble-bearded man in his forties with unkempt hair and a goiter the size of a pomegranate was standing there fixing a fishing net. As though I were carrion, he flinched at the sight of me. But he had a fat capitaine on a rope and we needed to eat. Desi called out a greeting and offered him ten thousand zaires for the fish, an acceptable price; he uttered a curt *te,* and demanded thirty thousand. Desi made a counteroffer. Shaking his head *(Te! Te!),* the fisherman refused to come down. We handed him thirty thousand, took the fish, and paddled off, with him shooting deranged looks at us.

"What's his problem, Desi?"

Desi was fully alert now. He shifted around on his seat and watched the man watch us as we made our way downriver. "I don't know. He's not of my people. I don't know what tribe he's from."

JJJ

By noon the river on which fishermen had hitherto passed by four or five times a day was flowing empty, and there were no villages. The open and swampy forest around Bumba had metamorphosed into a dark and snarled wall of vegetation, of serried gum trees and teaks and bombaxes rising hundreds of feet into the sky straight from the banks. A headwind wearied us, blowing hot and wet from the equator, where battlemented clouds of gunmetal blue massed above the jungle. Lightning tore loose over the horizon.

"Should we pull ashore?"

"We should not stop," Desi said, working his paddle hard. "Not here."

Soon the clouds were lowering, the palm fronds were hissing, blowing backward and showing their pale undersides; the wind was frilling the slate-colored water with white. We were approaching a forested peninsula. A long rumble of thunder broke into pealing explosions. We *had* to take cover. I looked back at Desi.

His eyes widened. "A boat!"

Rounding the cape at high speed was an oil-carrying barge, its deck manned by Bangala soldiers bearing automatic rifles. It came crashing through the storm-roiled water, and we ran lurching through its wake. As we regained our balance, two pirogues came around from behind the barge and shot toward us. The pilots— two men in each—were in rags, but they were muscular, paddling in unison, pitching and rolling expertly with the wake. They came alongside us, one port and one starboard.

"*Mbote!*"

"*Mbote!*"

Greetings were exchanged all around, but smiles were not, and no handshakes followed. One of the men put down his oar and shouted to Desi in Lingala. "We are *matata* [vicious]! Give us food! Give us cigarettes! You have a *mondele* with you—you have food for us!"

I looked at Desi. His face went blank and his eyes darted to the feet of these men, where there lay glistening machetes, heavy and murderously sharp.

"*Pesa ngai mbongo!*" (Give me money!), the leader shouted, growing impatient. He started leaning toward his machete.

"*Problem eza te,*" Desi said calmly. Take what you want.

The leader paused and, turning away from his weapon, began rifling through our provisions. The others held our pirogue firmly to theirs. We were being robbed.

Desi bent over as if to help him find what he wanted, but instead he reached under his bag and drew out the shotgun. He straightened up, expressionlessly waving the barrel back and forth across the four brigands. We bobbed on the waves, we drifted; thunderbolts broke free of the clouds to the south, flashing and crashing into the forest; wind gusted up the river. We swayed and tried to keep our balance on the mounting surf.

The robber abandoned our sacks and smiled. Desi smiled, too. I smiled. The brigands began half-bowing, rapidly uttering a supplicatory Lingala. Ngombe was mentioned over and over, as well as *likama* (danger) and *matata*. We were drifting toward a few huts under giant trees, and there were people outside them. Women picked up their children and ran off, and four or five men in rags came out to the bank.

"Come and shelter in our village," the leader said. He pointed at the sky. *"Mbula."*

Desi kept the gun trained on them. "No, thank you."

"Please, you and the *mondele* are welcome."

"Te. We thank you very much."

The leader shouted to the men on shore and one of them went running to the huts. A blast of wind hit us, and we all nearly toppled over. The man came running back with a handful of smoked catfish and crashed out through the water to the brigands' pirogue. We were directly opposite the village now, ten feet from the bank. The brigands took the fish—three shriveled black things—and passed them to Desi, who adjusted the gun in the crook of his arm and accepted them, nodding thanks.

At this point the leader began pointing at the forest and the river, gesticulating with passion, speaking loudly and with nasal flourishes, over and over saying *matata* and *likama* and Ngombe and much more than I could follow. Desi listened, his face a mask betraying no emotion, his gun remaining trained on them. Finally, they picked up their paddles and rowed back upriver toward their village.

Desi kept his eyes on them until they had vanished behind the trees.

"They warned us that they're Ngombe, they're vicious robbers and proud of it, and we're in their territory. We will have problems. No one who's not an Ngombe enters Ngombe land, and even the barges speed through, because Ngombe use gaffs to snare people off the decks. If we're seen we'll be robbed or worse. They told us to avoid showing ourselves to the villages ahead. And if Ngombe fishermen come up to us, they're not really fishermen—they're robbers. They said to shoot in the air or into the water when they approach." He held the gun high and gave it a proud pat.

"Our gun is a dud, Desi."

He lowered his eyes.

"But," I said, still not yet fully feeling the fear I knew would come once I had digested the incident, "no one has to know that. So, we have to hide from the villages?"

"Yes. We have to hide."

"Do you know where the villages are?"

"I . . . no, not exactly."

Any minute the storm would hit, and holding to midriver, which would help us conceal our identity from those on shore, would not be possible. I sat down in a clammy sweat. There weren't supposed to be Ngombe until *after* Lisala. I picked up the map. It seemed to show that we were following the bank of an island that terminated near Lisala—but then there were more islands here than anywhere we had been before, and the profusion of waterways could have confused us. The more I tried to make what we had seen today jibe with what was on paper, the less certain I became of our position.

Then I harked back to my pretrip readings. Stanley had described the tribes in this section of the river as "powerful, well-equipped, and warlike . . . hideously bepainted for war . . . remarkably superior . . . [entertaining] a singular antipathy toward strangers," but could his words really apply to the Ngombe of today? I also recalled the hierarchy and territoriality of the tribes he encountered, most of whom were cannibals. Many forbade strangers to enter their land—which accounted for much of the hostility with which he and his crew met, hostility that resulted in some forty battles on the way downriver and dozens of deaths. But that was all a hundred and twenty years ago! Could there still exist such people in the Africa of today? After all, barges passed through here. Isolated tribesmen did see outsiders; in fact, they relied on them for medicine and manufactured goods. How could it be— *could* it be?—that they were still so dangerous, as *matata* as the brigand declared? Then it occurred to me: if violent robberies were so common in Kinshasa, why wouldn't bands of thugs also roam the river?

I put away the map and started to paddle. Thunder broke once, twice, then lingered. Or was it thunder?

Desi froze. "Drums!"

Beats ominous and deep reverberated across the water. We listened.

"Could they be saying something about us?" I asked.

"I don't know. I don't understand the message. They are not the drums of my region."

"We have to stay away from their village, but where is it?"

The forest amplified the drumbeats and bounced them all over. They could have been coming from anywhere.

"There!" Desi whispered.

Smoke was billowing out from behind trees twenty yards ahead. It was too late to take evasive action: we would pass within ten feet of them. We quietly placed our paddles in the pirogue. Desi grabbed the gun, I seized the machete. Without steerage we started rotating, looping down along the bank.

We ducked. We revolved past the fire—but it was unmanned. The drums were resounding from somewhere else.

Rain began falling in heavy, single pellets. A terrible mountain of black thunderheads firing yellow bolts of lightning into the jungle filled the sky to the south, moving along the equator. It was three-thirty. We needed to find a secluded place to camp, and fast.

Despite the clouds, we coursed far out into midriver to avoid showing ourselves to a village on the left bank. The islands now were too numerous to keep track of: each had its own dark waterway with its dense jungle and kulokoko sentries. Conical wasp nests hung from high branches but there wasn't a wasp about. "The storm," whispered Desi. "It will be bad. Everything is hiding."

The rain was dappling the water with frothy ringlets of white, but the wind had died down; the storm was passing south of us. We drifted by a cove accessible through a narrow break in the trees—a perfect hidden campsite. We pulled up to the bank, and I stepped out and dragged the bow chain.

There was a gunshot. We ducked. Then another shot.

"Get back in! Let's go!" Desi whispered, "Let's go!" He dug

into the water with his oar, I pushed the bow back out and splashed along, trying to catch up to it, my bare feet slipping over the roots on the bottom. Cringing, I jumped aboard and we both began paddling. We saw smoke—the gunshots were from the opposite bank—and shouts of "Eeyaaah! Eeyaaah!" rang out from up and down the river. With these cries villagers alerted one another to approaching barges, to the unexpected presence of strangers.

We stayed within a yard of the bank. The rain turned heavy and gusts came rolling upriver, slowing us, raising breakers—it would soon be too rough to continue. We reached the rear of the island and started down the alley between two others.

We spotted a secluded glade at the far end of an island. It would afford us a with a view of the south bank, of the approach from the villages we had passed, so we chose it and set up camp in the soaking but now thunderless rain. We camouflaged our tents with tree branches, we dragged our pirogue behind the foliage, we abstained from lighting our lanterns or playing the radio. We spoke in whispers—when voices carried across the river we held our breath, and Desi tried to discern what was being said. But they were speaking Ngombe, and he could not understand.

I was determined not to give in to panic or break our routine. We had hundreds of miles to go to Mbandaka, and we would have to remain composed or we would destroy ourselves. I therefore shaved and bathed, albeit in the rain, and Desi did, too, and we felt better. At four-thirty in the afternoon I crawled inside my tent, Desi into his net. Desi spoke in a low voice.

"I'm a stranger here. If they see me, they will think I've come to steal, and they'll kill me. These people are robbers and killers."

I did not know what to say to him.

✧✧✧

Later there was a rustle, sinuous and faint, coming from the forest behind us, moving slowly and surely toward our camp. I held my breath and sat up. It grew louder and more distinct. The rain plopped from leaf to leaf, splattering onto the ground, into the

river; the river was now an expanse of running pewter glimmering
through the trees. I gripped the gun, squeezed its iron barrel, and
I waited, sweat pouring off my brow, for whatever it was to come
into view.

A python, ten feet long and as thick as a human thigh, scaly and
slimy, muscular and mottled brown and black, slithered by my
gauze tent door. It wended its way around our gear, slithered past
us, its tail slightly raised in a curl, and, at last, was gone into the
brush.

I relaxed and lay back, still listening but now breathing freely,
as the light failed and darkness, sultry and suffocating, settled over
the forest. Rain continued to fall in maddeningly resonant drops,
dripping down from the treetops.

Around midnight it ceased. For a while there was not a sound,
but slowly the forest began echoing with cries and wavering
hoots, with screeches that rang with the numbing terror we felt as
trespassers in this wilderness. We heard crashes in the bush, the
snapping of branches in nearby glades. Every snap or crash *could*
indicate the approach of an Ngombe murderer, but each time silence followed, a tense silence, as if the forest, frightened by an
intruder, were holding its breath. I woke up over and over again,
unaware of what had roused me, experiencing only a residue of
fear without knowing its cause.

Desi's cool and quick thinking during the attempted robbery
had saved us. But it occurred to me: might the Ngombe brigands,
in their chest-thumping explication afterward, have exaggerated
the danger for some purpose unbeknownst to us?

I pondered this during the long, long night, and waited for
dawn.

✦✦✦

At five in the morning we slipped out of our tents, tossed the
camouflaging brush from our pirogue, and shoved off, soundlessly
regaining the current, the sky hunkering low above us a black
cauldron of cloud. As day broke a headwind arose, rifling through

sopping leaves. Silently and assiduously we worked our paddles. Lisala had to be at the end of this island, it *had* to be. Noting that villages tended to appear in the southern reaches of the river, we stuck to the northern bank. The isle went on and on, and the sun came out, driving away the clouds and whipping up a headwind. We strained with each stroke of the oar, the calluses on our hands degenerating into blisters, then bloody-watery sores.

We passed only one village. The men came out and shouted, "Is that *mondele* alone?"

"No," Desi answered. "There are more coming behind us. *Touris.*"

They laughed and shouted a response in brazen Ngombe.

I looked back at Desi. "That was clever. Let them think we're carrying a veritable armory of Motorolas!"

Just then we floated by a cove. Two youths brandishing machetes came running out of the forest, leapt into their pirogue, and cast off, all in one balletic, lethal rush.

A surge of adrenaline coursed through my heart and I plunged my paddle deep into the muddy water. Desi scrambled and pulled out the gun. As the pirogue overcame us, he trained it on the youths.

"Ah, you and the *mondele* have a gun!" one shouted to us. "You win! We would have robbed and killed you both, and who would have ever known!" Laughing, they dropped back and returned to their cove, their laughter mocking and following us as we sped away down the bank.

𝆑𝆑𝆑

We lunched on the capitaine and the smoked catfish the Ngombe had given us, adding rice and canned tomatoes. This simple meal did more than nourish us—it distracted us, it gave us something on which to concentrate besides our wearying fear, and Desi's face showed fear as clearly as mine must have. I even managed to ponder for some time the putrid flavor of the catfish—which tasted the same as catfish I had eaten in the States. It took me back to the canal on which I used to fish as a boy; to mornings on the Potomac River; I recalled high school and friends I had not seen in years . . .

There was a glint in the distance far ahead of us, as of polished steel over water. Two pirogues were coming with three men in each. But as I bent around to warn Desi, who was washing his plate, I caught sight of two other pirogues approaching from the rear. He saw the look on my face, grabbed the gun, and shoved a cartridge in the chamber.

"That will do us a lot of good," I said, laughing.

"We have nothing else."

We were going to be ambushed. I could slash with the machete, I could strike with my oar. I could stuff a rag in the kerosene can, light it, and toss it like a Molotov cocktail. Desi kept the gun in his hands, his finger on the trigger; he steadily repeated a verse from the Bible. We were both going to remain calm. Until . . .

The sun gilded the river; a breeze blew cool and fresh; the coruscations ahead were rhythmic and slashing.

"I hate strong sun, Desi. I prefer the clouds. That's one reason I love Russia. The sun is soft there in the summer. In the winter, the sun is rare and welcome."

"Winter?"

Each set of pirogues was now twenty yards equidistant from us.

"When it snows."

"When it *what?*"

"Haay! Whooa! Whooa!" the men in the pirogues were shouting.

The pirogues from the rear reached us first. They paddled alongside us; their pilots, lanky youths, greeted Desi and ignored me. Then the pirogues from up ahead passed us, filled with families. The "machetes" turned out to be wet oars reflecting the sunlight.

In two craft next to us sat six people, men, women, children; in one, fish was being smoked in a miniature hut of bamboo sheltering a fire burning on a pile of earth. They had started out in

Bumba and tried to catch up with us to warn us about the route we were taking, but they lost us in the islands. Desi told them about our troubles.

The senior youth astern shook his head. "You are lucky to be alive. Anyway, what are you doing out here, Lokele? You're crazy to come out here with just a *mondele*. You need protection. You need to travel with Bangala or Ngombe. The people in these parts are *matata*."

He jumped aboard our pirogue. His head, wrapped in a turban, was angular, his jaw square; he was long-limbed and sinewy. He took my paddle and motioned me to rest, then turned to Desi. "And what is this *mondele* doing here? Looking for diamonds?"

We bucked heavy waves and a headwind. Tsetse flies, swarming above the hyacinth, dove into the air pockets formed by the gunwale of our pirogue; they tormented us, biting us behind the knees, on the backs, wherever we could not see to swat.

But it did not matter. In the company of others a millstone of fear had been lifted from our hearts. The youth said he and his companions were Bangala fishermen from near Mbandaka. Bangala! He would know about the abattoir—the place of slaughter—that the SNIP colonel in Lisala had told me lay between Lisala and Mbandaka. I interrogated him and Desi translated. The youth said he had seen two *mondeles* murdered in pirogues south of Lisala, and had a lot to say about the region. "It's very dangerous. We Bangala don't care for life. If we see a *mondele* many of us think only to kill him and take his things. After the murders I saw the whole area became a scandal for Zaire. Mobutu sent in troops and they wiped out the villages that killed them."

"Can we make it through?" I asked.

"You'll need to fire your guns. When the pirogues appear, shoot in the air before they approach you. You must scare them first, make them afraid. You will have to be alert and very careful, or you will have problems."

The day aged, the sun described its arc across the cerulean sky, the banks lifted the forest higher and higher. Lisala was not at the end of that island, or the next, or the next. At five, however, the youth announced we were drawing near.

I started getting ready. I put on the fresh Oxford shirt and trousers I had stashed in the bottom of my bag; I combed my hair; I checked my *lettre de recommandation* and passport and placed them in my breast pocket. Just before the sun fell Lisala appeared on the ridges ahead, and atop the ridges children popped up, running along and chanting *"Mondele! Mondele!" Mondele* rang out from hut to hut, along with cries of "Eeyaah!" The children raced the pirogue, shouting and skipping, now and then tossing stones at us. We paddled hard, riding the current, which was frothy and fast here.

The beach came into view. Soldiers were hoisting their guns to their shoulders and loping toward us, stumbling down the steps of the landing, their boots untied and flopping, their guns swinging. The youth hopped back into his own pirogue. I thanked him and he nodded farewell, then he and his company veered off down-river, leaving us to face the soldiers alone.

Lisala

"COME HERE! HEY! *LE BLANC!* YOU COME *HERE!*"

Like a ragtag lynch mob drunk on whiskey, seven or eight soldiers came bounding down the bank toward us, shouting in French and tripping on their bootlaces, waving their guns. As at Ngobila Beach, so here, there was something almost comic in the mix of swaggering bravado and exaggerated, no doubt, staged rage to which my appearance provoked them. But their sloppy speech told me they had been drinking booze or smoking *mbangi,* and they pointed their guns at us, which was not funny.

I stopped paddling and stood tall, preparing to ham-act here as I had done in Lokutu. We coasted up to the beach and the pirogue's bow scraped its way up onto the sand. The soldiers were dressed in khakis and yellowed T-shirts. They were enlisted men, and there was no sign of an officer among them. I stepped out, and they closed around me.

A man in full uniform shoved through the mob, kicked the last private aside, and thrust his face in mine. He was almost Arab in complexion, with a mustache and a long, stubble-encrusted mug. Epaulets on his shoulders marked him as an officer. Still, *mbangi* was on his breath and his eyes were murky red. His tongue moved around in his mouth like a squirming clam.

"Sh-show me your—"

I held out my *lettre de recommandation.* "I am on a mission sanctioned by the Chief of Staff of Military Intelligence of President Mobutu, as it says here. I will speak only to the Lisala base commander."

The officer shifted the gun under his arm. He squinted at the letter and reached for it, but I pulled it away. "I *said* I will speak only to the base commander," I repeated, staring hard into his sodden eyes.

He stepped back and dropped his gaze, and so did his men, who lowered their guns. He made a wary welcoming gesture toward the stairs leading up to the town. "No problem, *commandant*. After you."

Desi set about unloading the pirogue, and the officer and I started up the steps. The other soldiers tagged along, lagging well behind, as if I might crack a whip or kick an ass, and I tried to look as though I would. But along the way, still more soldiers fell in with us, and in no time we were leading a procession of slovenly, stoned, or drunk Zairean warriors swinging their taped-up rifles, scuffing their boots in the dust, nagging me for *mbongo,* beer, *mbangi,* or whatever *cadeau* they could cadge; they grew so insistent, pulling on my sleeves and whining, that I snapped to the officer, "Do something about these ridiculous men!" He flailed his gun at them and they dropped back a few paces, but followed us just the same.

We were in Lisala to hire a soldier for protection. I suddenly envisioned myself sharing the same pirogue with one of these louts, eating and drinking with him, and most absurdly, relying on him to protect my life.

Lisala was a torpid town with no charm. Its center was a mess of concrete buildings on dusty earth diminishing to huts with African-style courtyards in jungly suburbs. At the military base we were told that the commander was not in, that we had to come back in the morning. But on our way out we ran into the chief of SNIP, a potbellied colonel in his fifties wearing a Hawaiian shirt. Ignoring my proffered hand, he did not slow his pace to greet me, but instead pointed to a fellow waving at me and running up the road. "This man will take care of you," he barked, turning away.

The waving man, also dressed in a Hawaiian shirt (I was beginning to recognize a certain style of Hawaiian shirt as the Polo of the Zairean elite), grabbed my hand and pumped it vigorously. "Oh, pew! Hot today, isn't it? Well, I'm the adjutant. I got the letter from

Kinshasa. I'm responsible for your security. Anyway, welcome to Lisala! We have reserved suites for you! Where is your gear? At the beach? Ah! *Après vous!*" He grandly motioned me ahead, but then took my arm anyway and pulled me along in search of a pickup truck that could transport our belongings to the hotel.

The adjutant was sportily coiffed, and his wingtips were polished; he had an air of pleasant alacrity about him that contrasted with the malign torpor of most Zairean officials. His diction was clipped and suggested efficiency. All of this set me at ease and made him seem worth the price he was sure to demand.

Later, up at the no-name hotel to which he took us, Desi and I settled into our "suites." There was no water or electricity and the doors had no locks; in fact, most of the rooms had no doors. There were curlicues of feces scattered across the bathroom floors—only the toilets were clean. But the staff, a friendly family, did their best to make us comfortable, bringing water from the well for our baths and providing us with kerosene and kitchen space.

Night fell. Lisala after dark was all smoking middens alternating with the pale yellow flames of kerosene lanterns that illuminated the larval wares of sidewalk vendors. But it was not quiet: the air rumbled with generators powering the air conditioners and fluorescent lights of villas belonging to the local Big Men. Lisalans, Bangala, for the most part, were aggressive and blustering, and they made Desi and me nervous. It was not a friendly place, and we kept off the street.

rrr

Morning sun flooded through the window panes, flies buzzed in the dusty checkers of light falling on the floor. Mobutu looked rather peeved and put-upon in the portrait on the wall of the base commander's office, slumped on his throne and clutching his chief's staff, his Hawaiian shirt buttoned up to his neck and pinching him in the armpits. The commander, a clean-shaven man in spotless khakis, shook my hand and ignored Desi, and gestured to me to take a seat. Both Desi and I sat down in front of his desk.

"It is kind of you to receive us, Commander," I said. "I know you are very busy. I appreciate the time you will spend accommodating us, and I would like to present you with a token of my gratitude." I placed a brick of zaires—twenty dollars' worth—on his desk. (Desi suggested the amount and the wording of this address beforehand.)

His eyes on mine, the commander took the brick in hand, opened a desk drawer, and dropped it in.

"We will need a soldier to protect us on the way from Lisala to Mbandaka."

"There is no problem," he said flatly. "We have been informed by Kinshasa. The adjutant will find you a suitable man."

"Thank you."

I started to stand up and so did the commander. But Desi, slouched in his chair, did not move. He interrupted our rise. "Now wait ju-u-ust a minute. About this soldier. He must not be just *any* one of your men. He must not drink and he must not smoke. He must be a God-fearing Christian. He must love Jesus, and show that love in his deeds."

The commander furrowed his brow and eased himself back into his seat, as did I. He addressed me, as though I, not Desi, had just spoken. "Well . . . I don't see what Jesus or smoking has to do with your expedition. And I'm no less a military man for having a beer now and then . . . anyway, you talk to the adjutant."

Desi continued. "He must not smoke or drink because—"

I stood up and cut in. "Thank you for your time. We'll have the adjutant inform you of our progress." I grabbed Desi and led him out.

At that moment the adjutant came sauntering into the waiting room. He was beaming. "I have found *the* soldier for you. Meet Henri. You can reach an agreement with him right now!"

Henri was one of the *mbangi*-head privates who had pestered me on arrival. He was a runt with a pinched oily face—he looked like he needed a good scrubbing with antibacterial soap. He averted his eyes from mine and spoke only to Desi. I heard numbers being bandied around. Next thing I knew Henri was shaking my hand.

Desi was triumphant. "Henri has accepted your offer of two hundred and fifty thousand zaires."

"My *offer?* What are you talking about?"

"Well, the adjutant has approved him."

"I haven't made an offer. I don't know the first thing about this guy." I turned to the adjutant. "With all due respect, I decide here."

The adjutant opened his mouth, but Desi cut in. "Okay, what do you need to know?"

I was still upset about Desi's meddling in my talk with the commander. "Desi, you're not to talk on your own. You're acting on my behalf. Well, first of all, can this . . . Henri . . . swim?"

Desi asked him in Lingala. Taking a deep breath, Henri muttered an answer.

"No. Henri fears the water."

"Well, that's not good news if he'll be in a pirogue for the next two weeks, is it?"

"He knows that. He's very concerned. So he has raised his fee. To four hundred thousand."

"What happens if he should drown?"

"Drown?" Desi turned to Henri and translated my query. Henri protested, spewing forth verbiage in agitated Lingala, his forehead beading with fresh oil and more sweat. Desi relayed his words to me. "If he is going to drown he must raise his fee. He will now accept eight hundred thousand."

"Desi, I'm not hiring anyone who can't swim."

This truly upset Henri, who raised his rate to 1,500,000.

Desi grew grave. "You're frightening him with all this talk of water."

"Oh, for God's sake, he's fired!" I responded. Henri dropped his fee to 350,000. No. He then asked for severance pay. No again.

Desi turned back to me. "You are worried about his drowning. For your information the *Code du Travail du Zaire* states that the life of a soldier is worth the lives of one hundred and fifty civilians or fifty thousand U.S. dollars."

The adjutant perked up. "Is that so? Fifty *thousand* dollars?"

If I had had a club I would have clobbered Desi, and I told him so with my look.

The adjutant's eyes sparkled. "Fifty thousand dollars. Fifty *thousand!* But of *course!*"

"I'm not paying anybody fifty thousand dollars. No one is going to die on our expedition. We need a soldier who can swim and accept the risk in return for a suitable salary, food, and, if he does his job well, a healthy bonus." The salary alone that I would offer was more than twice as much as a soldier would normally receive in a month. It would be a good deal.

"You don't care about the life of a soldier?" Desi asked, frowning.

The adjutant interrupted. "You don't have to. You can simply pay an insurance premium and be absolved of responsibility if anything should happen."

"What sort of 'premium'?"

He darted into the commander's office, whence a bout of excited whispering issued. He darted back out. "Five hundred thousand zaires. Payable to the base commander through me. In advance."

"What sort of policy papers are involved?"

"Why, none at all! Just pay us cash—in advance!"

"With all due respect, no."

"But the commander has accepted your offer!"

"I haven't made an offer."

Desi took me aside. "You're acting as though Henri's life means nothing to you. You are acting *méchant*. You're—"

"Desi, please, stay out of this." Obviously the premium was a scam, and I wanted to talk no more about it. I addressed the adjutant. "Listen, if something happens to this soldier it will be in the line of his official duties; I have authorization from Military Intelligence for his services. In truth, I shouldn't have to pay him anything at all because he's still going to get his salary and he's simply doing his duty—the duty you are assigning him to carry out by ordering him to accompany me. Remember, my *lettre de recommandation* orders you to assist me. But I'll be generous with him—and with you—if this can all be satisfactorily arranged. And I'm not taking anyone aboard my pirogue who can't swim. Period." I walked to the other side of the room and looked out the window.

"*Bon,*" said the adjutant. "Okay. Wait here a minute." He hurried out the door, and Henri, realizing his services would not be wanted, slunk away.

A little later the adjutant appeared with another soldier in tow, a genial fellow who was just over five feet tall. His name was Amisi. Amisi held high his seventy-two-caliber FAL automatic rifle (a Belgian version of the M-16), and his uniform was buttoned and pressed. He could swim and knew Lingala and Swahili (he was a Swahili speaker from east of Kisangani), and not much French, he said, but he managed to converse well enough in that language that I got an idea of his character. He was not the fierce-looking guardian I had imagined, but he seemed trustworthy and that sufficed. I hired him on the condition that he sign a contract stating our terms. I wanted no misunderstandings to arise between us, and I wanted us both to operate on the assumption that we were mutually accountable. He heard me out and pensively nodded his assent.

The adjutant *après-vous*'d us into his office. "Yes, a contract! Now let's discuss the terms. The first term is that his entire salary is payable in advance. To me."

Desi rubbed his chin. "Sounds reasonable."

"Desi! I'm sorry, Adjutant. I will pay Amisi half his fee before the trip and the other half when he successfully completes his mission."

"Then pay me his bonus now."

Desi's forefinger stabbed the air. "Good idea!"

"Desi! I will pay *him* as I've said, Adjutant. The bonus will depend on an outstanding performance, as our contract will stipulate." I knew nothing would stop the adjutant from taking a cut later, but this was the most I could do now.

"Oh, his performance will be outstanding," the adjutant asserted crisply. "You can be assured of that! All the same, it will save us time if we dispense with the bonus and fee issues now, before such a dangerous journey."

"As I said, we will sign a contract and I will pay him as I've specified. That's my last word."

He fell silent, the pleasant expression on his face withering as he digested my intransigence, and, to be sure, the loss of the soldier's salary, which no doubt he would have simply seized for himself if I had paid it through him. "Listen," he said, "I absolutely *must* receive his salary in advance, or you can't have him. Your trip is too dangerous for us to wait until Mbandaka."

"Fine. Then I will call the Office of the President and tell him you are preventing me from carrying out my mission."

His smile returned, albeit in a somewhat sourer version. "Okay! All right! *Pas de problèèème!* Outstanding performance and a contract! *Mais oui!*" The adjutant rustled through the things on his desk and presented me with a sheet of paper and a pen.

Ten minutes later I had written out a straightforward contract in French. It stated that Amisi would receive his pay, his food, his return fare on a barge to Lisala, plus, if he did a good job, a hefty bonus. I would give him half the salary before we left so that he could go home and deliver it to his family. We would depart in the morning.

Amisi signed it, and I pulled the cash from my pocket. He took the money from me and looked at it, he *glowered* at it, as if it were an insult, then raised his eyes and glowered at me.

Why?

He again stared at the bills and recounted them, as if suspecting I had shortchanged him; then, apparently satisfied that he had indeed received half his salary, he hoisted his gun to his shoulder, paused, and walked out.

The adjutant stood expectantly with his hands in his pockets.
"You have helped us a lot," I said, offering him a modest brick
of zaires. I was not lying to be polite: I had expected far worse. He
was just another basically capable man warped by this horrible
system. He accepted the money with a dignified bow and agreed
to send a driver to pick us up at the hotel at five-thirty in the
morning.

***

Later, after we returned to the hotel, I fell ill in the debilitating
heat of late afternoon. Tormented by nausea, my intestines tight-
ening into knots, I rolled from side to side on the lumpy mattress
in my green room, weak and clammy, listening to the lizards crawl
up the walls and the parrots squawk outside my window. My
hands were blistered from paddling, my nose was burned from the
sun, my tsetse bites itched. On the river I had held myself in
check; here I could relax, but I felt that I might collapse into a
mass of maladies.

The last days on the water had been frightening; the worst, I
quailed to think, was probably ahead. Desi's meddling during the
day's negotiations had puzzled and irked me. How was he reason-
ing? Why was he siding with everyone against me? If I needed his
loyalty in a tough parley on the way to Mbandaka, would I be able
to count on him?

His talk of drowning and the Zairean Code of Labor served to
introduce a valid point, one I truly had not addressed in my bargaining: what if the soldier were to die? Fifty thousand dollars or a
hundred and fifty civilian lives—could this be true? And what if
Desi were to die? What would happen to his wife and daughter in
Bumba and his family in Lokutu? And how was I to interpret
Amisi's angry look on taking his advance? Could I trust him?
There were too many questions to answer, and I turned away from
them in that hot room, in my damp and suffocating net, feeling
pain knife its way through my gut.

I suddenly found myself fantasizing about finishing the trip and freeing myself of Desi and the soldier and all the fears I had lived with for the past six months. And then Tatyana came to mind and memories of her were too evocative to dwell on. It was incredible to think I was putting myself through all this, and I could not imagine why I should go on.

There was a knock on my door. I dressed quickly, hurriedly putting on my dollar-packed money belt beneath my pants, and answered. It was Desi. He had a towel around his shoulders; he had just bathed.

"Bonsoir."

"Bonsoir."

He tilted his head back and looked at me. "I want more money." His eyes were narrow and adamantine. "I have been thinking about it. It cost you millions to fly to Zaire from your country. You had money enough to buy a pirogue, and a good pirogue at that. You had money for a gun. You had money enough for charcoal and Cokes in Bumba, you have money for supplies in every town. You have money for a soldier. You have money for the base commander. You have money for the adjutant. You have much, much money. I want more money."

He poked his forefinger into the money belt bulging on my waist. (I had not had time to put it on properly.) "What is this? Your money?"

I stepped back, unsettled. "Come inside, Desi." I caught my breath, feeling the need to lie. "Most of my money is in the bank in Kinshasa. I would have been crazy to come out here with a lot of cash. The amounts I'm giving out are the amounts I carefully estimated in advance."

"Estimated?"

"I mean I have enough to get us to Kinshasa, and not more."

"So . . . can I have more money?"

"Desi, you signed a contract for a specific amount and I have given you half already, as we agreed. You will receive a bonus, too, as we agreed, once we get to Kinshasa."

"You are very harsh," he said, raising his head again, giving me his stony glare. "You were harsh with the adjutant. You were harsh with Henri. You seemed *méchant,* not wanting to buy him insurance. As if you didn't care if he lived or died."

"Desi, that insurance bit was just a ruse—a trick to get money from me. Couldn't you see that?"

"Well, I see how rich you are." His bony feet spread on the dirty floor. "I'm not rich. This trip is not so easy for me."

"You've done a good job, and if you keep up the good work I'll reward you well. In Kinshasa."

"Will you give me the pirogue?"

"Probably, but I'll decide that in Kinshasa."

"And all the things you've bought for the trip?"

"I'll decide that in Kinshasa. If all goes well, I'll be very generous with you, but in Kinshasa, as we agreed, and as is stated in the contract we both signed."

He mopped his forehead with his towel and sat down on the bed. "You are very harsh," he said again. With that he seemed to be saying, *Your world is your world, my world is mine. You are rich and I am poor. Have pity on me, because that will never change.*

I stepped back and looked out the window into the yard. In the lot stick-figure toddlers were running around naked, and a woman was pounding manioc root with a pestle, her arms little more than bones in loose dark skin. I had understood that Desi might not have had a clear idea of what signing a contract meant, but putting things in writing was the only way I could think of to prevent misunderstandings. I didn't want to give him more money (or not now, at least), and not because I was greedy: it was a matter of limits. I resisted giving more under pressure like this because I didn't want to look weak and invite further pressure, pressure to give *beyond* my limits. I had a certain amount of money on me, and there was no way in this wilderness to get more, if we should actually need it. But he might not believe me.

Then I thought again. Desi had just poked my stash of cash. He had watched me dole out *matabiches* to corrupt officials while he was used to living hand to mouth. I had everything I needed to survive in my world, but I was risking my life for nothing in his, and spending what to him looked like obscene amounts to do so. And in the end he would stay here and I would fly out. What loyalty *should* I deserve from him?

"So can I have more money?"

"I think you'll do all you can to get me safely to Kinshasa. In view of the dangers we're facing I'm doubling your pay." I could not refuse him, and not only out of pity. I *did* pity him, I *did* see how hard he was trying to do his job, but I also feared that if I appeared to be a greedy ogre, his loyalty would waver, and with the most treacherous stretch of river ahead that was not a pleasant prospect.

"Okay," he said in a low voice. "Okay."

I looked at him, at his bony feet. He was not just lanky—he was rail thin, and the skin on his legs was flaky. Had he grown this emaciated on our trip? I asked how he was feeling: fine, he answered. He didn't need any more worm medicine.

I wanted to cheer him up. "By the way, is there anything in Lisala you would really like to eat during the days ahead? Is there monkey here?"

"There's better: there's goat. I would really like some good goat."

"Then buy a goat so that we'll have meat on the river for at least the first couple of days." I handed him a wad of zaires. "Now, I'm tired and we depart early in the morning. We should get some sleep."

He walked out and I collapsed into bed, weak and shivering, and turned to face the wall. I found myself wanting to call off the trip. But it was easier now to just go on to the end, whatever that end would be.

Crisis

HEALED AND REFRESHED BY THE NIGHT'S SLEEP, I GOT UP BE-
fore dawn and knocked on Desi's door. He had not, it turned out,
been able to procure a goat the previous afternoon. In a groggy
mood he threw on his tracksuit and set out to find one. I sat down
on the porch and waited.

Five-thirty passed and there was no sign of the adjutant or his
truck or Amisi or Desi. By eight the sun was mounting a cloudless
sky, searing Lisala with incandescent light; pedestrians trailed
keen black shadows on the bleached dust road. I paced the porch, a
feeling of queasy unease spreading through me and mingling with
discomfort from the heat: we would not get out of here in time to
avoid detection. To distract myself, I took to double-checking our
gear and studying the map.

Finally Desi came jogging up the steps holding chunks of goat
wrapped in damp paper. "This is good goat. It will keep us strong."

But the sun grew hotter and hotter, driving away thoughts of
food, and still there was no truck. We set the goat in the shade, and
slumped by our things, weary already, and waited.

*　*　*

It wasn't until nine-thirty that a pickup truck came careening
down the road to the hotel. Soldiers, mostly the louts who had ha-
rassed us on arrival, were seated in the rear, guns raised. The truck
skidded to a halt, and its dust trail floated ahead to settle on our
gear. The adjutant, wearing a fresh Hawaiian shirt, stepped out
and waved. *"Bonjour! Allons!"*

He shouted in Lingala at the soldiers, who climbed down and
snatched up our gear and loaded it onto the truck. Ten minutes

later we were careening back down the street toward the landing. The late hour, the rumors circulating in town about who we were and what we were up to, and now this less-than-discreet ride to the river assured that our departure would be no secret; in fact, they guaranteed it status as the public event of the day. Near the landing we slowed and began fording a crowd. Half of Lisala had shown up to see us off.

Our pirogue was still there, locked by the bow chain to a mooring post, half-beached, the green river rushing frothy white around its wagging stern. Under the hectoring supervision of the adjutant, the soldiers started unloading the truck, grabbing our things and jogging them over to Desi, who packed them to make room in the middle for Amisi.

And then Amisi appeared at the edge of the crowd, staring disapprovingly at this mayhem, his FAL rifle sagging heavy on his left shoulder.

I went up to him. "Good morning. Are you ready?"

"Yes," he answered glumly.

"Ever been in a pirogue?"

"No. But I'll do all right."

Half an hour later, after having shaken fifty hands, paid the soldiers for their porter services, thanked the adjutant for his good offices, and seated Amisi in his chair, I poked my paddle into the sun-warmed sand and shoved off, and, with Desi's assistance, poled the pirogue out through the shallows. At the channel, the current picked us up and buoyed us downstream. Children followed us along the bank, shouting farewells, shouting and cavorting and cheering in the razoring, midmorning light.

✐✐✐

The river, studded with clumps of water hyacinth, spread glaring and glassy, surging southwest at the same time as it appeared to embody the very essence of equatorial torpor. We paddled slowly, overtaking and parting the hyacinth floes with our bow, sending the bees on their blossoms into angry flight, stirring up black flies and butterflies. The forest here was of palms; their fronds drooped, white with glare, heavy and still in the heat. We soon relinquished our paddles and retreated beneath our umbrellas. Ten miles out of Lisala the crumbling brick walls of an abandoned Protestant mission emerged on the north bank, covered with creepers. Even here there had been missionaries.

A screech shattered the tranquillity. "I once was lost but now I'm found . . ." Between verses Desi cleared his throat and piped his voice to decibels and notes it had (mercifully) never before attained on our journey.

I suffered the tune, but it grew more vigorous and intolerably strident, and it well seemed he might have the energy to wail on for hours. We needed to keep a low profile here; caterwauling like this could alert Ngombe to our presence miles in advance.

When I could stand it no longer I swung around. "Desi!"

"Quoi?"

"Desi, for the love of God, we're sailing into cannibal territory here!"

"You are right! Only with the help of Jesus shall we survive!" He laid his paddle in the bottom of the pirogue, and stretched his arms skyward. "Lord God! Listen to the words of Your humble servant! God, You love us! Jesus, You love us! Give us Your protection as we travel forth down this perilous river! Stay at our sides, be our light in the darkness of this jungle! Spare us from the dangers ahead! And save us from temptresses! Amen!"

He stood at the stern as if crucified on an invisible cross, then lowered his head and muttered a private prayer. Amisi, unmoved, shifted in his cramped quarters.

A word lodged in my mind's ear. "Desi, what was that about 'temptresses'?"

He grabbed the goat, unwrapped it, and with his machete started hacking it into bloody chunks. "Why, women have the powers of sorceresses—don't you know? When I'm away from my wife I always ask God to keep an eye out for the women."

"I see."

"Satan does his work through women. Satan comes to man through woman. I fear being alone with a woman."

I asked Amisi if he agreed.

"I don't fear anything. I'm a soldier."

Desi dropped the goat into the boiling *bambula* and sifted in rice. "I'm surprised you ask these questions. It's your prophets who tell us that Satan comes calling when an unmarried man and woman are alone together. But there are many kinds of sin. Amisi, you're a soldier. Soldiers rape and pillage. In God's eyes that is also sinful."

Amisi looked back at Desi and raised an eyebrow.

Desi stirred the *bambula*. "Do you follow God, Amisi, or do you pillage?"

Amisi said something under his breath, then, adjusting himself in his seat, picked up an oar and tried to paddle. "Amisi is trying to change," Desi said. "He does not agree with the ways of his fellow soldiers."

"So he doesn't rape and pillage?" I asked.

"No."

"That's comforting."

I suggested we tell Amisi about the problems we expected during the two weeks ahead, and Desi repeated the words of the fisherman from Mbandaka, with his own minor but colorful augmentations: "Mobutu sent his Division spéciale to punish the Bangala tribes here for murdering *mondeles* . . . the tribes had been cutting mondeles into little pieces . . . this was giving Zaire a bad name . . . the Division wiped out whole villages, killing and burning and looting everyone . . . the Bangala are thieves and murderers . . ."

Amisi listened but said nothing, his face remaining inscrutably blank.

By noon the heat exceeded anything we had experienced since Bolobo; the glare burned us from every angle. The *bambula* bubbled over, and Desi pulled it off the coals. The combination of the gamy aroma of goat meat and sweltering heat killed my appetite.

Desi ladled a fatty gobbet onto a plate.

"It's ready!"

He served us all. I took it and let it cool off under my seat, then, bite by bite, forced myself to eat every bit. Aroma or no, and not-withstanding a gag here and there, it was tasty, and most impor-tant of all, nourishing. Amisi enjoyed his portion. Desi, however, ate but a little, then put his plate aside, having trouble swallowing and complaining of nausea.

✦✦✦

After the meal we returned to the shade of our umbrellas, pulling our limbs within their protective and soothing circumference. We let the pirogue drift, and it performed lazy rotations among the hyacinth. As somnolent and serene as a Louisiana bayou, with the progress of the day the river shaded from green to satin blue, blue as the sky. Soon, my eyelids grew heavy.

But I struggled against sleep—this was not the time to drop my guard—and sat up. "Amisi, you should keep your gun on display. And Desi, raise the barrel of the shotgun so that it sticks out above the hull. Let no one doubt that we're armed."

Amisi sat alert with his gun on his knees; Desi dozed, his shot-gun lodged high in the crook of his arm; I kept my eyes on the banks of the islands, resisting drowsiness with every fiber of my body. Only swarms of bees broke the silence of the hot glassy river.

✦✦✦

I lurched awake to a scrape and a hiss and the giggles of children. It was after four o'clock. We were running aground in shallows amid a profusion of villages. Villagers were emerging from their huts and lining up on the banks to stare at us. Flustered, I shouted a friendly *"Mbote!"* but they did not respond. They stood still, their arms crossed, their eyes expressing nothing, neither welcome nor fear nor anger.

"Desi! Amisi! Wake up!"

They groggily opened their eyes and cleared their throats. Desi focused on the villagers and straightened up in alarm. He and I jumped out into the shin-deep water and dragged the pirogue off the shoal and back toward the channel, where we relaunched it and climbed aboard.

"Amisi, raise your gun."

Amisi hoisted his rifle and stood up, unlocking the safety. But we struck ground again and had to repeat the dragging procedure.

The banks by the villages were now lined with expressionless faces.

"These people are not good Christians," Desi said, paddling hard. "They are false Christians. These are people who can sing about God one day and rob the next."

A drumbeat sounded from one village, then from another. Despite the proliferation of villages, not a single pirogue was out on the water. *Why?* For an hour we continued, isolated by the stares, hoping to light upon a secluded spot to camp. But by five it seemed that there would be no seclusion, only eyes, drumbeats, and crowds coming forth to the bank from villages before we even reached them.

I asked Desi what he thought we should do.

"We should keep on. All night. We should not stop here."

With the mosquitoes and the loss of bearings night would bring, continuing in the dark might be even riskier than camping. I wanted to halt. But the drums were pounding, so we proceeded, eventually sliding into an uninhabited stretch.

Now the river behind us spread a pane of royal blue glass reflecting the diamond speckles of newborn stars, purpling at the edges where the forest met the sky; ahead, to the west, the fireball of the sun edged its way down into the water, filling the sky and river with molten lava light. We sailed into this widening lava reflection, scouring the banks for a sign of a suitable place to berth, finally descrying a solitary marshy islet surrounded by mangrove trees. Mangroves, we knew, meant swamp and bad air, but this spot had the advantage of facing uninhabited forest.

We veered toward its anvil-shaped head and poled the pirogue between two mangroves; the craft crashed and bounced against the root-entangled bank. Amisi and I hauled the pirogue into the brush, and we set up the tents behind the mangroves.

A stench of rot emanated from the mucky earth and the islet was buzzing with flies, crawling with beetles and biting black ants. Above the rising roar of mosquitoes Desi declared from his tent: "I am weak. I want to travel all day and all night. We won't need to paddle. We will just float. We—"

Voices.

On the other side of the trees a pirogue was drifting downriver and positioning itself in front of our tents.

There was a shout in Lingala: "Are you the *mondeles?*"

Desi answered, "There's no *mondele* here!"

"What are you *mondeles* doing here?"

"We are not *mondeles!*"

"Tell us who you are!"

"We are merchants traveling to Mbandaka."

There was a pause, then a swish as the pirogue turned back upstream, and the receding sound of paddles cleaving the water.

Moonless and hollow and resounding with drumbeats, darkness engulfed the river. A chanting arose from somewhere, followed by a clapping of hands. All through the night we had to fend off suspicious queries, and none of us slept well. An hour or two before dawn the queries and the drumbeats ceased, and the silence, unbroken by even the peep of a tree frog, a silence filled with suspense, not tranquillity, put us on alert. Sore with fatigue, we decided to break camp before light, but on rising we discovered that a dense fog had settled over the river. Nevertheless, we loaded the pirogue and pulled out into the enveloping vapor, quickly losing our bearings and any perception of where the bank was, aware of only dark and fog and the shifting current.

"That campsite had bad air," Desi said as we drifted along, sightless. "It has made me sick."

I closed my eyes but couldn't sleep, disturbed by Desi's declaration of ill health, and his suggestion—impractical and foolish—

that we travel all night. I had hoped he would have recovered in Lisala. But my own fatigue disordered my thoughts.

⚋⚋⚋

An hour later dawn was breaking. The burble and rush of water filtered into my drowsy purview; notions of brooks and streams mingled with fragments of faces, with vignettes from inchoate dreams. My eyes half opened, letting in a world of fog and pearly river, of warmth and encompassing wet, a world without lines or forms; there was only the sound of water, as of rapids, an ever-loudening splashing, as of water over rocks.

"Jeff!" Desi shouted.

Not thirty feet from us, directly downstream, a jutting black hulk materialized in the fog: the prow of a *pousseur* cutting a foaming V in the current. Amisi and I seized our paddles and threw all our weight into our strokes, Desi steered hard to port, we swung around and just evaded the steel monster. But the *pousseur*'s motion turned out to be an illusion: it was stranded on a sandbar, abandoned.

As we floated by, we stood up and peered inside, and Desi called out *mbote*. His voice echoed through the cabins, which, their doors hanging on hinges, their interiors stripped bare, looked to have been looted. Shattered glass lay all over the deck; trash covered the runways. Soon we slipped past the forsaken craft and returned to the world of pearly river and fog.

Desi stared at the fading shadow of the *pousseur*. "They must have lost the navigation route. The tribes around here looted them. The Ngombe are not good Christians, you see."

He paddled listlessly, then lay back in the stern. I thought about his words and grabbed the map. "Desi, if they lost the navigation route, what does that say about us?"

"We are near Bongela."

"But if they're lost, then so are—wait a second." Bongela was near Île Sumba: I remembered Paul's words about it being a robber village, about the treacherous *rivière* leading from Bongela behind Île Sumba. But the map showed them to be distant still. "Wait a second. What do you mean we're near Bongela? We can't be. We could not have not covered that much territory in one day. Île Sumba and Bongela are a hundred and fifty kilometers away."

"We are either near Bongela or the Mille Quarante marker." He was now slumped in the stern, clearly indisposed. "I don't know why you talk of Île Simba. There's no such place as Île Simba."

"Île Sumba, not Simba. Desi, we passed Île Sumba on the way up, and the first mate on the barge warned me about it. It's right here on my map. And Bongela is at its head."

He put down his paddle. "There is no such place as Île Simba." He doubled over with pain, clutching his gut. "I'm feeling ill today. You're asking too many questions. I rely on Jesus. Please, have faith in Jesus. My stomach is aching."

It was no use. I put away the map. I found I barely had the strength to paddle myself, and I lacked the skill to steer. Amisi sat impassive as ever, staring at the water, his rifle on his knees. The heat hit and snuffed out our spirits, and I decided it would be better to join Desi and rest.

Around noon, Amisi and I ate a meal of smoked fish and rice; Desi declined, declaring, as he had before Lisala, that he needed monkey to recover his strength. I was beginning to wonder if he would be able to make it to Mbandaka.

But seeing the *pousseur* gave me an idea: if we made it to the navigation route (or if we were already on it), the Colonel's barge would have to pass us somewhere on its way downriver. If the need arose, we could deliver Desi to it, and I could hire a healthy replacement from among its passengers.

There were no more villages that day. The sight of the *pousseur* seemed to have made an impression on Desi as well: he asked me what I would do if the Colonel's barge were to pass.

"I think we should wait to see if we come across the barge before making plans. But for now, you must eat. You *must*."

He did not.

The current carried us along, spinning us slowly downriver; the forest rotated around us; cool damp air flowed over us. Now and then, objections to Desi's assertions about our whereabouts formed in my mind, but I didn't express them. For the first time in my life, I felt myself inclined to surrender to circumstance—not to fate, because I didn't believe in fate, but to circumstance, to happenings without sense or purpose, without significance or drama. I pondered Stanley's descent of the Congo (or at least his account of it), the spirit of mission that imbued his orations to his crew. The descent was, he told them, "our work and no other! It is the voice of Fate! The One God has written that this year the river shall be known throughout its length! . . . Onward, I say; onward to death, if it is to be." In this wilderness nothing seemed more irrelevant than such high-flown words of mission and drama. All words seemed empty of meaning.

We drifted and drifted, until Desi felt well enough to paddle.

In the early part of the afternoon the sky blackened. Exhausted by forays this way and that, from one island to the next, in search of the navigation route, we erected our umbrellas and took to drifting close to shore. It began to drizzle, but there was no wind, so we kept on.

We were nearing the downriver end of an island. A thrumming distant whir evolved into the approaching chug of a motor. We perked up: it was a boat! Desi and I grabbed our oars and thrust them into the river. A hundred yards ahead, where one island ended and another began, in a stretch of river between the trees, suddenly appeared the rusty hull of a barge—the Colonel's barge!

We shouted and waved, we thrashed the river with our paddles. But the barge chugged resolutely on, passed behind the next island, and was gone, jealously dragging with it the echo of its engine, leaving us in aching solitude, drifting along the gloomy river, more alone than ever. Desi put down his oar, then sank to the bottom of the pirogue. Amisi raised an eyebrow.

"Well, at least we know where the navigation route is," I said. "Perhaps there will be another boat."

Desi looked at me, as if to say, "Not likely."

A boundless confetti of yellow butterflies was fluttering down around us. The river would give us no respite: they were set against a vista of thunderclouds churning in the east.

I took my paddle in hand and stood up. "Desi, we had better get ashore."

"That storm won't come this way," he answered, prostrate under his umbrella.

Like a supersonic missile of fire, lightning streaked from the iron vault of the sky and struck the forest; thunder exploded in deafening multiple claps. The wind hit and set the river aboil, and the gusts and rising waves nearly overturned us. Amisi grabbed his oar and did his best to help me pilot the pirogue toward the bank. The wind buffeted us into a wall of thorns and spiked ferns, and we became entangled in them; we had to relinquish one mooring spot then another, tearing our skin on the very bush we sought to approach.

Desi raised himself to steer us around the thorny thicket toward a sheltered break in a clearing. But as we drew near it, a crocodile, some twelve feet long, crashed out through the grass and launched himself torpedo-like into the churning river. Startled and frightened, nearly losing our balance, we backpaddled, skirting more thickets, and came to a second clearing. There a snag prevented us from landing; a particularly virulent blast of wind kicked up a wave that nearly pitched us overboard.

"We are in danger," Desi stated in a monotone.

Having seen the crocodile enter the water but having lost it from view, I felt totally exposed, vulnerable to ambush. Winds blew us past another clearing, and I, at the bow, had to jump into the shallows to drag the pirogue by the tow chain up to the bank, an ordeal during which I slipped in the clayey muck and banged my shin on a snag, all the while racing my eyes over the water in search of the croc.

With the rain washing over us in undulant silver sheets, we threw up our tarp amid giant spiked ferns sprouting from the forest floor, then crawled underneath to wait out the storm.

▰▰▰

The moon hung a giant pale orange orb that night, the forest echoed with hoots from monkeys, with the tumultuous splashings of hippos in the shallows somewhere behind us. We had bivouacked early in a malodorous and desolate bight of palm and rubber vines. Biting ants, fat and black, infested our camp, scuttling over our legs, chomping away before we could scrape them off, and we had to seek refuge from them in our tents. We had passed no more villages that day. The banks were uninhabited and the absence of hostile locals set me at ease, but I grew certain that we were somewhere on the river we should not be. Desi insisted he knew the way, but I was beginning to see he did not, this far from his home.

"May God's will be done. I place my fate in the hands of *le bon Dieu*," Desi announced, and crawled into his mosquito net pale and weak. Amisi sulked. I called him over to my tent to talk. "Desi is sick," I said. "We have to decide what we will do if he cannot continue."

"We should just keep on. I'm a soldier and a Christian. If God wills me to die here, I die. I can do nothing about it."

"We will have to think of something."

"What?"

"I'm asking for your advice."

"I follow God's will. What God decides will be."

Whence this indifference? *Was* it indifference? I glared at him, I felt a sudden urge to strike him, to slap him out of this torpor. But, turning into my tent, I did nothing more than say *bonne nuit*.

▰▰▰

"You must eat. You absolutely must."

"I will eat no more unless we can kill a monkey." Still pale and now more visibly weakened than ever, Desi stood trembling by his net at dawn, his eyes averted from mine. "I must have monkey, or, or . . ."

We had canned meat left, but the absence of fishermen meant it would be all we had for the next ten days to Mbandaka—sustaining, if monotonous, fare to be sure. But perhaps he was using this need for monkey as an excuse; he was sick and did not want to go on, or could not go on.

I did not know what to say. I felt I was to blame for having undertaken this trip, which now seemed like it could cost the life of this poor fellow, or leave him more debilitated than ever, which would ruin the lives of a dozen other people, given his position of breadwinner for an extended family. In all my preparations I had never imagined that it would be my guide whose health would fail, and not my own. But an isolating fear settled like a stone on my heart, isolating because, even in the company of others, we face death alone. If Desi gave up, Amisi and I would have a tough time making it to Mbandaka. This thought was too frightening to dwell on.

But I was overreacting. I grabbed my gear and tossed it into the pirogue. "We've got to move on, Desi. Let's get moving."

I looked to Amisi. His eyes registered no concern, only nonchalant comprehension. I finished loading the pirogue, Desi and Amisi got aboard, and we shoved off.

It was sunny but cool and fresh, a breezy day of luminous golden light, of soft golden light that saturated the forest and river without heating it, of comforting golden light that seemed to promise something good or to set the stage, conversely, for horrific evil: it was almost too idyllic to be true. The current came to our aid, flowing in a channel that cut across great silken-watered pools, dark pools spotted with mist. Just after noon, as we were drifting along the south bank, beneath a thicket low and dense, out of which protruded a second, jagged tier of broad-canopied trees, we spotted a monkey bounding away branch to branch. Desi livened up and steered us toward shore. Amisi unwrapped his gun, and the two of them stalked off into the forest.

After a while I got out, too. I walked in a ways and stood before the tangled creepers, the vines, the crisscrossing growths of ferns; I looked up at the dead palms, the soaring gum trees, at the maze of light and shadow, of green and green and bamboo yellow, here and there dappled with a vermilion blossom, a splash of violet petal. Save for the breeze rustling through the canopy, there was not a sound, and the silence boded desolation that accorded with what was turning out to be the barren reality of my hopes and plans, of the climax, the denouement that I had come to Africa to force upon my life. A denouement was taking place, to be sure—a stark and simple unraveling, as potentially lethal as it was mundane. Desi had taken on the job of guiding me to meet his obligations to his wife and child, his mother, his freeloading brothers, even his church. But it now was obvious that he had been ill since Kisangani, and I grew angry with myself for not recognizing it. Yet he would not resign or confess his condition: the specter of the Colonel (to whom he would ultimately answer for my safety) stood behind me, and no doubt he feared the consequences of failing him. Moreover, Desi was a man of his word, and rather than quit, he might simply die.

I began to understand Desi and Amisi's fatalism. If we perished in this wilderness, the forest would absorb us and continue silent and impassive, an eternal, if unfathomable, life force apart, endlessly renewing itself, indifferent to anything we feared, felt, or thought. For those on the Congo's waters, life was too filled with uncertainty, heat, disease, and hunger to permit resolution or defiance, to allow anything more than survival and gratitude for the scrawniest grubs, the smallest bananas. Fatalism was necessary here, as was surrender.

I walked back to the pirogue. It suddenly seemed clear that my expedition was not worth risking a life for, not Desi's, not Amisi's, not my own. If I could have called off the voyage at that moment, shot up a flare or radioed for help, I would have done so. But I had neither flare nor radio, and who would have come? There was no one to call. There was no turning back: the only way out was downstream.

Desi and Amisi returned, having had no luck with the hunt. We shoved off and let the current carry us.

⟋⟋⟋

The next day we moved on under clear skies. Around midday Desi plaintively asked me to take some photos of him with my Polaroid "for his wife," implying that they were to be remembrances of him. I agreed, and on an island we held a bizarre final photo session, with Desi donning his tracksuit and looking solemnly into my lens.

I thought of the sequel to my expedition. If Desi died and I lived, I would face the consequences: a grief-stricken family left without support; police and official inquiries; and guilt that I would carry with me for the rest of my life. But then the stone of fear pressed on my heart again: if he were to die, how would Amisi and I make it out? More than a hundred miles were left to Mbandaka, and we needed Desi's skill as a piroguist to cover them.

As we pushed away from the bank, I could not help but think about dying, about how there would be no closing ceremony to my life and no drama, just a cessation, as though it were a movie interrupted in the middle by the flare-up of a faulty projector bulb. Death seemed tangible and near; I felt distraught most of all because it might overtake me far from Tatyana, my parents, and my friends. I was afraid, but there was nothing to do except paddle and drift beneath the monster trees and vines.

⟋⟋⟋

That afternoon Desi's spirits lifted when he discovered two cans of pilchards (his favorite fish) hidden amid our provisions. He cooked and ate them with relish, and they somewhat revived his strength.

And now his strength would be needed. By four o'clock we had landed squarely in Ngombe heartland, passing village after village, unable to find a hidden spot to camp. He and Amisi took to raising their guns as a matter of course whenever we approached a village.

Darkness finally drove us ashore; we erected the tents as the mosquitoes descended. Soon pirogues were paddling up, invisible in the humid night, and baritone Lingala was booming in the blackness: "Is the *mondele* in there? What can the *mondele* give us!" Amisi would answer, "*Mbote!* Stay away. I have an FAL rifle and I'll shoot." It worked, but the hours dragged on, and none of us closed an eye.

The glow of the moon filled the sky and emanated from the water. I lay on my stomach, peering out of my tent's net door. Two pirogues bearing five people each materialized in the mists and moved toward us. I tried to warn Amisi, but I found my throat paralyzed; I couldn't speak or move a muscle. The piroguists pulled up to our camp and unsheathed huge machetes that glinted in the moonlight; I struggled to cry out but felt asphyxiated, immobile. As they stepped up to my tent I lunged into my net—and woke up. I had been dreaming.

On the river there were glints of silver—reflections of the moon—but no machetes or pirogues. Desi and Amisi had drifted off to sleep in their mosquito nets next to mine; the river lapped against the bank, flowing empty and silver far, far out into the channel.

Chasing the *Ebeya*

IT WAS AS IF THE RIVER GODS HAD CONSPIRED TO CONFOUND us: we awoke to despair at yet another dawn smothered under a pall of fog. We pulled up stakes and shoved off, Amisi and I having breakfasted on rice and frankfurters, Desi on nothing. We drifted in the dense white cloud, discerning no sign of our whereabouts, able to locate neither the north nor the south bank nor the navigation route, paddling only enough to avoid the snags that now and again poked up through the water and trailed wakes dark and tinkling in the otherwise silent, nacreous river.

When the fog lifted, it revealed a long and narrow water lane leading through a canyon of forest. The canyon went on and on, morning heated up into noon, noon baked us in glare, the glare passed, and the last hours of daylight began. We saw no one— until after three in the afternoon.

"*Mondele!* What are you doing here?" From a village of thatched straw huts a man was strutting to the bank, belly-first. Around him mothers gathered their children and ran into their huts. Desi looked up and exchanged words in Lingala with him. Our challenger quickly became agitated, shouting and thumping his chest. He was the *mokonzi ya mboka* (the village chief), he declared, and we were trespassing. Desi could not calm him; we drifted out of his sight, and no one pursued us. But within an hour there were more villages, and the shouts and angry queries multiplied.

I asked Desi if he had gleaned any information about our location from the villagers' complaints. He pointed to the forested bank on our right, and said, without reference to his previous denials, "Yes. That is Île Sumba."

Of all the possible routes we might have taken along our

eleven-hundred-mile journey, we had managed to stumble onto the only one we had been warned to avoid: the *rivière* behind Île Sumba. The *rivière* lacked sufficient breadth to afford us the mid-stream privacy of distance of the wider channels; I was on full display, the object of hostile cries and warnings to turn back. Among chiefs charged with protecting their subjects, the composition of my team could not but have aroused concern: an armed African not of their tribe and not of their region; an armed soldier of the hated regime; and a no doubt *méchant mondele* showing up in a place where none but locals were to be seen.

The map told us that we had some twenty-five miles of *rivière* to go before we would emerge into open river around the village of Makanza. I had seen a road at Makanza on the way upriver.

"Desi, that road at Makanza—where does it lead?"

"To Bonsambo."

"Where's that?"

"A few kilometers from Makanza." He got my drift. "There is no way out from there."

⁂

Toward sunset, as we pondered the unpleasant prospect of camping among irate villagers, a Ngombe fisherman in a Ford Motors cap came paddling upriver with his son. Smiling and staring at me, they pulled alongside us and ceased paddling, then drifted back downstream with us.

"What is this *mondele* doing here?" he asked Desi, keeping his bemused eyes on me.

Desi explained our mission, and he and the fisherman stood leaning on their paddles, trading questions and answers. During their parley a word I had not heard before in Lingala—*maswa*—sounded several times. Desi grew excited, and Amisi turned and listened with interest. Then came mention of the *Colonel Ebeya*: that was the *maswa*—the boat! The *Colonel Ebeya* would be passing by La Gare, the villager said, on the north bank, in a few hours, and he was going up to his village to get the fish he planned to sell aboard it. He still had a ways to go and might miss it; we, however, could certainly make it. But how were we to get across Île Sumba to La Gare? I asked him this in French and Desi translated, adding, "Is there a way to cross the island? Some sort of creek or channel?"

His response was clipped and dismissive: *"Te."* But making elaborate loops with his hand, he explained the way out by water, his voice rising and falling with what sounded like a complicated series of turns and reversals. I studied the map. There was no La Gare on it, but it showed four fish-shaped islands above whose pointy heads we would have to leapfrog in order to reach the north bank. From what he said, La Gare appeared to be just east of the Mongala River. The villager, smiling and urging us to hurry, pushed off from our hull. He and his son leaned back into their oarstrokes and were soon dragging their pirogue yard by lurching yard against the current.

We drifted. I looked to Desi. "What do you think?"

"I want to catch the boat. But I'm tired."

"Well, the choice is either paddle hard, with all your strength, no matter what, and reach La Gare, or do nothing and—"

Desi arose and steered us round, pointing us upriver. Amisi grabbed his paddle, as did I. After a brief prayer Desi thrust his paddle into the water, shouting, *"Allons-y!"*

With every last muscle we fought the current with our paddles, sweating and trembling with the exertion. I shifted in my seat for better leverage and was nearly lifted out of it by the power of my own strokes. We paddled past the end of the first island, then rested a minute, letting the current whisk us down a short distance. Desi gave up and retched, his face pallid.

"If you can't paddle, Desi, then steer. Amisi and I will do the paddling."

He shifted his oar right and left and added strokes when he could. Three times we repeated the leapfrogging maneuver. We ended up emerging onto a great basin.

The sun sank in a blaze of red and purple, and the mosquitoes flew up in roaring swarms, enveloping us in an impenetrable cloud, clogging nostrils, ears, mouths. We spat them out, we paddled, we swatted. Overhead the Milky Way stretched a glittering astral sea across the inky firmament, but nothing resembled the head of the fourth island, much less the bustling quay La Gare suggested, was to be found.

Soon, floating through the sultry blackness, amid dapples of starlight mirrored by the river, we concluded that we were lost again. It had been almost three hours since the fisherman spoke to us; the *Ebeya* would be coming along any minute now.

"I can't go on," said Desi. He vomited over the side. "I'm . . . I'm sorry. I'm exhausted. I'm sorry." He laid aside his paddle and slipped back at the stern.

I grew livid and leapt to my feet. "Desi, you have to paddle now or you'll die! We have no time left! You can't quit now when we're so close! Get up!"

I shot a furious look at Amisi. Amisi lashed out at Desi in Lingala and began paddling himself. Amisi and I paddled hard, but he and I alone could not sustain the effort necessary to find the final island. Our hopes dashed, we gave up and surrendered to the current.

Hours passed in despondent silence: there was nothing left to say. But around midnight a pale gray oblong in the gloom drifted near. Desi raised his head and spoke to it in a low voice. "We are looking for La Gare. Please, can you help us find it?"

A disembodied man's voice answered. "You are on course. This is the navigation route. La Gare is where I'm going. It's just ahead. Follow us."

The gray oblong was a pair of monster pirogues lashed together and loaded with stacks of smoked meat. Soon, from hidden estuaries flowing through the forest, other oblongs of gray drifted in. Altogether we formed a procession, silent save for the occasional low voice or swish of a paddle. But try as we did to keep up, we lost them to the moonless night.

Two hours later we perceived a white blur—a sandy clearing by a village. There were voices. La Gare. We moored amid a cluster of beached pirogues and set up our nets. Desi was ashen and curled up with cramps, sweating with fever. I looked out into the dark, hoping to catch sight of the *Ebeya*'s spotlight playing on the sky above the water, and waited.

◢◢◢

At noon the next day cries rang out upriver, joyful cries of "Eeyah! Eeyah!" that bounced from bank to bank, relayed by fishermen far and near. Desi raised his head. The villagers emerged from their huts. Children ran down the clearing and jumped into their pirogues. The *Colonel Ebeya*.

Lumbering around the far bend, doing an easy eight or ten miles an hour, was a hodgepodge assemblage of six or seven two- and three-story barges attached to a single ailing *pousseur,* the same ungainly craft we had glimpsed almost three weeks before on our first morning out of Kisangani. It would not stop, and to catch it we would have to perform a dangerous on-the-run docking maneuver—something far beyond my and Amisi's limited piroguing skills, and for which Desi would lack the strength.

I jumped up and ran to the villagers and extended a fistful of zaires. "Please, help us paddle out to the *maswa!* Please!"

They gave me a curious look and didn't budge.

"Please!" I shook the bills. *"Nalingi kokende na maswa!"*

Finally, the sturdiest man among them stood up and nodded assent. He called a comrade out of a nearby hut. Desi and Amisi disassembled their nets and tossed them into the pirogue, and we hopped aboard with our two aides. One took up position at our bow, the other climbed astern and paddled for Desi.

We were not alone in setting out into the channel. Like a school of jittery fish, pirogues were swarming and circling out into midriver as the *Ebeya* approached, darting to position themselves for mooring on the port side of the huge vessel.

The sturdy villager, perched on the bow and crouching low for balance, shouted directions in Lingala to us, waving us to paddle now to the right, now to the left. As the *Ebeya* drew near, its features grew distinct: it was a floating tenement of rusty barges with laundry hanging out of cabins, decks teeming with merchants and tied-up antelopes and chained monkeys; it trailed dozes of pirogues loaded with crocodiles and pigs, fish and fruit. Even the roof was packed with passengers. We gained on it, riding across the cresting wake, following the directions of the man at our bow.

He pointed to a free spot on the *pousseur* and shouted, *"Kuna! Kuna!"*

We accelerated our paddling, hunkering low, bouncing across the waves. Passengers rushed to the railings, shouting encouragement. The water adjacent the vessel churned and thrashed, threatening to overturn us.

When we were a couple of feet from the *pousseur*, the villager, holding our bow chain in his left hand, sprang to the deck and clutched the railing with his right hand. The lagging pirogue consumed the slackness in the chain and jerked his arm, but two other men on deck grabbed the chain and held it fast, looping it round a post. Finally, moored fast, we bounced against the hull.

Hands reached out and pulled us aboard. A crowd surrounded us and hustled us up to the first mate's office, where, after a long wait for the appropriate *Ebeya* official, I purchased two tickets to Kinshasa and one (for Amisi) to Mbandaka.

Thus, four hundred and seventy miles out of Kisangani, my expedition ended.

Mbandaka Again

THE SUN COATED THE *COLONEL EBEYA* WITH GLARE. ROACHES scampered up and down the walls of my mold-splotched cabin. A rat dwelt in my toilet; a lizard leapt out of my clothes dresser. The food I ate in the dining room made me ill. There was no safe and open rooftop on which to camp, as there had been on the Colonel's barge. There was none of the solitude of the pirogue trip: the *Ebeya* carried four thousand people; there were no quiet quarters, only endless warrens of merchant racks, beer tables, garroted antelopes, crocodiles lashed to logs, bats and rats and fish for sale, ill-tempered soldiers and brazen whores. All this, and it would be a week or two to Kinshasa, or longer. Definitely longer: our first night aboard, one of the barges snapped free of the *pousseur* and drifted away, bouncing from bank to bank. At the time the captain did not notice, nor did the crew, so we spent a while searching for it in the morning, chugging upriver and down, until we came across the hapless vessel lodged against an island. There was, in short, no relief aboard the boat, and I found myself leaning on the railing and staring into the forest, be-numbed, wanting it to end.

But Desi made a full recovery. Having treated himself with powders purchased from women on the deck, he was feeling happy and healthy. For his sake, I knew I had made the right decision in calling off the expedition. Still, I found myself stung by my fail-ure and trying to deny what I would later come to see as obvious: that I had exploited Zaire as a playground on which to solve my own rich-boy existential dilemmas.

✐✐✐

Three days after our rescue Desi knocked on my door. His mood was still nothing short of buoyant. I did not know how to react to him, to his new bubbly cheer. Seeing him, I was suddenly filled with selfish anger—why had he not simply confessed at the beginning that he was ill? I could answer my own question right away— I would not have hired him, that was why—but it bothered me just the same.

He stepped inside. "Are you upset?"

"I'm glad you're okay."

"Are you angry with me?"

"Desi, please . . ."

"But are you upset with me?"

"Oh, Desi, come on! I spent five months preparing for this trip, thinking about it, planning it, and dreaming about it. I hired you to guide me to Kinshasa. I'd prefer to think that this was God's will, as you would say."

He looked despondently at his feet. "So . . . so . . . so you're not going to pay me, are you?"

Hence his despondency.

"Of *course* I'm going to pay you! We had a deal, didn't we?" I got out our contract. I handed him his fee, the extra money he had wheedled out of me in Lisala, plus zaires for food and the return fare on the barge. He counted the bills and looked up.

"And . . . and?"

"And what?"

"And what will you do with the pirogue and your gear?"

"It's all yours." I handed him the key to the pirogue chain padlock. The rest of the gear, aside from the personal things I had brought with me to Zaire, was in his cabin anyway.

Saying nothing more, he turned and walked out.

There was soon another knock.

Amisi walked in and sat down. I paid him his fee, a bonus, plus barge fare back to Lisala and money for food. He took the zaires, counted them twice, and stuffed them in the side pocket of his fatigues. But he stayed seated.

"Well, Amisi, thanks for doing a good job."

His gaze was sullen, his eyes heavy.

"Do you have something you'd like to say, Amisi?"

He pulled out the money and counted it again, examining it with something akin to disgust. "Give me more."

"I have given you what we agreed to, plus your bonus."

"But I want more."

There was yet another knock on my door. This time it was the first mate. "Monsieur, we have a problem with some *mondeles* up at the bridge. Please come with me and help."

Amisi sighed and walked out, shaking his head. I locked the cabin and followed the first mate to the bridge.

゛゛

Up on the bridge, three young Spaniards were trying to converse with the captain, who knew only French. The bearded one among them stepped forth and addressed me in English. "Please, translate! We have an urgent problem. We keep trying to tell the captain we're going to miss our flight to Spain if we don't arrive in Kinshasa in three days. He says the barge will arrive in a week, but it's already two weeks behind schedule. You see, we got a special deal on our plane tickets. If we're late, we lose them. And we have no more money. We'll be stuck here."

The captain sympathized with them, but, he said, there was no way to speed up the *Ebeya*. As if to prove his words, one of the barges snapped free of the *pousseur* and began twirling slowly off toward shore. A hubbub arose among the crew; the captain issued orders; the *pousseur* started swerving to catch up with it. The Spaniards rolled their eyes, and the bearded one spoke again. "Well, this is the last time we'll spend our holidays in Zaire! Can't you do something?"

I found out from the crew that there was a flight once a week from Mbandaka to Kinshasa on Air Zaire. It occurred to me that I would like to take it myself—I had had enough of the river. We would arrive in Mbandaka tomorrow and the flight was the day after.

"We'll all go to Kinshasa together on the Air Zaire flight," I told them.

The *Ebeya* caught up with its runaway barge and reattached it. I set out to look for Desi (I wanted to thank him and assure him that I harbored no grudges about his falling ill), but I could not find him, so I returned to my cabin to pack, thinking he might stop by my cabin.

✦✦✦

He did not, and I could not find him by the time the *Ebeya* motored into the dock at Mbandaka the next afternoon. After mooring, the usual riverboat landing scene ensued: soldiers flailed whips; passengers got their noses bloodied; porters stumbled under impossible loads; there was screeching and shoving, sweat and fistfights. Using our bags as rams, the Spaniards and I disembarked and pushed our way through the melee.

Up near the dock offices we broke free of the crowd. But there was a timid tug on my arm. It was Desi. He had the pirogue key in hand; he appeared oddly diffident. Now that I was in the presence of other *mondeles* he was shy of approaching me.

He looked at his feet. "Hello."

"Hello. How are you feeling?"

"I'm fine. But an army officer here thinks someone died on our expedition. There are rumors."

"I'll tell them that no one was harmed. But Desi, I want to say something to you. I feel . . . I—"

He turned away and darted back into the crowd.

"Desi!"

He was gone.

The Spaniards asked me to hurry—we had to find the Air Zaire office before it closed for the day. I obliged them, torn up with regret and not wanting to think, for the moment, of why he had run away, desiring only to get out of Mbandaka and away from the river as quickly as possible.

I was never to see Desi again.

✐✐✐

We made our way up the embankment to the Air Zaire office, a modest storefront on a palm-lined and carless central street. Chalk writing on a blackboard sign by the window announced that the flight to Kinshasa would leave tomorrow at two in the afternoon.

A small pert man in dark glasses and a dapper safari outfit came running up. He introduced himself as the Mbandaka director of Air Zaire. "Would you like tickets! Excellent! Please step into our office! I'll be happy to sell you tickets to Kinshasa!"

He ran inside and slipped behind his desk. The Spaniards made merry, with elated outbursts of staccato Spanish and a collective wiping of foreheads; finally, their problem was solved.

The director wrote out the tickets by hand, taking great care with the orthography, the spacing of the numbers, confirming codes with his handbook and checking prices against a tariff schedule. Then he took out a stamp, huffed on it, and plunked it down on the tickets. Everything was in order. Did we need a place to stay? Why, yes. He could put up two of us in his house next door. A local preacher would take the other two. The Spaniards emitted a gleeful chorus of *muchissimas gracias*.

We stood around in front of the office savoring our good fortune while the director closed up shop. An Indian man in blue robes was passing by. He stopped and said hello, and in a melancholy way asked if he could be of service.

"No thanks," I said. "We've just bought tickets to Kinshasa."

"What kind of tickets?"

"Plane tickets. On Air Zaire."

"Who told you Air Zaire flies to Kinshasa?"

"The director himself."

"The director sold you tickets? Ah, well he does that some-times." He bobbled his head. "But my good sir, the plane does not fly, it certainly does not. Try to get your money back quickly—quickly—and return to the *Ebeya*."

Just then the *Ebeya* hooted farewell from the river.

"Ooooh, my good sir!" the Indian said, frowning, "I feel very sorry for you now!" His head bobbling, he continued on his mel-ancholy way. "Veeery sorry!"

That crazy Indian didn't know what he was talking about, the director snapped when I asked him if what he had said was true. And how did we feel about a night out at Chez Tatine?

✂✂✂

The next morning, our heads aching from Chez Tatine, we hauled our bags around to the office for our eleven-o'clock ride out to the airport. Eleven came, then eleven-fifteen. Then eleven-thirty, and there was no car, no truck, no bus. I went inside to the director's office and asked what was going on.

He gripped his hair. "Not to worry! I'm on the radio now try-ing to find our plane! What could they have done with that plane?"

"Find the plane?"

"It was due to arrive an hour ago. But, *pas de problème!* We will find it! It was supposed to have left Kisangani, but now there's some confusion over whether it left Kinshasa. Or whether it made it to Kinshasa from Lubumbashi. Or for that matter whether it is still in Gbadolite. But we will find it, we will! And you *will* fly to Kinshasa! Do not listen to the Indians!"

By one o'clock the Spaniards were pacing circles around their bags in the stultifying heat. Each time I had walked into the office to see whether the airline had located the plane, the director had uttered frantic assurances that the flight would depart as sched-uled. This time, however, he admitted that, ahh, well, hmm, it appeared the flight would be, as he delicately phrased it, *"un pé en retard."* Under other circumstances I would have been upset, but now, after my ordeal on the Congo, it just did not matter to me. I shrugged and walked out to the Spaniards, who chattered away in rising panic. Certainly if there was no flight it looked as though they might not make it back to Kinshasa today, next week, or even next month. I joked that I had learned to pilot a pirogue, and offered my services. They were less than amused.

Just then the Indian came shuffling down the road and accosted me with expressions of sympathy. *"Un pé,* indeed!" he responded, after having heard my story. "My good sir, there will be no Air Zaire plane now or ever. Just ask him when the last plane was."

I walked inside and did that.

"Okay, okay, you've been talking to the Indians again," the director said. "So we've had some problems in the past. They'll never let us forget it."

"Well, when *was* the last flight?"

He held out his fingers and counted. "Give or take a few days, the last flight was, oh, well, roughly, ah, let me think, umm . . . well, it wasn't last month, and not the month before that, but ahh, it might have been last year, but then again . . ."

The Spaniards greeted the news with incredulity and an explosion of expletives; the director mournfully refunded our money. The Indian, by contrast, was unperturbed. "Please, sirs, there is City Express. It is run by a Belgian. You can fly City Express to Kinshasa today at three. I will arrange it for you."

"Why didn't you tell us about City Express before?" I asked.

"Why should I have, sir? You believed Air Zaire."

✦✦✦

At three the City Express jet lifted off from Mbandaka, with us aboard it, and banked southwest toward Kinshasa. I settled into my seat and looked out the window. The Congo, the color of café au lait, resembled not a river, but a lake broken up with many strips of forest, and beyond the café au lait the green of the forest swept on and on, without variation, toward every horizon. It was as if there were no such thing as humankind or civilization, as if we were taking off during the Jurassic period and we might suddenly spot the head of brontosaurus amid the canopy, or the bulk of a *Tyrannosaurus rex* crashing through the bushes.

An hour and a half later, just before we landed, the river reappeared below, here wide and blue at Malebo Pool, but farther ahead winding on and away toward the cataracts to the south. Then we dropped into the haze of Kinshasa, the haze of rubbish burning in bidonvilles, veered toward the Quonset huts and runway of the airport, and leveled off for landing.

Epilogue

WHEN I ARRIVED IN KINSHASA THE COLONEL WAS STILL COM-
ing down the Congo on his barge, and he had not landed by the
time I left. I did see Marc, George, and André at the bank, and we
said our good-byes. They would not allow me to face the Beach
alone again; they provided me with their besuited and gold-
bedecked *protocole* (a high-ranking former Zairean military officer
whose job it was to deal with officialdom on behalf of the bank),
who, brandishing his automatic rifle, escorted me quickly and easily through customs and put me aboard the ferry to Brazzaville.
And that was it: I was out of Zaire.

For the first few months after I left Central Africa, I revisited
the Congo River in nightmares, in visions of endlessly unfolding
watery lanes and shouting villagers and thunderhead skies flickering with lightning. When I awoke I remembered the pain and regret I felt for Desi: I thought I had been too hard on him. Why had
he turned away from me so abruptly in Mbandaka? Why had I
never managed to understand or truly accept him? Why had I not
been more generous with him? He had risked his life in my employ, and then I had just flown away. I wanted to do something
more for him (I did not know what); I wanted to help him. Had I
seen the Colonel again, perhaps he could have located Desi or
passed on a message or a gift from me. But that was not to be, and
in any case, I lacked the resources to do anything that would have
been of lasting benefit to him. He would remain in Zaire, living
hand to mouth, struggling to provide for his family and church,
knowing only his river and his faith.

Still, my regrets, combined with the sting of failure, prompted
me to find a way to return to the river, to mount another expedition

and try the descent again. There was no reason why it should not have succeeded if it consisted of many men, more pirogues, and ample reserves of food. I would hire Desi as my Lokele-region guide and find a Bangala for the Bumba-to-Mbandaka stretch. But when I reflected on what I had gone through, an attempt to repeat the undertaking seemed a frivolous tempting of fate. Moreover, I thought back to the reactions of the people along the river: the mothers grabbing their children and running; the invincible suspicion and hostile inquiries about my intentions; the general assumption that I was a *méchant* diamond hunter, mercenary, or Motorola-wielding *touri*. Being seen that way troubled me and pressed home the fact that history between Europeans and Africans, between blacks and whites in Africa, has left a mark that at least in part of the continent has barely begun to fade. And if the fears urban Zaireans entertained about cannibalistic Ngombe and Bangala seemed exaggerated to me after my time on the river, poverty and hatred rooted in history might have motivated attacks on us. Traveling safely unarmed would have been impossible, yet taking along a gun and soldier turned me into a redoubtable invader. That being the case, it seemed better to stay away. If people wanted privacy I would leave them alone.

In 1996, a war broke out in Zaire and scuppered notions of a return anyway. (An unrelated civil war erupted in Brazzaville, too, and destroyed that city.) An ethnic rebellion in the eastern part of the country, supported by Uganda and Rwanda and led by Laurent-Désiré Kabila, a Marxist-Maoist protégé of Lumumba's, the prime minister whom the Belgians and Mobutu had had assassinated in the 1960s, gained momentum and metamorphosed into a national campaign to overthrow Mobutu. In March of 1997, Kabila's forces took Kisangani, and in May they reached the outskirts of Kinshasa. Mobutu, who was ill with prostate cancer, fled to Gbadolite, the village of his birth, in the jungle north of Lisala. Kabila's men walked into Kinshasa almost unopposed, and days later, Mobutu, with bullets pinging off the sides of his hired

Antonov jet, flew out of Gbadolite—and Zaire—forever. Later that year he died in exile in Morocco.

Kabila's revolt was a rout (for who would fight for Mobutu, who no longer even paid his own army?), and he came to power with much popular support. Western mining companies were quick to court Kabila, and several Western governments declared that with the departure of Mobutu a new era was dawning in Zaire. Such statements could only ring absurd considering Kabila's Marxist-Maoist ideology, his past as a *chef de guerre,* and his ascension to power via armed rebellion—factors that presaged only more turmoil for Zaire, not prosperity. Not surprisingly, Kabila's first move was to suspend the constitution and ban all political activity; the support he had enjoyed among Zaireans eager to taste democracy after thirty-two years of dictatorship quickly dissipated. Ironically, he also restored to the country the name it had born before Mobutu dubbed it Zaire—La République démocratique du Congo—when now as ever the former Belgian Congo would be anything but democratic.

These events gave me reason to worry about the Colonel's safety. (He never responded to the letters of thanks I sent him after my return to Moscow. But then the Zairean postal service was barely functioning, and I have no way of knowing if they reached him.) During Kabila's takeover of Kinshasa, Tshatshi, the district where he and Mobutu had their residences, was looted. Many members of Mobutu's elite escaped by boat across the Congo to Brazzaville, but Kabila's men gunned down others as they tried to flee, and an untold number of Mobutu's cronies were tortured, shot, lynched, or torn apart by vengeful crowds.

Then, a little more than a year later, another revolt threatened to unseat Kabila, this time one supported by Rwanda and Uganda, which he had snubbed after coming to power. The revolt continues: the battles between Ugandan- and Rwandan-backed rebels on one side and Kabila's forces on the other ebb and flow, and have resulted in the de facto partition of the country. Now, in

late 1999, the northeastern half of the former Zaire is in the hands
of the rebels, and Kinshasa and the southwest of the country are
under Kabila's control. Barge traffic up and down the Congo
River has been suspended—the dividing line is north of Mbandaka, in the great forest—and Kinshasa has suffered food short-
ages as a result. Desi, if he was in Lokutu, Bumba, or Lisala when
the rebels came, is probably trapped there now.

I shall return to the personal to close this account. Before my
trip I entertained visions of Zaire's wilderness that, if they did not
resemble the oil-painted visions of European romantics, were false
in their own way. The alien in Zaire had seduced me; the threatening had challenged me; and I had pictured its wilderness as a
bourn where I could rejuvenate myself through suffering and
achievement and the conquest of my fear. But my drama of self-
actualization proved obscenely trivial beside the suffering of the
Zaireans and the injustices of their past. That it should have
seems obvious to me now, but I learned this only by buying a
pirogue and attempting the descent.

Yet my endeavor taught me something positive: to value what I
have and to strive to preserve it. As I write these last words, the
crows are cawing in the frost-glazed birches outside my Moscow
window and the winter solstice is at hand. The Russian night has
become long, long in a comforting way unknown in the tropics.
Tatyana and I are married, and I am at home now and happy
about it. If the boundlessly auspicious *vozrast Khrista* is behind
me, the promise of youth, despite some losses and disappoint-
ments, has proved true in many unforeseen respects. I do not, after
all, regret my time in Zaire. The best we can do is exorcise our
demons through action, for time will always be short, and there is
always much to be learned from living—even when the lessons
prove to be deeply painful.

Kiev, November 1998—Moscow, December 1999

Illustrations

page

2   Map of the region

16   Merchants

30   A one-hundred-zaire banknote

42   The barge from onshore
Paul and Jilly

58   Deck life

76   Danger de Mort (left)

86   The *pousseur*
A village

92   Palm grubs and monkeys for sale

112   Pirogues alongside the barge

128   Approaching Kisangani (the Zairean flag is in the foreground)

138   Desi on the river

154   Sunset near Lokutu

168   A village along the Congo

176   Campsite scenes

190   Mirrored river

208   Send-off from Lisala
The view from our pirogue

222   Amisi (foreground) and Desi

240   The *Colonel Ebeya*: docking and rescue

248   Sunset on the Congo River